PRODUCT MANAGEMENT

George S. Dominguez

American Management Association, Inc.

International standard book number: 0-8144-5238-8
Library of Congress catalog number: 74-134720

FIRST PRINTING

To
my wife, Shirley Jean
my son, George Samuel
and
my daughter, Shirley Jean

Preface

THIS preface, like all prefaces, was written after rather than before completion of the book it is meant to introduce. There is an inverse logic in such a situation, because it is only after the author has completed his work that he has enough perspective to determine whether he has accomplished his purpose.

There has been—and there will no doubt continue to be—a vast increase in both number and diversity of books dealing with management. This book, however, is intended to fill a definite gap in the information on the relatively new management technique known as product management and the product management system. A careful, thorough search through the existing literature made it apparent that despite widespread interest in the product management system and its techniques, no detailed statement of either the premise or the practice existed.

This book is not a typical survey of experience, either personal or as known in various companies. Valuable as this approach may be, it presupposes that the reader has at least basic familiarity with the subject and is able to make judgments about the material. However, since there is little fundamental information available on the tools, techniques, and practices of product management itself, it was felt that a better purpose would be served by providing such background. The book therefore presents the pragmatic basis for product management and then details in depth the organization, climate, and business conditions requisite for its introduction, implementation, and, most important, success.

Because many neophyte product managers have not had the benefit of extensive management training—a lamentable but all too common situation—there is extensive treatment of basic management techniques, but with emphasis on their relation to the specifically delineated tools and techniques of product management. Of necessity, coverage has been broad. The product manager certainly cannot be all things to all men, but he must at least endeavor to attain perfection in the multiplicity of areas that involve his product. It is hoped that he will find guidance in the following pages, and while some of the areas reviewed may seem fundamental to experienced product managers, other areas will not be so familiar and should be applicable to his own particular product management situation.

A brief word to brand managers is in order. Although the title of the book is *Product Management* and most of the direct references and terminology relate to product management, the principles involved have very direct applicability to brand managers and brand management. In order to better relate the similarities and dissimilarities of product and brand management, several of the chapters contain specific comparisons of the implementation of management techniques in the differing climates of the product and the brand management situations. Brand managers too, therefore, will find their unique problems discussed and, I trust, will forgive the use of product management terminology in their special field.

Most prefaces close with long, grandiose thanks and appreciation to publishers, friends, business associates, aunts, uncles, and whomsoever. A vote of thanks is due to one and all of the aforementioned, but even more importantly it is owed to you, the reader. Product management is still evolving. Its success and future depend upon efficient, effective, and, above all, creative product managers themselves, and so if any appreciation is forthcoming, it must be to those actual and potential product managers who will build the product management of the future.

George S. Dominguez

Contents

PART ONE

Theory and Practice

1

The Origins
of Product Management

Seven years ago an article appeared in the *Harvard Business Review* entitled "Product Management—Vision Unfulfilled." Seven years later, while the vision is well on the way to being fulfilled, substantial confusion still prevails despite the ever increasing number of product managers and acknowledged role of product management in contemporary business operations. Product managers constantly hear such questions as: What is product management? What do product managers do? Why do we need product managers? What can the product manager do for me? What contribution can product management make in my operation?

While these are the questions most often posed by general management, the product manager himself faces many personal operational questions. With the lack of information on product management techniques he, too, has often been left with no answers. Therefore, both overall management and individual product managers have suffered from the age-old communications gap, a gap that must be bridged if the vision is to be fulfilled. And so this is not only a book but a bridge, a bridge on the road to successful, integrated management.

There can be no doubt of the progress made by product management within the past few years. The number of articles dealing directly or indirectly with it attests to the interest and development of this concept. There is hardly a business concern today that does not employ and apply product management techniques. In a world of continuing economic pressures and profit consciousness the cost versus contribution of product management (and product managers) has been evaluated, reevaluated, and "re-reevaluated," and repeatedly substantiated.

From this emerges a clear pattern not of static, contained, staid product management but of an always dynamic product management, creating a situation in which the product manager finds his responsibilities in corporate life constantly expanding.

To say there has been some confusion without providing some overview of product management does not help clarify the situation. And attempting to define in a few words what a product manager specifically is and does painfully confirms the difficulty. The product manager has been compared (somewhat invidiously) to a "little general manager." While this certainly evokes a precise image in some minds, it is hardly valid, for, as we shall see later, the duties and responsibilities of the product manager are somewhat more and, at the same time, somewhat less.

One of the main problems is that too many old-school business management techniques prevail. The newer principles of management, while promulgated freely and widely, are still viewed with a certain skepticism, and by natural and logical extension not universally applied. But the product manager can function efficiently and effectively only when allowed to operated within the broader scope of contemporary management approaches in the new, freer organizational concepts. This means that management had best recognize this obligation, be certain that it wants effective product management, and be willing to pay the price, not in dollars, but in the operation commitment that this entails.

Now that we have admitted the problem of definition, we cannot beg the question. We must at least define what a product manager is and does. Fortunately, doing so also largely provides the definition—in general terms at least—of product management. So, taking faint heart in hand, we erect one of the main pillars of the bridge:

> The product manager is the central focus for all information relative to his product or product line. He is the repository of all such data, the source of information about his product, the planner, the profit controller and motivator, and the center of a large sphere of product influence that permeates every aspect of the business operation necessary for the accomplishment of his primary duty—the successful

introduction, marketing and sale of profitable products and the continuous review and analysis of his product or product lines to assure continued overall profitable growth and marketing position.

Quite a challenge, no matter how it's phrased.

Product and Brand Management

Another but fortunately lesser source of confusion and, hence, difficulty is the relationship between product and brand management. The problem of distinguishing one from the other is primarily semantic for while the duties of both may differ, the brand manager ultimately has the same functional responsibilities and profit goal orientation just identified for the product manager.

Brand management, as we shall see shortly, is the elder of the two, but in many respects the application of product management techniques is operationally more understandable in the brand management position. The product manager has clearly delineated responsibilities in certain areas, but frequently these become somewhat tenuous and defy precise delineation in others—a problem less often encountered in brand management. The brand manager usually has a role whose parameters are more precisely indentified, and his functions fit within more clearly defined, if not more circumscribed, limitations.

Later we will explore in detail the specific differences between the product manager and the brand manager. Essentially, we have seen that the product manager deals with a larger totality and, in many instances, has a broader sphere of influence than his brother brand manager. What should be clearly recognized, however, is that the fundamental techniques of product management apply, whether the product manager is just that or whether he is a brand manager. To be more precise about it, brand management is concerned primarily with the controlled distribution and marketing of a specific brand within a given corporation. The brand manager may be controlling several products that are being marketed under the same brand designation, or he may, in effect, be dealing with only one product and one brand.

Since brand management almost universally involves the sale of the product by the manufacturer directly to the consumer or primary distributor, the brand manager is extremely consumer conscious, and in many instances is himself directly involved with the consumer. The product manager is often involved with an intermediary using his product, which finds its way to the consumer market not as the original product he sold, but as the component of some later fabrication. While he is, therefore, concerned with the consumer, as we all are, his primary interests are usually industrially oriented.

While both product and brand managers deal with many similar internal functions, it is outside their corporate environment that the distinctions between the two become apparent. Later, we shall see a second, important distinction involving the emphasis each places on the principles of product management. This means that, functionally speaking, both product and brand managers have basically the same tools at hand, and are charged with essentially the same responsibilities, but the degree of emphasis and the proportionate amount of time spent in the pursuit and accomplishment thereof varies greatly.

In this book we deal with both the product and the brand manager. There is little doubt that both these subdivisions of the product management concept will continue to change. They will change as the individual manager's involvement within the corporate structure changes; they will change as the role of marketing changes; they will change as the concepts of business in society change; and they will change as men change. But whether we call him a product manager (as we do in this book, meaning, unless otherwise indicated, both the product and the brand manager) or a brand manager, the same principles apply, and he will have to be capable of change. In many cases, he will find himself taking leadership in advancing these changes.

This is vital, for in years gone by, change in business organization has often been painfully slow. But few people today will say that it remains so. No longer does the lethargy and relative inertia formerly manifested continue. One of the new developments in the business world is that of the product management concept. It is a challenge to product managers to continue building upon this foundation. In order to do so the product manager must firmly and fully understand what his functions are, will be, and can be.

Product Management—History and Development

Sometimes it seems that product management, like Topsy, seems to have just "growed." Before one is accused of too harsh a judgment, however, it must be admitted that many intriguing hints exist to indicate that product management had its origin some 40 years or so ago. The initial credit must go to Procter & Gamble, which had a brand manager for Lava soap in 1928 and, subsequently, pioneered in product and brand management for some time.

Despite this early beginning, many years passed before any semblance of a spreading influence was to be found. We owe most of the subsequent development to two major industries, the chemical and the detergent fields, and to a handful of pioneer companies: General Electric, General Foods, Monsanto, General Aniline and Film, and Johnson & Johnson. All these firms were successful in their initial endeavors to apply product management philosophy to their operations. Still, most industrial and consumer goods firms adopted product management on a wide scale only within the past 10 or 12 years. As a management technique, product management is a young discipline indeed.

DEVOLUTION AND EVOLUTION

Essentially, product management evolved from the need to centralize all data relative to individual products or product lines in one area to optimize operation and profits. It was the obvious outgrowth of the limitation of previous organization structures wherein manufacturing, sales, or other major functions exercised virtually monopolistic control over the organization. Such dominating influences almost invariably created an untenable imbalance between the objectives of divergent groups and their realistic limitations. The resultant compromises often were not to the best corporate advantage.

A close look at the operations of a typical firm so structured reveals this imbalance and an intrinsic crippling, stultifying lack of coordination between responsible functional, support, and management areas. In Figure 1, the straight line represents any given product in a hypothetical company as it is fed through the structure from conception to sale. From this we can see that although there is ample provision for research, development, marketing, manufacturing, engineering, accounting, advertising, promotion, sales and distribution, nowhere is there any one group or individual concerned with integrating all of these divergent functions. Moreover, there is no one involved from initiation through to finalization as a manufactured product, and on to concern with the product once it is in the marketplace.

The illustration also indicates a lack of specific corporate interest, ironically enough, in the product itself. While it is self-evident that

FIGURE 1

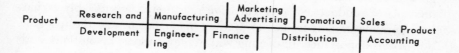

without a product there cannot be a sale, in the frenzy of all the other activities, the poor product seems to be a second class citizen.

Certainly, we are all aware that once a product is sold, it does not magically disappear. People have problems with products. Even the most ideal product, once in the marketplace, develops its problems and difficulties, taking on a subsequent consumer life of its own. Reapplication of what is learned about the product in the market after its initial introduction, or even after years of availability, is fundamental and vital. Often such subsequent developments lead to product modification, forming an integral component of the product modification process. In order for this information to be effectively utilized, there must be a source for its collection, interpretation, and useful implementation.

Someone, somewhere, some time took a long hard look at this situation and wisely said that there should be a definite, finite, coordinated, cohesive interrelationship among all these factors, and they should be oriented from the product viewpoint. Why the product viewpoint? One might expect sales to dominate, or that manufacturing should take precedence, or any one of a number of other areas, depending upon the proponents of any individual school. But since it is the product that must be sold, and it is the product that in the final analysis is the vehicle by which the corporation is or is not successful, then, obviously, it is the product that is central to all functions and that forms the nucleus of integrated orientation.

Nothing has yet been said about profits. In looking over our small, hypothetical company, one is clearly struck with the fact that there is no profit centralization. This does not imply that people were not profit motivated. It does imply that contribution of individual profitabilities was not known and that profit or loss was dispersed over all functions. Many companies had absolutely no knowledge of individual product profitability, nor was there any central control over the totality of profitability and the resultant profit or loss either in the aggregate or as it derived from the individual product.

Logically enough, then, the product manager has become the profit center, or is at least responsible for product profit. Later we will discuss in depth this profit responsibility concept, which is also a great source of confusion, and just how it applies to the product manager's job.

Suffice it to say, however, from the historical standpoint, product management is quite young, and its basic development was the outgrowth of the limitations already discussed. Over the years the basic precepts of product management have not altered appreciably. What has altered is the importance of product management and the recognition of this importance. In dealing with the evolutions, involutions, and convolutions of product management, we are also faced with the additional difficulty that, pragmatically speaking, companies do have people charged with what are essentially the responsibilities of the product manager (in greater or lesser degree), but without the title. While this may confuse history and management, it nevertheless lends further credence to the validity and value of the concept. Whether called by the proper name or not is relatively immaterial, for it is the application of the concept that is important, not the titles given.

What does all this tell us? It tells us that product management is young. It is dynamic, and it is growing. As the corporation grows, so, most often, does the number of products, their nature, the extent of market involvement, and the nature of the marketplace. All of these factors create the dynamics in which product management changes. Where product management is today is one thing; where management and product managers will take it tomorrow is another.

2

The Product Manager's Job

Now that we have theorized extensively on product management and the function of the product manager, we should like the product manager himself to answer the question: What does the product manager do?

Naturally, the product manager's job varies to a significant extent, depending upon the organization where he is employed. We have already seen that there is a division in responsibility and a very clear distinction in emphasis between the functions of a product and brand manager. Further differences, however, exist depending upon the interpretations placed on product management by specific organizations, and even within the same company having multiple product lines or multidivisional structure.

Requirements for the management of a product brand or divisional series of products vary substantially. Depending on these needs, as well as the feelings of general management, and even those of the individual product manager, differences in approach will occur. This is a good thing, for a substantial part of the product management challenge is the effective application of technique as required for the particular product and circumstances. No two products should be managed in exactly the same way; and no two product managers will ever manage the same product in the same way. Because of this, the product manager may find himself involved with more than those duties and responsibilities normally associated with product management.

However, if the concept in its totality has any validity, we should be able to set forth a logical range of typical things that product managers do. When we do so, not only will these differences be clarified, but some of the questions over and above what the product manager does (such as those posed in the beginning of Chapter 1) will also be answered.

Before we begin, let's understand one more thing. As with any management function, authorities disagree on specific details concerning product management. But some of these differences are thankfully more semantic than real, and with all good conscience we can ignore them. The following list of product management responsibilities reduces a number of details and trimmings to the few key elements. These elements contain what is thought to be the sum and substance of the product management functional concept. They are the building blocks from which the edifice of product management is built. Once constructed, the product management system can operate, and from it flows all the specific, tailored devices and procedures required for operational efficiency.

The Product Management Hexagram

People expect product managers to be individualistic, and a certain degree of nonconformity is both anticipated and accepted. Considering the tendency toward objectivity, automation, and the application of dispassionate scientific techniques in the management sciences, this is certainly refreshing. That such a situation prevails is probably because product management is a relatively young technique; and it is fortunate for many product managers that such latitudes and attitudes are afforded. What we must concern ourselves with as product managers, however, is not that we are allowed to be highly individualistic in our approach both to product management and business life in general, but quite the opposite: namely, that there are certain areas and principles which we, like all others in managerial positions, should conform to, or at least comprehend before we elect not to do so. After diligent searching, careful analysis, and a distillation of many divergent opinions, it is possible to condense the essentials of product management into six principal areas.

In a temporary fit of conformity, we can follow the trend of reducing polysyllabic nomenclature to mnemonics and call this the PMH (pronounced pimh)—Product Management Hexagram. To further conform let's examine the hexagram diagrammatically, as shown in Figure 2.

From this we can immediately see that there are six elements that must be analyzed in more detail: product, market, profit, forecasting, coordination, and planning. Now that we have them all neatly listed, let's again pause to reflect for a moment on some psychological problems that always arise when things are put into lists. First, these are words we are all familiar with and which immediately evoke certain images, responses, and connotations. We all have our own interpretations of these words as they relate to us as managers. Next, we will examine each thoroughly and refine our understanding of them in a somewhat new light. Rather than consider them as mere verbs, we will think of them as adjectives in the context of the product management concept. In doing so we will find that we have vastly expanded the parameters of their definitions, and that the multitudinous aspects involved in these six simple key words provide the nucleus of the product management concept theoretically and functionally.

As if this problem were insufficient, we have to contend with another phenomenon: the tendency to conceive of a list as ranking items

FIGURE 2
Product Management Hexagram

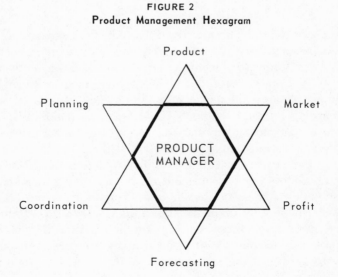

in importance. This is perfectly natural, even if it is not necessarily the intention, which it certainly is not in this instance. One of the reasons for illustrating the Product Management Hexagram diagrammatically was to emphasize that while we are dealing with six separate entities, they are directly interrelated and have continuity. No one has any greater significance than another, although the emphasis given each provides the basis for variation in product management technique and will be subject to the dictates of the management situation.

Now that we can assume all to be equally important and recognize the interdependency of these separate elements, we should also consider that in contradistinction to the rigidities of mathematics, the sum here amounts to more than the total of the parts. As we examine each of these principal areas, we should keep firmly in mind that individual knowledge and experience enable each product manager to augment them. And the specific practices employed in their application by that product manager provides an aura of personal creativity. Through an effective balance of these elements, as they apply in any given situation, unlimited possibilities for endless permutations exist, each of which will have its particular advantages in a given management situation. It is the sum and substance of the imaginative, creative product manager to implement them as only he can.

Product

Many product managers rightly consider the product to be central to their concerns as product managers. The difference we should establish is that this is usually conceived of exactly as stated: the product itself rather than a consideration of "product."

Naturally, the product manager is concerned primarily with the product itself, as this is essential to his functions in the management area. The product, however, is usually limited to a concrete entity that has a definite initiation and termination. As we shall see later in discussing products as such, this approach relates to measurable identities, cycles, prices, market trends, segmentation, packing, advertising promotion, distribution, and many other specifics. What is meant in considering the product here is to imply that the product manager should be thinking about the theory of product, and product far outside the confining limitations imposed by restrictions of physical criteria and his specific product entities alone. It is the philosophical difference between essence and is.

The product manager should be a total authority on the individual product, yes; but he should also be an authority on the theory of product, and recognize that product is frequently something intangible but nevertheless valuable. For example, customer service is in reality, although not usually considered to be such, a product. It is admittedly a rather ill-defined and tenuous substance. It is difficult to analyze the cost and contribution of customer service in many instances, and it clearly does not have a finite delineation, but it is an active product of the company, or at least it should be. Similarly, the image of the company, created via the contribution made by the product and the product manager, is effectively a product of the company and certainly a product of the product manager's effort.

In the assumption of his duties as they relate to product, the manager is being asked to be not only a practical, active, businessman, but simultaneously a somewhat impractical theorist. Predicated upon a clear recognition of the necessity for thorough, fundamental knowledge of the dynamics of product theory, as they pertain to effective introduction, sale, distribution, and profitable marketing, the product manager creates from tangible and intangible elements the harmonious blend leading to the success of his specific product, range of products, or brand.

What emerges from this is a commitment to comprehension of total product. Here, too, we should realize that such concerns as product mix, product control (addition, deletion, attrition) are involved, and the product manager must take these into account as they relate to any individual product, as well as the total product offered by the corporation. The intereffects of individual products upon each other, and the additive effects of product lines on other product lines and brands upon brands are facts that all experienced product managers have encountered. Yet this is very much a part of the total product-involvement concept being discussed. All too often it happens that in a given situation, in the haste of developing, releasing, and marketing a new product, sufficient thought is not given to these effects on existing products. This can result in very serious repercussions on either the new product, the existing product, or, in more peripheral areas of relationship, to total product.

Consideration of the product in relation to corporate capability concerns again not only factors that affect manufacturing, engineering, total capacity, intrinsic capability, and capitalization, but less obvious aspects such as overall economics, consumer credit, customer service, technical service, support effort, administrative functions, finance, effect on market, dilution of effort, and over or under extension; all must be weighed in the balance. To say that many of these concerns are outside the sphere of the product manager's job, *per se*, is assuredly correct, particularly in a larger corporate structure where separate departments exist that are responsible for each of the factors. But this is not to say that the product management concept does not make a thorough commitment to the necessity for understanding, optimizing, and giving each of these factors the consideration it requires. Later, in our discussion of the coordinative responsibilities of the product manager, his role in applying his concerns in these specific areas, as they relate to him and as he relates to them, becomes apparent. It is just because of this overlapping of interest and concern that he becomes effective in the integration of all that results in fostering the product and profit. However, in order to function effectively and to exercise the influence and judgment required in his duty as product manager, he must have a definite feeling for the interplay of these forces and their ultimate effect on his product. On this basis, he then assists in directing the effort judged to be most conducive to optimization of manufacture, distribution, marketing, accounting, and all of the aspects we have mentioned to provide the epitome of operational effectiveness and economy.

Before we leave this area, one more factor is important. We have already mentioned that product management is dynamic. It seems that in no other management position are so many changes taking place so rapidly. In this we are not referring to changes in product management, but to changes constantly occurring in products themselves, in the market place, with customers, in internal corporate operations, and by extension in the myriad circumstances that involve him and his product. Again, in concerning himself with *product* as opposed to *the* product, he must be concerned with these dynamics and their resulting influences. Therefore, a sense of priorities, timing, and responsiveness are exceedingly important. If he does not have them, he should cultivate them.

Market

To ask the product manager for effectiveness and efficiency and then divorce him from the market may seem a patent absurdity. But foolish as it seems, how often do we see just this happening. The problems here are not that anyone disagrees with the need of the product manager to be fully acquainted with the market, nor that there is any substitute for first-hand contact, but rather confusion and misunderstanding: confusion between marketing and market, and misunderstanding between sales and product management, which leads to objection, restriction, and limitations imposed on the product manager, crippling him in his ability to go forth and personally ascertain those circumstances prevailing in his market.

Indubitably, marketing has its own, unchallenged, specific responsibilities. While it may be all-pervasive, product management is operationally only a phase of marketing and an effective support and adjunct to the total marketing effort. The product manager is not out to usurp the marketing prerogative but to augment it through his market knowledge. To do this, however, he must first have the market knowledge.

The market in this context is the specific entity in which the product is to be sold. Therefore, it is evident that the product manager must be fully knowledgeable of his market and responsible for this knowledge. It is obvious that if he is marketing-oriented also, so much the better; but marketing is not his primary responsibility. This, however, is gradually changing and is undoubtedly one of the areas for growth of the concept. Again, as a practical reality, we are all aware that most often the product manager is involved in marketing to some extent and certainly involved in marketing plans and programs. When we discuss this planning function in more detail, we will distinguish between the planning function as a passive marketing role and active sales activity.

Therefore, the product manager is not a marketing manager, nor is he an active selling instrument (except in a very circumscribed sense); but he is the central, focal point for marketing planning responsibility, since we are involved with passive marketing duties. Now, since we have firmly established this point, we can also definitely state that he is and needs to be involved in the market, both as the base for his activities as product manager and as planning manager.

The market is vibrant and viable; it is actually analogous to a living thing. Subject to constant change through the influences of a number of forces, it is constantly shifting in its responsiveness to them. One moment, like a living organism, it builds upon itself; and it is unique in that it can create itself. The market becomes not only the subject, but the object of the external forces brought to bear upon it in the marketplace; but in itself it is a force that self-actuates activity and perpetuates the dynamic. The chemists and physicists among us will understand that this is an equilibrium, a balance between interacting and sometimes opposing forces; but as with many equilibria, it is a constantly shifting and changing one, which keeps the balance effected only temporary. When the distribution is altered as one force changes in intensity or direction, it is met with a response reestablishing the equilibrium, only for the cycle to be endlessly repeated. Into this vortex plunges the product manager with his product. Naturally, he is therefore concerned with the variations encountered as well as the possibilities of these variations since they dramatically affect his approach to the product in terms of marketability and sales. Clearly then, this represents a basic precept in the concept of product life cycle, marketing, and marketability.

In his concerns with the market, the product manager will examine factual information: population, population density, geography, demography, social and psychological factors, gross national product, expendable income, politics, legal and trade restrictions, and innumerable other specifics. But more often than not, he must exercise subjective judgment to blend the measurable, observable, quantifiable factors with those that can only be "felt," from which he then distills his market analysis. This he employs as the matrix for product activity.

Profit

Almost everyone agrees that the product manager should be the profit manager. But even here, that old ubiquitous confusion clouds the issue. This time it stems from what is meant by profit and how responsible the product manager should be. It may be obvious that profit is the money the corporation makes in any given period of time; but because we employ this one simple word "profit" to encompass at least two major ideas, and what are really many overlapping aspects of corporate income, the nature of profit and the extent of the product manager's involvement become a trifle complicated.

In traditional approaches to profit and profit centralization, the responsibility has always been placed with corporate officership. And in the final sense this is undeniably correct, for corporate management must be charged with the basic responsibility for earnings of the corporate body. However, even in such a structure many functional organization groups have responsibility for certain profit areas, which in the aggregate constitute the profit totally derived. This, again, should not be confused with the creation or existence of profit centers, analogous to cost centers, but should be construed as those functional groups controlling certain aspects of the company business that generate profit or play a determinate role in total profitability.

GROSS PROFIT AND NET PROFIT

A very simple way to clarify this distinction is to consider the difference between gross profit and net profit. Most commonly, gross profit involves a statement by percent of earnings, based on the difference between total cost of goods sold and total sales dollars. Of course, there are differences of opinion on exactly what should be contained in cost of goods sold. Assuming classical factors employed (which is good enough for our nontechnical purpose), regardless of the precise specifics employed, it would be the relationship of selling price to cost of goods sold that determine gross profit.

Net profit is derived from the gross profit (one way of doing it), after subtracting all overhead expenses; again, the exact nature of the expenses included in overhead determination or operational expenses varies, and here we encounter fixed as opposed to variable expenses. However, for our purposes we are not concerned with meticulous detail, as applied in accounting and financial procedures, but rather with a clear distinction between two principal types of profit and how they apply to the product manager.

This very simple distinction is important because it provides the ground upon which we construct a meaningful understanding of the product manager's responsibilities in the profit area. It is the basis upon which we can delineate the authority and responsibility that will enable him to perform and provide for a meaningful coexistence in the corporate framework.

All of this leads us to say that the product manager is fundamentally involved in gross profit. Seen in this light, he is accountable for the cost of goods sold. The exact nature of influence will vary from corporation to corporation, depending on the factors used in the determination of cost of goods sold and upon the extent to which the product manager is expected to extend his efforts in this sphere. Gross profitability then becomes the concern of those who are and should be charged with it, since they are in a position to control and direct those factors which determine it.

This appears to be a very satisfactory resolution of the problem. Active product managers know from experience, however, that rarely are things so clear-cut, and many of their activities and influences are in areas that affect net profit as well. There is no real reason for concern over this actuality, for the essential element in effective product management is the optimum operation that yields the best profit for the least cost with lowest possible overhead and distribution, thereby creating greatest profit. As long as management permits his activity in these areas, there is no need to impose the rigidities of the gross or net profit concepts. However, it is a useful differentiation in those situations where an apparent conflict arises, providing management with proven workable guidelines.

Since, ultimately, the profit generated by a given product, series of products, or brands is the *raison d'être* of business, the product manager's profit responsibilities must be fully comprehended, and he must be given the latitude to discharge these obligations. Therefore, this rather deceptively simple distinction bears further elucidation. Figure 3 shows gross and net profits, and those areas in which the product manager has primary responsibility: gross profit and those in which his role is secondary net profit.

Considering the multiplicity of elements that go into the determination of either gross or net profit, it is a seeming contradiction that the product manager, who is rather remote from most of these elements over which he clearly exercises little or no direct control, should be charged with the ultimate responsibility of the gross profit that is created by these very factors. The reason for this is based on the pragmatic considerations that we have discussed. It is a logical managerial evolution that arrives from the concept of product management itself.

Figure 1 illustrated, by use of a horizontal bar, the mechanism of managing products without product management. While such functions as research and development had their separate responsibilities, none of them was involved primarily with profit as related to individual products, brands, or lines. While manufacturing and engineering were concerned with determining the cost of manufacturing a specific item, and the sales group with selling it later, the sales group seldom, if ever, was involved in the determination or serious consideration of the cost of manufacture; nor were the manufacturing and engineering people concerned with the cost of selling the product. Similarly, logistics or inventory people, while deeply involved in determining and controlling inventory costs and handling expenses, were divorced from both direct product manufacturing costs and sales and distribution expenses.

FIGURE 3
Profit Factors and Responsibilities

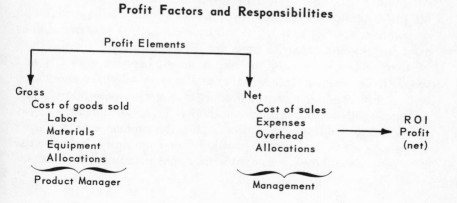

Corporate management was, of course, concerned with the eventual net profit, but often the determination of the net profit was predicated upon an across-the-board profitability approach, resulting from analysis of cost of goods sold and applying those controllable and uncontrollable expenses to the total, thereby providing net profit in the aggregate. No one argues that this cannot work, but one can argue about how well.

In this entire horizontal scheme, no one was concerned with the determination of product-by-product analysis to ascertain the effect of all these factors on the product, each other, and the inescapable extension of this concern, namely: correction of excesses, inefficiencies, or exorbitant elements. Obviously, no one really knew if a product was profitable; could be made profitable; or should be eliminated. This control over individual profit, if effected, could not help but lead to profit improvement.

The product manager is the corporate octopus with each of his tentacles reaching out to improve profit when and wherever this can be done, while keeping ever-watchful for the next situation to be corrected.

Coordination

At last we come to an area of almost complete agreement, for virtually everyone says that one of the product manager's main jobs is to be a coordinator. That few, if any, say what or how he is to coordinate is inconsequential, for at least they agree that he should be doing it.

This is a real blessing, for it is in his role as coordinator that the product manager can bring to bear all of the personal, individual creativity that he can contribute to the job. There are no specific boundaries set up for this phase of his operations, no externally applied restrictions. Rather, he is virtually given unlimited latitude to expand his range of influence, both vertically and horizontally, within the corporation in order that he be most effective. This is a tremendous asset and, simultaneously, a tremendous responsibility.

Later, when we discuss the old argument between authority and responsibility, we will face what a number of people have considered to be a serious problem for the product manager: responsibility in certain areas without commensurate authority. This is mentioned here because, within his function as coordinator, the product manager faces a cogent conflict between responsibility and authority. To advocate increasing his authority is fraught with serious potential complications.

To say that he cannot function without this increase is manifestly untrue. This, then, is another of those challenges for the future of the system. At the present, however, it is practical for him to operate effectively within the limitations of his authority.

Any active product manager knows that the lack of specific authority does not render him helpless. In certain situations authority vested in the product manager would be a specific aid in the accomplishment of a given duty or the resolution of a specific problem, but usually the situations in which unequivocal authority is necessary are not the coordinative situations. The difficulties here stem from confusion over what is involved in the coordinating function. The product manager, as a coordinator, is serving as a central focus for information on the product. He is in this instance acting primarily as a communicator and interpreter. It is his function to assemble all the loose threads in any given product, in all those phases we have seen in our horizontal chart; digest, interpret, and analyze these; and then, using the judgmental options that he alone is capable of making, since he alone has all of these facts, communicating with the specific functional area in order to accomplish profitable results.

Forecasting

It may seem strange to include forecasting as one of the major responsibilities of the product manager. Until recent years, management sciences were not advanced to the point of taking forecasting beyond the point of saying that one specific individual should be responsible for it.

More recent understanding, however, of just what forecasting is, what it does and what it can do suddenly creates an awareness of its significance and has forced management to do something about it. Many of you are already aware of why forecasting is important. But just so that we all fully comprehend its significance, we should realize, first, that forecasting means far more than just the limitations of forecasting sales and profits, whether on an individual product or line; just as important, it involves the forecasting of the market in toto and by segment and the corporate position in the forecasted market. In addition, forecasting relates to the following, but by no means total number of important considerations:

Contributory factor to effective planning.

Establishment of inventory levels.

Establishment of turnover rates.

Establishment of cash flow.

Factor in committed capital, assets on hand and employed.

Controllable expenses.

Contribution to profit (via adequate manipulation).

Coordination with manufacturing and engineering.

Establishment of potential for new or modified products.

Identification of areas of opportunity.

Hidden profit contributor or consumer.

Market identification and segmentation.

Areas of attrition.

Opportunities of expansion.

Causes for retrenchment.

If we look at these and consider their implications, we see that they are extremely important, and it would be difficult to attribute any greater significance to one over the other. Yet each requires accurate forecasting techniques for quantification and evaluation. When we are confronted with a situation such as this, it is difficult to deny the value of accurate, rapid forecasting.

Forecasting costs money, and the more accurate the forecasting, the more expensive it becomes. This is something that we must clearly recognize initially because, in many instances, no existing systems for accurate forecasting prevail. It will be part of the product manager's responsibility to assist in the development of such systems. However, since we are principally concerned with profit, we should see the application of accurate forecasting from the product manager's standpoint as ultimately returning to this basic concern. He must also, therefore, be concerned with the expenses involved in developing and maintaining the forecasting system. We realize again that often a balance or compromise is necessary—a balance between adequacy and accuracy in the forecasting system relative to the amount of money available for commitment to the system.

In such compromising situations the goal is to develop the most comprehensive, accurate forecasting system in a given situation for the least money. At the same time, we must not fall into the trap of self-deception that false economy alluringly poses. There is no question that good forecasting can save many dollars and hundreds of hours. These dollar savings sometimes cannot be measured. As we all know, it is those subjective and indefinite factors that lead to so many problems in justification. We either tend to overjustify or underjustify based on these intangibles. To say that they exist in forecasting is true. How to measure them is the problem. However, it is evident that we must consider them in the contribution that forecasting can make to the effective business operation, but the situation must be approached realistically. To do justice to the subject, we must examine those situations that provide an even further challenge. Not only are they difficult to measure but they sometimes cannot even be foreseen. Nevertheless, they are there and, depending upon the specific nature of the business involved, will manifest themselves to a greater or lesser degree.

Forecasting techniques will be discussed in greater detail later in the book. It is apparent from what we have said, however, that forecasting is a very important factor in modern business management. However, while electronic data processing has greatly simplified some of the problems that previously existed, we should acknowledge their existence and understand that computers in no way replace the necessity for individual personal judgment. It is usually the product manager who is final arbitrator. This is another of those many instances where his accumulation of knowledge serves a function nowhere else obtainable within the organization.

While forecasts, particularly those based on the use of computers, have become more accurate in recent years, the line about computers—"garbage in, garbage out"—should keep us on guard. The computer, and any forecasting technique, is only as good as the information input. It is implicit in any such system that accurate, timely information be available. The product manager is concerned not only with the ultimate forecasting system itself insofar as technique is concerned, but with accumulation of data and continued informational input. Considering the output, an expenditure of effort is clearly worth the reward.

While on this subject, a word about courage. Often in forecasting the product manager will face the inevitable situation in which he must have the courage to crawl way out on that proverbial limb. Without the courage of these convictions, no product manager can be effective. While it may be a soul-searching experience, he must have the fortitude to exercise his judgment. Let us hope that he is more often right than wrong.

Planning: The Marketing Plan

The last of our six major responsibilities is planning. It is impossible to overestimate the importance of planning in the modern corporation, for it involves dedicated commitment by all those involved in formulation and execution. It is the result of the product manager's unique product knowledge and broad, basic knowledge of the corporation that makes him the ideal person to be charged with responsibility for the planning operation. Even in those instances where he is not primarily responsible for the total plan, his portion thereof is one of the most important elements. To be a useful, workable instrument, he must be fully involved in the total formulation of the plan, even if only in an advisory sense.

Because companies vary in size and number of personnel, the exact participation of the product manager varies. It can be anywhere from responsibility of the total market plan (where he functions primarily as coordinator, assembler, and final drafter of the plan that subsequently receives management approval and then implementation), to merely being responsible for the product planning segment of the total. Taken from the standpoint of either extreme, or any of the in-betweens, the product manager finds himself very deeply involved and concerned with planning.

While we are considering only formal marketing planning, we should digress for a moment. There are many other plans on a smaller and sometimes larger scale than the marketing plan in which the product manager also becomes involved. He is constantly planning on a smaller scale for each of his products, and may be called upon to contribute to an overall operational plan in which the marketing plan would then only constitute a segment.

Therefore, when thinking of planning, the product manager should give due thought to the totality of this concept. In any event, there are several problems inherent in the planning concept, and it can be either (and usually both) bane or boon to the product manager, depending very largely upon the corporation and the product manager's attitude toward, and eventual use of, the plan.

It is an irony that all of us constantly plan our own individual activities, but many seem to balk at the necessity of forming a corporate plan. No doubt a good deal of this stems from the fundamental misunderstanding of what a marketing plan is, as well as the cultivation of the proper atmosphere in which the formulation of the plan occurs.

The ultimate use to which the plan is put is also exceedingly important. No one can feel a serious identification in the construction of a vast and meaningful plan when he finds that it is neither used nor seen. A very obvious but necessary excursion into the psychology of getting people to do things—something that the product manager is constantly worried about—tells us that the job to be done should result in something useful and usable. It sounds rather simple and self-evident, yet how often is such a fundamental rule broken only to result in disenchantment with the planning operation in succeeding years.

As a planner, the key to his contribution is the ability of the product manager to cross lines of vertical and horizontal authority and collect data from every stratum within the organization. He alone really has the ear and the mouth of his co-workers. If the rapport is there, everyone in the corporation is his co-worker; he is in a position to develop a knowledge base second to none.

Recognizing that the product is central to the company's best interest—for no one will argue that with nothing to sell no profits can be generated—the product manager has to develop a product plan that will support the efforts of the existing modes, as well as provide research and development of new products, lines, or brands and see that they are successfully introduced in the marketplace. Additionally, he must provide guidance to the research and development groups. This would be predicated on anticipated changes in the market and the need this may create for the modification of existing products or the creation of new ones.

Like forecasting, planning requires a very definite financial commitment. It is deceptive to think that a marketing plan can be generated without the expenditure of substantial funds. The extent to which this expense is incurred is in itself hard to identify specifically because too many intangibles enter into the composition of the final plan and its cost. The product manager had best recognize this and provide the necessary funds in his budgetary developments. As far as personal time is concerned, most product managers spend a large percentage of their job hours on planning. Some experts estimate that more than half the product manager's time should be spent in the planning function. But most product managers will say that they are not able to devote more than one-half their activities to it. At first glance, this may seem an insoluble problem. But the problem, which stems from a misunderstanding between expert and practitioner can be resolved.

A very basic element of planning is the assimilation of information, and here is the key to the problem. The product manager is in reality functioning as a planning manager every working moment that he is involved in his business activities. He is always garnering information, whether it be consciously or unconsciously, and assimilating this data, which is later translated directly or indirectly into the plan. In this sense he is operating as a planner for more than half his time. Viewed in this light, both the planning operation and the product manager, as a planner, become more meaningful concepts, as they become synchronous and complementary.

Considering the formal aspects of planning, namely, the writing and development aspects as they relate to the planning cycle, will help us to establish more definitive time parameters. Even here, it is artificial to impose any time restrictions; these will vary substantially, depending on the size of the product line, number of products involved, and the depth to which planning is executed in any given situation.

Suffice it to say that the product manager is a central figure in an operation that has planning as the issue, not time, although whatever time is devoted should be meaningful. Later in the book, we will comprehensively deal with planning and include some plan outlines, guides, and cycles.

One last thing to remember in planning: Don't plan to plan; *plan.*

A Job Description

It is best to avoid the rigidities of a formal job description for the product manager whenever possible. Where this is required, based on standard corporate operating procedures and the mandates that job descriptions will exist for all, then we must, of course, conform. And indeed, several firms have published job descriptions for their product managers with varying degrees of success. In examining these, however, one finds that they essentially revolve around our product management hexagram. If we keep these principal duties in mind, the more lengthy, detailed descriptions contained in formal job descriptions are merely local expostulations, predicated upon these responsibilities as they can be applied within the specific corporate structure. For those who wish to compare and analyze some of these, we have included three job descriptions in Appendix A.

In either event, with or without a job description, if the product manager is aggressive, efficient, and effective, he will eventually find himself deeply involved and committed to the basic operations we have discussed.

Assessing the Product Manager and His Job

After investigating the major elements of the product manager's job, we must in all candor ask ourselves: How do we know when we are doing a good product management job? This is an instance where the product manager finds himself in the unenviable position of having a job that basically has no criteria for evaluation. There should be no misunderstanding here. There really are no specific quantifiable criteria by which we are able to measure accurately the product manager's productivity and contribution. We can study profitability figures or gross sales; or number of products added or deleted; or implementation of forecasting techniques; manufacturing and quality control; or we can examine improvements in internal service functions, particularly those that involve products; or the informational flow, and the speeding up of product conception to marketing cycles. But meaningful as these may be, most defy precise quantitative assessment.

This is no blessing to the product manager. It is the lack of specific criteria that makes it sometimes difficult to build a case for product management or the product manager. So long as his attributes cannot be computed in strict dollars and cents, his justification remains nebulous. Either a salesman sells, or he doesn't. Examination of neatly printed statistics based on monthly, quarterly, or annual assessments, enables one to see at a glance whether he has or hasn't. The efficiency of the plant manager can be gauged through his production figures and the comparison of improvements and cost increases or decreases over a given period; the operations manager, in the increase of delivery speed, control of expenses, and curtailments of inventory or handling and shipping expense; the sales manager, through the control of cost of sales to cost of goods sold and the increase of sales per se. But the product manager must rely on less tangible benefits for the assessment of his worth.

Knowing that this problem exists doesn't exactly help us. Product management is not a form of management religion that can be taken on faith or moral value alone. Fortunately, this is not a totally dismal situation. Certainly, the subjective criteria are here, and with the sophistication of modern management, the significance of intangibles is more appreciated every year. More concrete assessments are possible, however, by examining these aspects:

Achievement of planned profits.

Cost and profit control.

Product line control.

Product life cycle, analysis and capitalization.

Product development and success of new products recommended.

Improved communication.

Improved supplies and sourcing.

More and better market information.

Wider competitive product knowledge base.

Increased market response and increased potential for response.

Centralized product planning.

Interestingly enough, these are just a few of the factors that can be considered. They do provide, however, the nucleus for assessing the product manager and his performance. Clearly, each becomes more apparent as he progresses in his particular firm, especially in those areas deemed most important by the company and to which he devotes most of his time.

3

Organizing
for Product Management

How do we implement effective product management either in an existing organizational structure or as a new function? The problems inherent in these situations differ considerably. If the product manager is to succeed, he must give careful consideration to all factors involved in the creation and fulfillment of his position.

Psychological considerations have great impact on the success or failure of a given operation. The real or imagined threat of obscurity, professional insecurity, resistance to change, resentment of that which is new, and suspicion of an unproven management technique are some of the factors that may be anticipated.

The product manager must be prepared to play a vital role in determining the success of the product management operation. He must be ready and able to be a personal salesman. This is vital to his overall effectiveness and, more especially, influential in certain specific areas. Obviously, it is particularly applicable in his coordinating function, as it is apparent that he is at the mercy of others when operating in this sphere. As a product management salesman, he must also be an educator, constantly bearing the product management banner. Without being a zealot, he must have zeal.

It is imperative to realize that product management must be integrated into the organization and, therefore, carefully planned for. It is unrealistic to decide that product management can be added to staff functions simply by adding a manager one day and having him operate the next. Both management and the product manager must be aware of the need for preliminary spadework and proceed accordingly.

Implementation of Product Management

When implementing product management within a given corporation, it is important to realize that there is no single approach. Rather, we are faced with a selection and have to determine the method best suited to achieving optimal results, consistent with management objectives. Again, this puts the burden clearly on management. It is its responsibility to determine what approach best fulfills its requirements—marketing, technical, financial, manufacturing, sales, research, development, or whatever—consistent with corporate objectives. Product management must then be used as deemed most effective, consistent with the attainment of these objectives. This ultimate authority is vested in top management; but it is the duty of the product manager, either initially when product management is being introduced or in those situations where it is being upgraded, to recommend organizational approaches suited to the attainment of these goals. The reasons for this may be stated:

1. As the nominal product expert he should be able to analyze the management structure as it exists and relates to the product and develop the most effective management operation structure to meet, or better, to exceed expressed management product needs.

2. The product manager is most knowledgeable of product management limitations and capabilities; therefore, he is better able to give objective formulation to organizational approaches.

3. He has the most intimate understanding of that rather ephemeral web he can weave, enabling him to attain group or departmental success. He therefore knows what he needs and what internal interconnections are required.

4. By participating, he creates his own effective, self-generated goals, which are often above corporation expectation.

5. As a member of fairly high-level management, but as one with little or no direct authority, he requires overt recognition and implicit

backing in the structuring of his own operation and in the establishment of departmental interrelationships.

After examining these claims, it may be easy to state what the product manager should do. Admittedly, it may still be difficult to see how we can do this within an organization without disrupting an apparently effective operation.

How do we, then, install a product manager, or produce the conditions for an existing product manager to come to grips with his responsibilities? Frequently management recognizes the problem but does not effectively cope with it. This is a critical but fair statement. Management is occasionally reluctant to face the problems that are inherent in trying to accomplish this. As a result, everyone remains confused, and the *status quo* prevails.

In considering product management within a given corporation, one must give careful scrutiny to all existing areas—whether functional or otherwise—not only from an organizational standpoint but with psychology and personalities included. Management should pause to reflect on whether or not it really wants product management. This question may seem irrelevant at this point, but nonetheless it is one that must be faced squarely by both the product manager and the general management. Implementation of the product management system involves a mutual commitment. It requires certain managerial latitudes that we have already seen transgress classical, functional, operational, and authoritative lines. Management must realize this and its potential impact on the rest of the organization. In giving this due thought, management should examine the questions raised in the following section as they relate to the organization of the business, organization of the product management group, the number of product managers, the expenditure to be made for product management, and, finally, whether to have product management at all.

Factors to Be Considered

Each of the factors should be examined in the context of corporate and, more specifically, marketing objectives and their translation into specific product management capabilities:

What do we want out of product management?
What do we want our product managers to do?
When do we want our product managers to do their jobs?
How do we want them to do them?
What, if any, restrictions are to be implemented?

What operational guidelines are to be established?

What expectations do we have for the specific contribution of product managers and product management?

What price are we willing to pay?

What general and what specific duties and responsibilities will be assigned to product management?

What authorities will be assigned?

What are the number and nature of products and brands?

What are our product objectives?

How long will we give for the job to be done?

How will we measure the effectiveness of our product management?

Since the answers to these questions are highly individual, relating as they do directly to specific corporate objectives, it is hardly worth considering them in more detail. Each is clear in its implications and involves nothing more complex than the application of several traditional criteria to product management, specifically as it would be required in a given business. Therefore, further elaboration is obviated.

However, a careful, objective analysis of these questions is required to enable both the product manager and top management to formulate a realistic product manager program. Such analysis will further provide for the structuring of an effective product management system that starts from a clear base.

Once this base is determined, prompt announcement of the product management operation follows. The initial introduction of the product management system will be vastly facilitated by this simple and inexpensive technique: Let those in the organization know about it. Communications is the number one problem of management. Properly handled, it is also the number one problem solver and problem forestaller.

Now that we have given due respect to the dangerous thought of challenging the necessity for product management, we can safely assume that top management will say yes; the only difficulty still confronting us is deciding just how to set it up. As this book is predicated on the assumption that its readers are already advocates (or partial advocates) of the system, we will not deal with further justification but proceed directly to a consideration of organizational approaches and their relationship to product management.

Organizational Approaches

Now that we have dealt with the broad background, we can attempt specificity. However, bear in mind that use of any one specific approach requires judicious consideration. We will examine some of the techniques that have been used in implementing product management within the "organization." In general, these will be appropriate with new or old organizations, or if product management is new to them or just being reevaluated for justification, expansion, or elimination.

Before we go on, one more vital and practical thought: We must learn to divorce ourselves from the rigid structural strictures that for years have represented the bases and parameters of organizations. Inflexible, established line and staff relationships have, in recent years, been subject to critical reexamination, as has the functional management organization. One is certainly justified to question rigidities where they exist, and more significantly, whether they should exist. There is no doubt that a staff or line function can be constructed and imposed within an organizational framework. It is even admitted that operationally this can be justified, but this does not mean that the structure does not deserve challenging.

This inflexibility may insert an artificial constriction, the imposition of which depends more or less on the constriction placed on traditional line or staff relations and responsibilities. This is of special concern since we know that we are not dealing with a fixed entity when we consider organization and business, but rather with a dynamic; and this dynamism conspires to place responsibility on management for constantly reexamining and revising its structures and managerial relationships.

The Challenges to Marketing

No one seriously questions the fact that marketing is a vital and dynamic force. But one of its failures is a lack of responsiveness within the demands of immediacy. Time lost because of this lack can be— and has been—incalculable. A constant reassessment of marketing in relation to the market and the total business operation must be made in order for a marketing group to remain successful.

This represents a considerable management problem as it implies that once an organizational relationship is established, it must be prepared to change. Moreover, such change is inevitable. A constant state of flux will prevail whence come the elements of stability and continuity required. The answer to both these questions, fortunately, is not negative, although it differs.

The first is answered by the objectives and operational guidelines established for the total business organization, the second, by the goals set to meet these objectives. This indicates that we give organization the position it warrants, but are aware that organization serves a purpose—the purpose of enabling the effective implementation of functions and services required to accomplish goals and objectives.

Organization is not the end. In a real sense it is not even the means. All of which means that it is far from sacrosanct and should be as fluid as the dictates of objective attainment require.

Similarly, from the management viewpoint, old precepts must be challenged where inadequacies are evident. This possible management heresy is nowhere more applicable than in product management, as it is a patent inadequacy to consider product management a mere staff or line function. For that matter, neither can we feel that once established and operational, the product group should not be re-examined constantly or be altered in the same sense in which the organization must be subject to examination and change.

The product manager is in the unique position of being simultaneously in a staff and a line position. His is primarily a staff position (as staff positions are usually defined), but he also has direct line authority, or should have, in the management of his own brand or products. This is a tenuous situation, close to the heart of the perennial controversy between responsibility and authority. To have line responsibility he must have line authority. We say that the product manager should have little or no authority, yet he does hold line responsibility—a patent contradiction.

We will attempt to clarify this by advocating the implementation of an authority and responsibility index. The index is based on a simple product management formula wherein we balance the product manager's line and staff functions with his responsibility and authority. Thus we can derive an authority flexibility that is really a dynamic relative absolute. This enables the product manager to exercise authority within reasonable guidelines established by management. He is therefore able to operate with responsibility and authority outside the restrictions normally conceived in the staff and line relationship. He could even exercise authority, albeit limited, in other functional areas. This dogma, reduced to management pragmatics, means he will function simultaneously as a staff and line manager; but his exercise of authority is a variable. The use and extent of authority will depend on extrinsic factors; the degree to which it is applied must be consistent with particular situational requisites. For our mathematicians here are two formulas for the Product Management Authority Responsibility Index (PARI), one for the staff and one for the line functions:

Staff Function: $\dfrac{\text{Responsibility}}{\text{Authority}} \times \dfrac{\text{management guidelines}}{\text{dictates of situation}} = \text{results}$

Line Function: $\dfrac{\text{Authority}}{\text{Responsibility}} \times \dfrac{\text{dictates of situation}}{\text{management guidelines}} = \text{results}$

Implementation of PARI places a very heavy burden on the product manager since it is imperative that he not exceed the authoritative limits of this delicate balance. It also represents a burden to management because its confidence, once placed, must be sustained. Without an all-out management commitment, product management cannot succeed.

Upper management is already conditioned to respond to such an operational necessity because product managers have been given overlapping line and staff responsibilities internally and in functional areas outside their normal spheres of direct operation. They could not have done this were the old line and staff parameters in force. The fences built around certain functional groups are gradually being lifted, allowing intercommunication that must be effected in order to have a dynamic marketing organization. When the product manager is allowed to function outside these narrow confines to make his influence more pervasive, it is a logical corollary that he have certain operational responsibilities outside his regular product or brand responsibility. It is extremely important that he use discretion in his approach toward these peripheral duties. He must also be cautious about overextending his authority.

Recognition of this need is evidenced by creation of the product director, product group manager or marketing director. This position is the outgrowth of limitations experienced in allowing additional authority to individual product managers. It permits additional authoritative function in the so-called product group, and is a portent of the future.

We cannot conclude this important subject without pointing out that vesting complete authority in the product manager is self-destructive and would probably prevent him from accomplishing his job effectively. For one thing, there are psychological barriers inherent in boss-subordinate relationships. For another, there may be conflicts where multiple product managers are involved. Unequivocal authority also has the effect of restricting a man from making completely objective, impersonal explorations of conditions or situations in which a nondictatorial resolution is required.

Once we understand these factors we can appreciate the practical need for a device such as the Product Management Authority Responsibility Index, because it provides a modicum of authority where essential without defeating the intrinsic value of an essentially nonauthoritative relationship. In this sense even the group product management approach does not violate the fundamental necessity for a nonauthority position, although it overcomes some of the severe limitations of too little representation and attenuated authority, which lies with the higher managerial echelon involved.

Now let us return to the point of organizing for product management.

Traditional Organization

We should not be awed by the word "organization." Organization is nothing more than an assembly of people which functions systematically in a manner suited to the accomplishment of business objectives. We may read in management textbooks that there are five basic organizational approaches:

1. Line
2. Line and staff
3. Pure functional
4. Line and functional staff
5. Line, functional staff, and committee

However, there are in reality as many variations as there are managers. These five major approaches relate to the organization of the total business entity. At present, the most common approach is probably the line, functional staff, and committee. This general concept should be kept in mind when considering the following remarks regarding the product management group.

While we consider product management as one segment of a functional area—marketing—marketing is integrated into the totality of the business operation through the organizational structure. This, as a practical consideration, means that much of the intraorganizational relations that will be utilized by the marketing group and by the product manager will to some extent be dependent upon the total organization structure. The structure of the overall organization then becomes at least the frame of operation. Many operational guidelines exist within the total structure and will provide the president with interdepartmental contact on a day-to-day basis in lower echelon product management operations.

This book is not intended to delve too deeply into the theory and practice of organization; therefore, we cannot theorize in much greater length. However, lest it be thought that only these approaches exist, or should it be confusing since few companies appear to be structured on any one of them, we must admit that in practice we seldom see a pure form of any of these five; conversely, we appear to see an endless variety of approaches. As business objectives vary, it is logical to find these variations; ultimately, the organization chosen must be the one suited to accomplish these objectives.

The Marketing Organization

Do not be confused by this term. This refers to the entire concept of a marketing organization, whether we are dealing with an essentially marketing-oriented business or merely with the marketing segment of a total enterprise. As already stated, we usually find product management reporting to the chief marketing executive and functionally associated with the marketing operation. From two viewpoints this is logical. In the overall marketing concept we see the needs of the marketing group having representation in every facet of the business operation from research and development to customer service. The product manager's job, while not restricted to a marketing operation, is by its very nature and evolution essentially a marketing technique. Either of these facets leads us back to integration of the product management operation in the marketing area.

However, a distinction should be drawn. If the product manager were to be concerned with nothing more than the traditional concerns of marketing, we would face the absurdity of having a product manager who does little more than the chief marketing executive could do directly, and either one could be obviated. It is inherent in the product management concept that the product manager is given far wider contacts and influence; primarily of importance in this context is his ability to cross organizational lines and operate in other functional areas such as manufacturing or finance without consideration of the limitations of the marketing function alone. This explains the caution signs on authority; even with PARI, we must be careful to establish management guidelines since other functional areas are involved.

Product Management in the Marketing Function

If we now attempt to sift all the organizational approaches to marketing, we can grade them roughly into three piles representing three principal approaches. Because product management may flourish in a variety of marketing organizational structures, we would be dealing with far too many if we did not attempt rough classification and then expound on the product management function within these divisions.

We can illustrate with traditional organizational charts the three main marketing organizational techniques: the general manager approach, the functional approach, and the product manager approach. This is done in Figure 4, and it will clarify the role of product management and its implementation in the marketing operation and, by extension, into the total business operation.

FIGURE 4

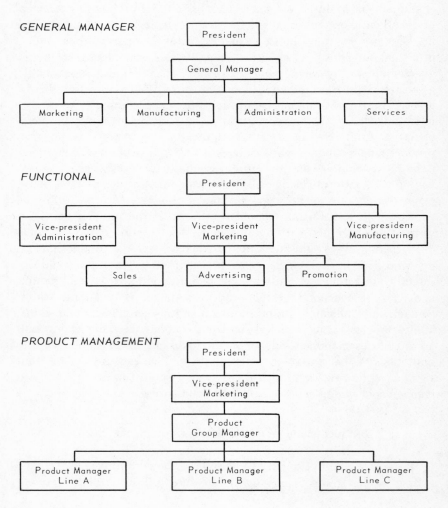

An organization, new or old, will fall into one of these three rough groupings. We must briefly reexamine each to understand them and the potential role of product management in them. Notice too that we have included identification for "the product manager approach." The relationship of this to other approaches will be clear from the descriptions that follow.

THE GENERAL MANAGER APPROACH

We deal with this approach first because it is the oldest and most readily understood. Product managers, if they exist (and they seldom do), report to marketing directors, who report to a general manager or directly to the general manager himself. The general manager, in turn, reports directly to divisional or higher level management in a non-multidivisional corporation.

The general manager is responsible as an individual profit center for either a divisional group of products or a specific series of products or brands within the total marketing entity, representing a subgroup of the complete line. In smaller companies he may have direct control over all the company's products. As such, he has direct or indirect lines of authority in all functional and operational areas.

This approach has been used for years and at one time enjoyed great favor. Today it is seldom encountered and when found, usually is not in its pure form. There have been comparisons made between this concept and the product manager in the sense that product managers have been represented as small-, medium-, or large-sized general managers, depending upon the number of products they manage. However, this comparison has to be made with the limitation that he (the product manager) functions in this capacity relative to his specific products or brands and has essentially no influence outside these parameters. Unlike the general manager, he would have no authoritative lines direct or indirect to other functional areas.

The general manager approach certainly brings to mind the Napoleonic image; and while it might be quite successful in certain situations, it does not possess the flexibility and subtlety necessary for modern business. In multidivisional and nonintegrated manufacturing or marketing organizations the general manager was found wanting on the scales of efficacy. The advisability of using a general manager as the vehicle by which to implement product management implies a modification of the normal general managership to allow the flexibility required by the product manager. Although not ideally suited to implementation of product management, the staid general manager approach can be livened up somewhat with the installation of a product manager, provided that sound rethinking of the general manager's relationship to the product manager and the product manager to the rest of the operation occurs first.

However, considering that general managers are marching off *en masse* to the great elephants' graveyard of management, we need not be concerned with implementing product management in this atmosphere.

THE FUNCTIONAL APPROACH

The second structure is based on a functional approach. This is a functional suborganization within a functional group. It is probably the most commonly encountered technique in contemporary marketing management. Just as in the functional approach to general or overall management, it is predicated within the marketing group on the same principle of specialization. In this structure the marketing unit is subdivided by the type of work done.

Figure 4 indicates most areas of traditional subdivision. We have provided a subdivision for product management, although a separate product manager and the product management approach itself may not necessarily exist in a functional marketing organization. It is indicated merely to llustrate the structure as it would prevail if product management were contained therein.

A very commonly encountered technique, the functional approach, is employed in both consumer and industrially oriented concerns. It also lends itself to those corporations that are dealing with government marketing as well. It is quite flexible and has served well in its adaptability to many organizations. There are some obvious coordination problems, where product management is not present, but it is an excellent foundation upon which to build, and provides optimum atmosphere in which to introduce the product management concept.

This versatile and productive technique has gradually become one of the most commonly encountered in effective marketing organizations. With the increased needs for flexibility and immediacy of response, division of marketing duties, based on specialization coordinated via product management, would appear to provide a solution to many marketing problems. With an intrinsic capacity for enlargement, this approach also enables expansion to meet added products, lines, or marketing operational needs, including such functions as market research and analysis, separate planning personnel, advertising specialists, and even administration or technical support people when necessary. Considering the accelerated rate of market change, this capacity for meeting the needs of change augur well for the future of the functional approach.

THE PRODUCT MANAGER APPROACH

In effect, the third approach is an expansion of the functional approach to include a full-scale product management system. It represents the evolution from a strictly functional marketing organization to one in which product management has been fully integrated. As such, the product manager's responsibilities and duties should be crystal clear from the product management hexagram and the details of his functional marketing responsibilities. It should also be clear that in a full-scale product management-oriented marketing group the extension of product management activities into other corporate functional areas is not tolerated but mandatory.

In this structure we are now prepared to take full advantage of the product manager, and he should be in a position to exercise the full spectrum of his abilities in the conduct of his job, thereby fulfilling all the potential inherent in the system. With these factors in mind, it is easy to visualize exactly what the product manager can do for the marketing group and the corporation. It is also easy to grasp the full nature of the interplays that must prevail in order to capitalize on his full range of contributions.

OTHER APPROACHES

There are numerous other approaches to organizing the marketing function. Their application depends largely upon the basic organization of the corporation, whether single or multidivisional, research or development oriented, marketing oriented, consumer or industrial market oriented, sales or product oriented, service or real product oriented, the short- and long-range corporate goals and objectives, and the self-conceived image of the corporation as a total business operation. All these factors must then be construed as they relate to management's approach to management.

Of the three primary alternatives that have been reviewed, it would appear (with no bias) that the product manager approach lends itself best to almost any type of organization emphasis. Regardless of the specifics of structural relationships or the general nature of business orientation, this concept serves its multiphased purpose. What would vary is the emphasis placed upon the product manager's specific responsibilities, just as the specific responsibilities and emphasis of the entire marketing group must vary, depending upon corporate orientation. One of the main distinctions is that market orientation would relate back to the three classic market segments long used in their identification: consumer, industrial, and government.

To further comprehend the relationship of product management as it would be integrated into a marketing organization operative in any one of these three markets, we can consider the major duties of the product (or brand) manager as they would be emphasized or de-emphasized. This will also serve to distinguish further between product and brand management. While it may be a rather broad generalization, it is not too simplistic to consider that in the majority of instances we find product managers, as such, operating in industrial and governmental marketing operations, whereas the true brand manager is primarily involved in consumer marketing.

The following tabulation of duties, which is a little more specific than the broad guidelines of the product management hexagram, serves the twofold purpose of showing this relationship in these three areas and identifies the major differences in product and brand management as they would apply to such segmentation. In actuality, they also would apply in the basic distinctions between product and brand managers regardless of market identification. In this list, the plus sign signifies major emphasis and the minus sign means minor emphasis.

Responsibility	Industrial (Product Manager)	Consumer (Brand Manager)	Governmental (Product Manager)
Profit	+	+	+
Coordination	+	+	+
Sales			
Development	−	+	−
Promotion	−	+	−
Assistance	+	+	+
Direction	−	+	−
Planning	+	+	+
Consolidation	+	+	−
Customer service	−	+	−
Merchandising	+	+	−
Competition	+	+	+
Manufacturing	+	−	+

Responsibility	Industrial (Product Manager)	Consumer (Brand Manager)	Governmental (Product Manager)
Engineering	+	−	+
Training	−	+	−
Market			
Analysis	+	+	−
Research	+	+	−
Planning	+	+	+
Forecasting			
Profit	+	+	+
Sales	+	+	−
Market	+	+	−
Inventory	+	+	−
Distribution	+	+	−
Advertising	−	+	−
Promotion	−	+	−
Product			
Research contact	+	−	+
Development contact	+	+	+
Test marketing	−	+	−
Introduction	+	+	+
Planning	+	+	+
Packaging	−	+	−
Control	+	+	+
Modification/			
improvement	+	+	+
Pricing	+	+	+
Quality	+	+	+
Legal aspects	+	+	−
Technical service	+	+	−
Consumer research	−	+	−
Operations research	+	+	+
Purchasing	+	−	−
Systems	+	+	+
Computer applications/			
services	+	+	+

It is also worth noting that the product manager's reporting level is extremely high within the organizational structure. He usually reports directly to the chief marketing executive or a product group manager (product director, marketing director) who, in turn, reports to the marketing chief. This is a cogent consideration since it implies his elevated stature within the managerial hierarchy as visualized by upper management. Operationally, this is a distinct advantage, putting him in the position of being able to communicate constantly with higher management without recourse to intermediaries. This status is a direct consequence of the importance attributed to the product management function and is indicative of the relative position product management enjoys regardless of organizational specifics.

Before leaving this subject, we should also realize that despite the way organization charts are written or drawn, it is what is not written between reporting lines that is often more important than what is communicated in the little black boxes. No one knows this better than the product manager, and certainly he will more often find himself functioning out of "his box" than in. Someone once aptly said: "He must have the ability to cross managerial lines without crossing managers."

Organization of the Product Management Function

Having dispensed with the overall complexities of where to place product management within the organization, we must turn our thoughts to organizing the product management function itself. Naturally, the exact approach will again vary, depending largely on the number of products and brands, as well as marketing objectives and managerial preference. It also depends on the capabilities and abilities of the individuals involved. In a highly individualistic management area, this is inevitable. While it may defy some traditionalists, "the man makes the job" is a valid premise in many cases; it is most assuredly true in the product management field.

In considering possible selection of organization for the product management function, reference should be made again to many of the factors recommended in the original analysis of the needs for introducing product management. The conclusions reached in this connection will indicate general requirements for number of managers and a basic idea of division of labor. When initiating product management, bear in mind that it is mandatory to pay careful attention to the required number of product managers and support staff. Also essential to successful performance is the built-in ability for expansion.

It behooves us to consider broad principles rather than detailed specifics since the product management approach can be tailored to meet the highly individual needs of companies. However, we can distinguish three approaches:

1. An individual product manager reporting to the marketing executive.

2. Several product managers reporting to the marketing executive

3. Several product managers reporting to a product group manager. The techniques can be illustrated accordingly, as shown in Figure 5. Before we consider the characteristics of these structures, we should realize that the product manager, although he deals with products or brands, can be assigned products predicated on several criteria:

By specific products—pure product assignment.

By industry—specific products for specific industries.

FIGURE 5

INDIVIDUAL PRODUCT MANAGER

SEVERAL PRODUCT MANAGERS

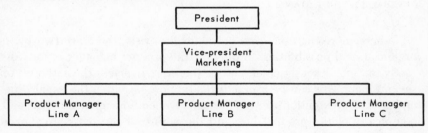

PRODUCT GROUP MANAGER APPROACH

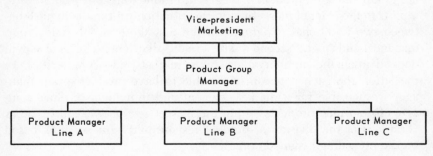

By market segment—specific products for market segments.

By geographic distribution—products in specific territories.

By consumer—direct sales, resale, co-manufacturer, distributor, retail, wholesale, etc.

Whichever basis is employed for dividing the product lines, which obviously only occurs where there is more than one product manager in a specific marketing group, the effect on the structuring of the product management operation is obviously there. It is conceivable that in a large multiproduct line operation two or more product group managers or product directors can exist, each of which can have one or more product managers reporting to him.

Individual Product Manager

Where only one product manager exists, he will report directly to the marketing executive or general manager. No difficulties of intermediate communication usually prevail, and this constitutes the simplest expression of the product management operation.

Several Product Managers

Where more than one product manager exists, there are two basic organizational possibilities. In the first, the product manager reports directly to the marketing chief, and he therefore oversees the activities of several men. This can be a practical situation, provided the usual principles of overextension are not broken. Depending upon the size and complexity of the product line and the nature of the marketing function, it is a tenable situation.

In the second instance, several product managers report to a product group manager, product manager, or product director, who, in turn, reports to the chief of marketing. In this situation we can distinguish between two additional variations. In the first there is only one group manager, and in the second there is more than one. The choice will depend upon the number of products, markets, and complexities. In the latter approach it becomes possible to have product group managers responsible for a market segment and individual product managers for specific products within the market section. Of course, other variations of the division of product responsibility are possible, based on the preceding assigned criteria.

In either event we are dealing with a more complex operation, one in which the product group manager is to function more as a manager of men than of products. He becomes truly the management expert in the field of products rather than the true corporate product expert.

THE PRODUCT GROUP COORDINATOR

The evolution of large-staffed product management groups has led to a recently created product management position: the product group coordinator. If we visualize the product group manager as being primarily responsible for the efficient operation of the total product group, acting in a managerial capacity relative to this group, we can see the product group coordinator as that person responsible for the internal integration of the operation.

As the size of the group expands, uniformity of operational approaches becomes increasingly important, as do internally developed systems particularly suited to the special needs of product management. It becomes the responsibility of the coordinator to develop and implement them. He also acts as a central clearinghouse for those functions that may require the action of specific managers, thereby alleviating confusion in direction of incoming work from outside the group. The coordinator collects and compiles these diverse efforts when more than one product manager is engaged in a project that requires consolidation. It is also possible for him to assume many of the more routine administrative duties of the product managers, thereby providing them with more pure product management time.

While to some extent this may appear to be a duplication of services already available on an accommodation basis, employing the normal administrative support facilities contained in other operational or functional areas, this is not really the case. The turn-around time required for reaction and action in product management is critical. Reliance on other than self-contained services, readily available and fully knowledgeable of special requirements, can be disastrous. Also, the product group manager is often an experienced product manager elevated from the ranks that provided him with essential technical experience. Ultimately, the product group becomes its own best administrative instrument, requiring the proper staff to accomplish these added duties.

Since we are now dealing with two additional managers in the product management scheme, it may be helpful to contrast their major duties by summarizing them:

Function	*Major Responsibilities*
Product group manager Group product manager Product director	Group administration Product profit Product marketing policies and strategies Planning
Product group coordinator	Departmental services Consolidated activities Planning Coordinated functions Departmental administrative functions
Product manager	Product Market Profit Forecasting Planning Coordination

After giving full weight to all factors, one should be able to implement the product management approach in virtually any organizational situation. In light of the variations possible within the specific structure of the product management group itself, management is provided with a viable instrument capable of meeting the needs of change.

Product managers too have an obligation. Change challenges them as well as management. Product management must remain alert to the needs of marketing and management, and the far-thinking product manager will ponder the requirements of the future.

4

The Product Manager
as Manager

Up to this point we have considered product management from a standpoint of structure and organization. Now it is time to discuss its actual implementation. Once the product manager has been installed either individually or as a member of a product group, he departs from the lofty realm of management theoretics and comes to the practical challenge of his daily tasks. This poses three problems. The product manager must be (1) conversant with overall management principles; (2) able to apply them in the context of his position; (3) capable of functioning with responsibility in both line and staff areas. This is clearly a complex situation.

Product Manager's Sources: Past, Present, and Future

Sometimes the newly appointed manager is so product centered in his thinking that he tends to lose sight of his managerial responsibilities. No amount of product expertise can take the place of fundamental management principles and a clear recognition of the need to use them in product management operations. Of course, it is somewhat difficult to translate many traditional attitudes into the requirements of the product management function, for there are several aspects of product management that defy conventional management approaches. We must not overstate the case either way.

In addition to the principal duties and responsibilities enumerated in the product management hexagram, the product manager has customary managerial responsibilities relative to his corporation, supervisors, co-workers, and subordinates. Occasionally, product managers have been criticized for lack of balance, the problem being an overemphasis of their product functions as opposed to fulfillment of their more broadly based managerial obligations. This is excusable to the extent that most product managers are not recruited from experienced management personnel. They have been selected from sales, finance, manufacturing, engineering, or marketing rather than from the hordes of business management graduates. This practice has been based on a sensible rationale, for the experience required for effective product management can only be obtained through annealment in the fires of business experience. Specific academic training has also been lacking, a situation that contributes to the difficulties of recruitment from business schools. In the future this will probably be less of a problem, first because the product manager's function, which until now has been somewhat vague and misunderstood, is becoming crystalized; and second, because product management courses in business schools, management training programs, and in-house educational facilities are becoming increasingly available.

While it now appears advantageous to favor experienced men, it is harsh judgment indeed to say that a business graduate is less qualified for the simple reason that product management, per se, has not stabilized to the point of establishing clear educational or functional criteria. Recruitment practices will change as greater management expertise becomes essential to the product manager's job. At present it is easier to train the product manager in the necessary intricacies of management operations than attempt to train an academically oriented management graduate in the technical areas normally involved in effective product management.

But the day is soon coming when product management science will require management specialization of the product area, enabling specific product management training. When this occurs, the shift from pragmatic, experience-based product managers to expert product managers, academically trained and practically experienced, will occur. Naturally, the product manager will always need a deep knowledge of his product and market, this is the core of his existence. However, the harmonious integration of product management expertise in a specialized management discipline coupled with requisite technical knowledge will ultimately constitute the optimum product management background.

Naturally, the managerial-technical balance that is required will vary in relation to both product management application and the nature of the total business operation. This equilibrium is inherent operationally in the organization and can only be determined and implemented on an individual corporate basis. Neither concept negates the other; rather, optimal emphasis and selection will synergistically create the whole. The total would exceed the sum of its parts.

Of primary concern in the approach taken toward organizing the product management operation is the nature of the market being served. We are all familiar with industrial, consumer, and government market segmentation. Each of these markets has its individual characteristics, and the nature of the marketing effort is distinctive in each. Product managers should be thoroughly familiar with the basic nature of these markets so that they are able to approach them with a fundamental awareness of suitable techniques. This does not mean that there is no room for innovative marketing tactics. It is, however, necessary to be knowledgeable first.

The nature of the market has changed vastly in recent years, both relatively and absolutely. Perhaps more important is the exponential acceleration that is occurring with an incredible and unpredictable effect on scientific, technological, and sociological evolution, with a resulting impact on the marketing operation. Clearly, the evolution of marketing precepts and the relationship of the marketing effort to the total business effort has been revolutionary. This was predicated on just such changes and a resultant pressure on business to find new ways to respond, survive, and prosper.

The awareness of the average consumer (whoever that may be) in areas that were completely unknown only a few years ago creates extreme demands on the marketing executive, and the marketing effort must alter to keep pace with these trends. Service, quality control, brand awareness, advertising consciousness, and the tremendous improvements in reciprocal communication between the consumer and the manufacturer have all been factors in this change. The sum of this is the development of dynamic marketing that with anticipated change can only become more frenetic. Marketing is faced with the challenge of anticipating market conditions and then devising the internal managerial and external marketing regimes that will be best suited to cope with these situations, capitalizing on them when possible.

This is a growing problem because the market is expanding through population increases, and technological achievements create alterations at a dizzying rate. Subsequent to World War II, which seems to be a turning point, scientific change and the impact of technological attainments on the social structure generated an unprecedented culture of change. And the rate of this change has increased, with no reasonable expectation of alteration in the future. Quite to the contrary, we can be assured that the future will be different from the present and past in respect to both market availability and volatility.

All this has far-reaching impact on the role of business in society, which will undoubtedly cause it to alter more than it has in the past two generations. The marketing structure that will ultimately survive is the one that has the capacity to meet the demands of these changes.

These factors are of grave concern to everyone involved in the marketing activity. While there is little reason to suspect that we will ever differentiate in other than industrial, consumer, and government market segments, there is certainly every reason to believe that the mechanisms by which we market in these areas will continue to change as they have in the past. The broad-based operational criteria that have long prevailed in doing business in these segments are only to some extent true today. While we must consider these basics as a foundation for orientation, the specifics may alter as well as emphasize change, as do the socioeconomic conditions and the technistructure. Business will continue regardless of change, but it is from these contemporaneous models that future actions will be initiated.

INDUSTRIAL MARKET

While we can argue whether or not the industrial market existed prior to the Industrial Revolution, no one can deny its contemporary significance. As a major classification, the industrial market includes those goods that are not classified as consumer products or those products that are usually required in the production of other goods. Examples are manufacturing equipment, operating supplies and services, raw materials, chemicals, building materials, agricultural products, parts, and fabricated and semifabricated equipment.

The industrial market is also characterized by goods that are generally purchased in large quantities, and the ratio of producers to consumers is relatively small. Selling is frequently direct from producer to industrial customer, and purchases are often made on contractual bases.

Although competitive pricing is a reality in some sectors, the industrial market has a relatively stable price structure. Because of contract customer relationships, many industrial products are specifically geared for individual large customers, making this a highly specific industry in many instances. These considerations are quite important to the product manager since they mean that he often operates on low profit margins and high volumes; the value volume relation of cost to unit is extremely critical.

Also, since he is dealing with few customers, gains or losses of individual accounts can severely affect total sales and profits with the correlated impact on manufacturing, inventory, warehousing, distribution, and the entire gamut of integrated operations. There are, of course, exceptions, particularly where heavy equipment at great expense is involved. In those cases, large profits may be generated on a single or on a few units sold. However, the sensitivity of profit to units sold, though inversed, is just as critical. The product manager must closely follow all of his major accounts. The concept we will discuss later—management by exception—is an important principle for the industrial product manager.

In Chapter 3 we itemized several major responsibilities, contrasting them by industry segments relative to product and brand management. In considering the role of the product manager in an industrially market-oriented company, we can elaborate somewhat further by examining the functional responsibilities of the industrial product or brand manager. The number of plus signs indicate the increasing responsibility or involvement.

Activity	Emphasis
Product	++++
Planning	++++
Forecasting	++++
Market analysis	++++
Profit	++++
Competition	++++
Advertising	++
Promotion	++
External contacts	++
Sales contacts	+
Purchasing	++
Control functions	+++
Travel	++
Training	+

CONSUMER MARKET

As we are all consumers at one time or another, we tend to think that we know what the consumer market is. However, since it is one thing to know it as a consumer and another as a supplier, it is worthwhile to consider the subject in more detail.

There are three general subdivisions of the consumer market from a consumer-purchaser standpoint. Each of these is extremely important in relation to marketing and selling consumer goods.

Specialty goods. As the name states, specialty goods are those premium items that are usually identified by brand name, and the customer will often go to great lengths to seek out the particular product or brand he wants. From a selling standpoint, specialty goods are easier to sell because they meet a specific demand—real, imagined, or created. Their identity must first be created through consumer consciousness, and in order to keep them in the specialty range, specific marketing tactics are required. However, once customer demand has been created, it is difficult to displace. Being sold usually on a brand-name basis, it has a definite imagery of its own. Distribution of such a product is often limited to recognized dealers or "specialty shops." This further enhances the prestige aspect and illustrates the marketing mystique at its finest hour. More recently, the somewhat opprobrious but accurate label "snob appeal" has been attached to those products that appeal to a hauteur that lurks in the hearts of many.

Not all specialty products, of course, fall into this category. Thus the marketing effort must be oriented accordingly, and different distribution and promotional activities employed. The product manager must assess market potential, market share, and product life cycle in a manner that he would not use in approaching other market segments. Competition in this market is more often indirect than direct. He must also be seriously concerned over problems in marketing his new products since it is not easy to establish a new specialty product, and such a market can be readily saturated. There are only so many Cadillacs.

Shopping goods. The shopping goods market is comparatively large. It includes those products that a consumer buys with relative frequency. Examples are furniture, clothing, jewelry—in other words, general merchandise. Market fluctuations are frequent and characteristically involve such transitory factors as fashion and social trends. Consequently, product life can be short, particularly if the product involved is based on the ubiquitous fad. On the other hand, there are many reasonably stable areas in this market, such as foods, clothing, and furniture, which of necessity are relatively durable in terms of "need." This is predictable, as many of the products included are fundamental requirements and represent items that are repeatedly purchased. While individual products may be short-lived, there is the corresponding advantage that product innovation and total product substitution by new product addition is readily feasible; and as a technique, product managers can continually replace old products with new to perpetuate their position. Packaging "eye appeal" is exceedingly important, and the prudent product manager must recognize the importance of impulse buying and take full advantage of it.

Because it is such an available "open" market that depends directly on the public, it is dynamic, fickle, and highly competitive. Advertising and promotional aspects are of basic concern, and successful companies spend money to make money. The product manager must be sensitively attuned to the heart of his market, and it is an erratic pulse indeed.

Commodity goods. Another large segment of the consumer market is the convenience or commodity goods area. This segment involves products that individual consumers purchase repeatedly; they usually require relatively small personal expenditure. Such items might be newspapers, books, tobacco, personal products, and comestible items. Many of the marketing problems and opportunities parallel those in the shopping goods area, and again we deal with a highly competitive, brand-conscious market.

On the positive side, however, this segment is so large that there is room for continuous entry of new products and suppliers. This, of course, is a mixed blessing, as it means that all motivational and behavioral techniques developed and used in recent years must be constantly refined and reapplied to maintain a position. Wide product diversification and far-flung customers require careful consideration of geographical distribution and costs. Often the producer will be supplying through a distributor or wholesaler, which involves whole new series of marketing contacts. Dealing through distributors or wholesalers entails well-known obligations and often involves contractual relations predicated on a sales-supplier basis. The product manager will, of course, be involved in these aspects, both directly and indirectly. Where he controls distribution, his role is obvious, where control lies elsewhere, he functions as counselor or coordinator.

As a last word on this market, we should mention price. All consumers are bargain hungry, which means this is a highly price-conscious, price-sensitive market. The product manager often makes or breaks his product through price. It is a difficult but critical balance between profit and volume related to selling price. Manipulation through price strategies is one of the most elemental tactics the product manager can use in his techniques of marketing in this field.

THE NEW CONSUMER MARKETS

While the foregoing have been the traditional consumer market segments of importance, there is a recent trend toward the identification of two new major sectors. The first, and ultimately the larger of the two is the convenience market; the second, the familiar entertainment market. Both of these are outgrowths of sociological changes; the advent of vastly increased leisure hours and relative affluence make it possible to couple time and money, thereby creating an entirely nonutilitarian consumer market. These areas combined encompass what could become the largest segment for market expansion in the future.

1. Convenience market. In many respects the convenience market owes its origin to the social evolution of the female. The changing status of women in our society has been radical, and we now find the phenomenon of a working housewife not only common, but almost expected. While originally this was necessitated by a relatively higher earning capacity for young women as opposed to young men, this practice gradually expanded to encompass the nonessential working wife, wherein additional monies are earned merely for leisure-time activities or out of housewifely ennui.

Either way this resulted in internal household pressures that have been relieved through the availability of prepackaged culinary goods and easy care products, to mention two obvious examples. A revolution in the textile industry was generated through such requirements as minimum or no-iron clothing, permanent press resins, soil release finishes, and a whole host of accelerated, improved cleaning compounds. While these have had a tremendous impact on the consumer market, they have also had a less apparent but incalculable influence on those industries supplying the products that are used in the production of these consumer goods. The impact on chemical, textile, and allied industries is immeasurable. This is a good example of a correlated impact on the total economy that can be the outgrowth of just one major consumer market innovation.

There is no indication that the trend toward convenience products will diminish. Quite the contrary, while originally the main purpose served by such items was directly utilitarian, they are now household expectations. As the family becomes more accustomed to less effort, it refuses to go back to old ways; there is thus vented a self-generating interest in convenience articles that portends a fantastic growth potential. This provides an increasing and profitable market, for premium prices usually prevail; also, the consumer seems to be more than willing to pay for his new-found ease. This can mean more profit as well as more opportunity.

A segment of this segment is the "do-it-yourself" market. We are all familiar with the available household "do-it-yourself" products and projects, the appeal of which does not always rely solely on the notion that it is cheaper to do it yourself. Consumers are even more persuaded by the satisfaction of having "fixed it themselves," the simple "hobby" aspect, and their inability to find skilled labor to do the job in the first place.

From whichever vantage, it is an important market, and one in which the elements of both convenience marketing and the appeal to the fix-its can be combined; the easier we can make the project, the more appealing it is.

Again we have premium pricing. It is a market that is vital, vibrant and increasing at a rate far beyond expectation. The challenge to the product or brand manager in these markets lies not so much in channels of distribution and the more conventional marketing concerns, but in the need for innovation and creativity. No one would have thought of packaging half the products we now package in aerosol containers until a daring few tried it and met with such success that we can now buy anything from toothpaste to contraceptives that save us the trouble of squeezing the tube. Although new products are constantly fed into the consumer stream, more are demanded. A creative marketing organization that can anticipate market needs and offer products in either convenience or do-it-yourself forms generates for itself an assured position. However, as with many other market areas, it is highly competitive and requires alert, responsive management.

2. *Entertainment market.* In the second of our new market areas we again deal with a viable entity. The recent emphasis on leisure activity and the need to be entertained has created a whole host of new product possibilities.

It wasn't too many years after the turn of the century that the be all and end all of existence was the expectation of a chicken in every pot on Sunday. It now seems to be two cars in every garage, one portable radio, one nonportable radio, two TV sets, one phonograph, one "home entertainment center," several cameras, projectors, and assorted sports paraphernalia. This is not an entirely unexpected situation since people are intrinsically energetic and simply do not like having nothing to do. The void of work time therefore has to be made up for with play time.

It is easier to find entertainment outside one's self than to generate it for one's self. Hence the creation of this market.

Again, the existence of this market is extremely challenging. Product or brand management is now in a position where innovation and creativity are the key words—fertile ground, indeed, for the modern marketing concept to flourish. This market is exciting and rewarding since profits are reasonably high. An excellent example of a company that capitalized magnificently on both segments is the Polaroid Corporation when it added convenient self-developing film for its entertaining camera.

While on the subject of new markets, let's not forget the youth market. Probably the most volatile and dynamic of all markets, we had better not dismiss it lightly. Predictions for a population shift to the below-25 group, with a consequent alteration in spending distribution and power, are awesome.

Actually, directing product activities geared to the teenage or youth markets applies to all segments of the consumer markets we've discussed. They have created a spillover into every part of the market and therefore constitute a double concern. How do we sell to young people, and what effect will they have on consumer products and policies in the adult fields? The impact of youth has been great and will probably continue to grow. Product managers take note.

From all of this we can see that consumer marketing requires an orientation substantially different from that required in the industrial or government market. These requirements are summarized as follows, with the addition of plus signs showing increased responsibility or involvement.

Activity	Consumer market	Industrial market
Brand identification	++++	+
Advertising	++++	++
Promotion	++++	++
Test marketing	++++	++
Trials	+++	++
Personal contacts	+++	+
Innovation	++++	++
Dependence on fads	+++	+
Price sensitivity	++++	++
Controls	++	++++
Quality	++	++++
Specifications	++	++++
Travel	++	++
Product	++++	++++
Competition	++++	+++

GOVERNMENT MARKETING

The term "government marketing" immediately evokes the image of dealing with a vast bureaucratic organization. Too often however we think only in terms of the federal government and lose sight of large similar markets in state and municipal agencies. They too, of course, are government operations and require application of the basic techniques applied in dealing with governmental institutions. Some prime requisites are substantial emphases on contractual obligations, which very closely relate to quality specifications and time limitations. The product manager who functions in this industry must be technically oriented and an expert in some scientific or engineering discipline. This is one of the main distinctions between product management operation and industrial or consumer operations.

Often the product manager finds himself involved in the government's product much in the manner of a project manager. He will be responsible from initial research and development stages through to completion and offering of the final product. He will also negotiate its sale and remain closely allied to the continuous programs of quality control and engineering requirements necessary to maintain the product after acceptance.

The successful government bid involves many negotiations and a substantial commitment of time and money. While we are dealing with a market that has competition, as all do, it is usually of a somewhat simpler nature. There are fewer competitors, the limits and capabilities of the contenders are known to one another, and countermeasures, strategies, and tactics can be developed. Also, once the contract is awarded, it is in a sense guaranteed business until it is time for the next negotiations or the opening of new bids.

In another sense, government business is unique because it is usually on a bid-and-award basis, meaning that industry can or cannot participate to the degree it sees fit. Profitability is a problem, and the product manager is in an unusual position since his profit is essentially predetermined and fixed with little variation after the business is obtained. If, for unforeseen circumstances, profit alterations arise, the company will gain or lose, depending upon appropriate management or mismanagement. This is a very critical factor since once the price is established it is not alterable. Therefore, there is a very heavy investment in preliminary planning and a thorough and absolutely accurate costing. All of these commitments are expensive.

While many of these negative aspects militate against bidding for government business, it must be understood that this business can be quite profitable and extremely valuable to the bidder. The vast sums expended by the government certainly indicate the magnitude of this market. It is clear that in order to participate in such an activity, the product manager must be more scientifically and technically oriented than he is in many other marketing areas. He becomes, in effect, a product or project engineer, and his more traditional managerial duties are subordinate to primary technical or engineering requirements.

As we have done with both industrial and consumer marketing, we can summarize the distinctive features of government product management, using the same hierarchy of plus signs for degree of involvement:

Activity	Emphasis
Product	++++
Planning	+++
Forecasting	+++
Market	++
Profit	++++
Competition	++
Advertising	+
Promotion	+
External contacts	++
Control	++++
Specifications	++++
Tolerances	++++
Quality	++++

Product Management Assignments

Assignments of specific product management responsibility can be predicated on several criteria. Selection depends on the nature of the business organization, number of products or brands, and allowable financial expenditures. Where economics permit, the maximum number of personnel should be employed, consistent with business requirements. As stated before, product management requires a definite commitment in order to be effectively implemented, and this applies as much to staffing as to other factors.

Our concern here, however, is that the correct approach will be taken in assigning product responsibility, assuming that the appropriate number of product managers are available. Assignment can be based on several approaches.

Product. This is a pure and simple case. A product manager is assigned all the company's products or, in those instances where there are multiple product managers, each is given responsibility for selected products only.

Product line. In this case product managers are assigned specific lines of products and individual product managers are then responsible for the entire but specific line.

Brand. Here the manager is assigned a brand or series of brands and is responsible accordingly. We have already contrasted product and brand management, and by now the basic differences should be clear.

Trade. This is another way of saying that the product manager is oriented by the market served. In such a structure products marketed to specific trades are segregated and the manager then handles those within a segment—the agricultural chemicals product group, the cosmetic product group or whatever the categories are.

Geographic. In this instance the product manager is given a range of products as offered in certain defined geographical areas, such as eastern district or southern district.

Source. In this case the product manager is responsible for products predicated upon their source within the company. Examples are product manager for purchased products, distributor products manager, agency product manager, or self-manufactured products.

Project. Product management by project is not often encountered. It best lends itself to highly research-oriented organizations or situations, or in government marketing. In this instance it is apparent that the product manager assumes responsibility for those products associated with a specific project—one that is naturally highly product-oriented.

New product development. A product manager assignment based on the needs for the development of new products is a relatively new concept indicative of the sophistication evolving. It clearly recognizes the needs for special management to insure the success of the new product. When one considers the high cost of researching, developing, and marketing new products in many fields, it is hardly an expensive insurance policy. In this structure, once the product reaches preset sales or maturity levels, it is usually transferred to the more normal product management area.

In addition, it is possible to have combinations of the foregoing approaches, particularly when a product group manager or product director system is involved. In such a situation the product director is responsible for the total management operation offered by the firm, but his individual product managers can be structured on a brand, trade, product, or other basis. This is often the approach found in large concerns operating in diverse markets where there are a number of products offered to several distinct trade segments or separate markets. In such a structure the individual product managers will be responsible for those products directed to that particular market or trade segment, thereby combining the approaches of both total product management and segmented responsibility. This can be further refined by having the specific product line manager serve under a market-oriented product group manager.

Organizational Relationships

We have already stressed that the product manager must be fully aware of the total organizational entity; and he must understand corporate as well as marketing objectives. By now it is obvious that he must also maintain a close relationship to the total operation in order to accomplish his own strategies and objectives

At the same time, the product manager is not working in a vacuum, his department is also a service group. This is a somewhat ironic situation since it is admittedly difficult to visualize a line and staff function that can also simultaneously operate as a service unit. This is, thankfully, a problem more semantic than real, as we do not mean to imply that the product manager is a serviceman as we traditionally think of it. Rather the product manager in the discharge of his duties does in effect serve other functional areas, in particular those within the marketing group. In this way he provides product information and documentation to the sales and marketing forces; and he distributes sales and marketing data both internally and externally. The product manager is also a constant source of information on competition, market, and the relative interactions thereof; and he formulates countermeasures on product and market response.

He also operates in a service function where he acts as planner, since he is often the source of relevant information in the development of the total plan. Service relationships can further be envisioned when we consider him as the channel for product modification or for the resolution of product claims and complaints, an activity that we will review in some detail later in the book. And, lastly, he is both seeking and rendering service whenever he functions in his coordinative responsibilties.

The streets of interrelationship, however, are all two-way; never totally self-reliant, he needs as much as he gives.

Coordinating Responsibilities

The role of product management in coordination is so fundamental to the product manager's position that we have indicated it as one of the principal areas in which he operates; and we have identified it as one of the key elements in the product management hexagram. The enormity of this responsibility can more readily be appreciated by examining some of the areas in which the product manager touches base with other functional groups. Whether he becomes involved with each one and the extent of such contact depends on the size of the corporation and the nature of his responsibilities. However, all areas must be considered, for often the product or brand manager will find himself involved with each one. Moreover, he may have to deal with them simultaneously on different levels and to varying extents.

In the next chapter we deal in depth with the tools and techniques of product management. One of these is personal contact. It would be well worth the time to refer back to this section after reading that chapter.

Remember too that these functional areas will be calling on the product manager for information and services essential to their operations; this give-and-take is the epitome of the interrelationships that form the nucleus of effective product management.

Here are the operational and functional areas of product management concern:

Marketing	Personnel
Market research	Legal
Product management	Patent
Planning	Trademark
Sales	Application
Advertising	Manufacturing
Promotion	Technical service
Inventory control	Administrative services
Research	Engineering
Development	Accounting
Electronic data processing	Finance
Office services	Traffic
Systems	Library
Purchasing	Sales service
Intercorporate relations	Toxicology

At first glance it may seem redundant to indicate that the product manager is involved in some areas in which he is also a direct component, for instance, marketing, market research, advertising, sales, promotion, and product management. However, in a multiproduct or multidivisional entity the product manager is frequently not only involved in these areas as they relate to his specific product(s), but as they relate to all products of all divisions. This means that he must consider his efforts and activities in the totality of the entire corporate effort; hence the reference to such areas.

Since most product managers have at least a general familiarity with the functions of these groups and their relationships, there is little need to go into specific detail. Some general indications of the duties of these departments as well as indications of the key relationships to the product manager can be helpful. These factors are listed below.

Key Functional, Operational, and General Areas
of Product Management Contact

Area	Relationships
Marketing	Strategies, planning, pervasive contacts, sales, all aspects.
Market research	Problems, types of markets, information gathering, market segmentation, valuation, analysis, forecasting, model development, consumer needs, new product recommendation trends.
Product management	Objectives, goals, strategies, interrelationships, conflicts.
Planning	Objectives, goals, strategies, action programs, corporate and divisional, interrelationships, coordination.
Sales	Organization, expenses, selections, motivation, territories, compensation, evaluation, as sources of information as technical guidance, product selection, key product emphasis, profit.
Advertising	Role in marketing, possibilities and limitations, budgeting, media selection, assessing effectiveness, planning, product selection, coordination, control, and direction.
Promotion	Role in marketing, possibilities and limitations, budgeting, media selection, assessing effectiveness, planning, selection, coordination, control, and direction.
Inventory control	Inventory control theory and practice, criteria, minimum and maximum, turnover, performance levels, relationship to product management, to sales, to promotion, to accounts, critical areas, forecasting, contact with manufacturing, economics.

Area	Relationships
Research	Basic and pure, direct and indirect, applied, product, process, influences of product management, sales, marketing, the new product planning committee, need analysis, duplication, coordination, marketing estimates and potentials, planning, reporting to and from, testing, test marketing, trials, costs, patents, secrecy.
Development	New uses for old products or processes, product modification, process modification, marketing development versus product development, field trials and testing, pilot plan responsibilities, promotional responsibilities, critical elements, coordination.
Electronic data processing	Product-oriented reports and reporting, overall utility, sales reporting, marketing reports, models, information storage, manipulation and retrieval, control procedures and functions, studies, contribution, input requirements, systems development.
Office services	Equipment, information storage and retrieval, personnel, general contribution.
Systems	Studies, control and review procedures, model development, processing and procedures.
Purchasing	Cost, sources, specifications, acceptance rejections, delivery and supply, tolerances, advantages, limitations, coordination.
Personnel	People, policies.
Legal	Rules, regulations, allowables, limitations, labeling, pricing, deceptive practices, advertising and promotion review and approval, marketing, mergers, acquisitions, agency agreements, secrecy agreements, licenses, advice, implications, legislation, liabilities.
Patent	How to obtain, what to do with after obtaining, filing, protection, limitations, violations, agreements, inclusions and exclusions, uses and abuses, expenses, marketing coordination, literature searches.
Trade mark	How to obtain, how to protect, violations, agreements, inclusions, exclusions, coordination.
Application	Use of product, market, relationship of product to use, development, testing.
Manufacturing	Coordination, informational requirement, capacity, forecasting, problems, alternate sources of supply, contingency manufacture, role in plans and plan-

Area	Relationships
	ning, relationship to customer and marketing effort, specifications and tolerances, acceptance, rejection, rework, cost control and review.
Technical services	Testing, control, service, cost, contribution, value, use and abuse, marketing relationship.
Administrative service	Relationship to marketing, sales, technical service, customer service, internal organizational functions, office procedures, policies, personnel, equipment, operational requirements.
Engineering	Product requirements, processing requirements, problems, cost control and review, contribution, coordination, limitation, capacity, alternative process, critical areas.
Accounting	Costing, direct, allocation, contribution, record keeping, accounts receivable, accounts payable, relationship to sales and marketing, data source.
Finance	Balances and statements, control, cash flow, budgets and allocations, allowances, planning.
Traffic	Rules and regulations, savings, bulk rates, commodity rates, distribution, customer service, liaison, U.S. Customs.
Library	References, documentation, research, literature searching.
Sales service	Cost, relationship to marketing, sales, product management, product requirements, critical areas.
Toxicology	Legal and medical relationship, product, process, internal external, rules and regulations, new product, product development, liabilities.
Intercorporate relations	Objectives, goals, strategies, policies, approaches, common points, differences, reconciliation, coordination, direction.

Communication

Communication is a part of coordination and therefore a very close part of the product manager's life. Without a constant informational flow, modern product management cannot exist, and it is incumbent on the product manager to foster communication wherever he can.

It is unrealistic to expect the product manager to surmount communication obstacles by himself, but he must be willing to exert tremendous energy in this field.

When we examined the number of operational areas involved in the average large corporation, it was apparent that the magnitude of the communication problem is beyond the scope of this discussion. And the number of books and articles written on this subject is almost astronomical. There are, however, two concerns especially close to the product manager's heart that bear elucidation. The first is the necessity for total or integrated information, which is termed "verti-lateral communication"; the second is the need for face-to-face communication.

The facilities available for communicating today are virtually unimaginable, and from a physical standpoint, the existence of a communication problem seems inexcusable. This is not to say that the psychological factors of making oneself understood have been obviated. But the devices and mechanisms for communication do exist. The problem is how to make people use them properly. Obviously, these problems cannot be discussed here in detail. It is imperative, however, that product managers avail themselves of known physical techniques. Simultaneously they have to take it upon themselves to bring the message to others.

VERTI-LATERAL COMMUNICATION

Figure 6 diagrams the traditional pyramidal concept of management, which shows the top, middle, and first line management structure. Regardless of florid terminology, in this organization, which was most often found in line operations, information flowed from top to middle to bottom in just that sequence. There was little or no communication from bottom to middle to top and equally little from middle to middle or bottom to bottom—essentially vertical communication.

FIGURE 6

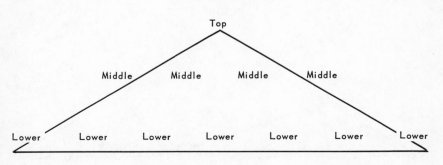

FIGURE 7

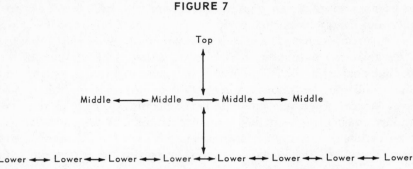

From this evolved a slightly more sophisticated approach which, in a way, related to staff and functional management in which we find a lateral information flow structured as shown in Figure 7.

In this situation we find again that top, middle, and first line management are involved, but there is now an improvement for top management while communicating to middle and first line management. Also, middle management and first line management communicate directly with each other on a lateral basis. Unfortunately, there is still a gap, since all too often middle management tends to communicate only with certain areas and most first line managers follow this example and suffer from the same limitations. It is, however, an improvement.

Still more can be done via the introduction of a verti-lateral communication system, which, by preference, should be called "verti-lateral information flow." The word "flow" is a key since it implies, as the diagram illustrates, that information not only goes in one direction but in several—top to first line, vertically and within levels—laterally and both downward and upward as well as tangently and obliquely. This enables all management echelons to communicate with each other directly or indirectly as the case may be. Figure 8 shows such a system.

FIGURE 8

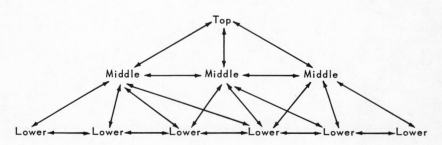

There is inherent danger in such a structure since there are no safeties or guards to prevent unnecessary communications; just as we can be overorganized we can be overcommunicated. However, being practical, it would appear that there is much less danger in being overcommunicated than in being under, and that while too much information may provide a problem in interpretation, analysis, and distribution, it would behoove us to have more than less.

Also, top management may not wish to be accessible to other management levels. This can be controlled by the introduction of specific channels for information flow and proper management direction on the nature of the data desired. Once this is accomplished, some of these difficulties can be eliminated without defeating the basic purpose.

In any event, a verti-lateral information flow system permits an exchange of information far beyond that possible in any other way and is an unavoidable necessity in endeavoring to operate successfully on a functional staff basis. Even if the total business organization cannot or does not wish to sustain such an extensive communications network, the marketing group within itself can and should.

One important role of the product manager is to ensure the flow of this information. In many instances he will be the repository for a great amount of the data flowing both ways and will in effect serve as a two-way funnel, or better yet, an hourglass. The product manager would be the constriction in the center from which he directs the appropriate information. A word of caution to the product manager: Be a constructive constriction and not the bottleneck that both literally and figuratively could result. This is a big responsibility and one which, at least within the marketing area, should be within his purview.

Training

Product managers, like all management personnel, require training and continued education. Since they operate in a special area, their training carries with it a special need. The irony is that this specialization is generalization. The active product manager is involved in so many different operations that his training must cover multiple areas, and he can readily profit from most management training activities.

Product management education, therefore, should include the specifics of product management and its techniques, the philosophies and disciplines of other functional management areas, and the general theory of management itself. The product manager, especially where he is involved in industrial or government work, must keep abreast of pertinent scientific and technological developments. Therefore, he must also maintain scientific or engineering expertise.

Of course, with the availability of both management and scientific courses, as well as those special programs offered through specific professional societies or trade associations, he has a host of potential sources. In-house training programs, however, require additional comment since all too often these do not concentrate on product management per se. Of course in-house training dealing with special product management sectors would be somewhat impractical considering the limited audience. But, conversely, it is not necessarily unrealistic since the product manager could function as teacher and the object would be further expanding of product management knowledge in other areas, an asset to product managers later.

Teaching

From the preceding we can see that one area where the product manager can operate as a teacher is the in-house training program. More than this, however, he functions as a teacher in his day-to-day operations as they relate to expanding the horizons of product management in the shop, in external contacts, and in the clarification of product management as it relates to the corporate activity. Often the product manager is called upon to assist in sales or marketing training programs. He is frequently asked to make personal presentations to customers. In all these situations, he performs as a teacher.

An effective product manager must familiarize himself with general techniques involved in teaching: visual aids, presentations, preparations, public speaking, the psychology of learning; in short, he should learn all those techniques that will aid him. Such training will assist him in both formal situations and in those informal contacts that foster his coordinative and communicative activities.

Product management is provided additional challenges in the scientific or technological realms. We have already noted that the product manager must combine his particular expertise with a fundamental grasp of management techniques. Striking a harmonious balance between the two is difficult but necessary.

Getting the Job Done

Considering the diverse and numerous activities of the product manager, both in the overall organization and the marketing group in particular, it would seem that, like actor Lon Chaney, he should be dubbed "the man of a thousand faces" or, better, "the man of a thousand jobs."

In order to approach this problem realistically product managers must concern themselves with division of time, and thoroughly plan their own activities. The budgeting of time should be based on the particular operation of his product activities and on the product management hexagram, which provides a basis for analyzing relative time spent on major responsibilities. To this, however, we should add some additional factors: external contact, training and sales, and marketing participation. There are many to consider, but only the more meaningful aspects can be delineated. Figure 9 indicates others—not to be all-

FIGURE 9

Activity	Time Budgeted	Time Actually Spent
PLANNING		
PRODUCT		
Monitoring		
Development		
Cycle analysis		
Pricing		
PROFIT		
Development		
Improvement		
Monitoring		
COMPETITIVE ANALYSIS		
FORECASTING		
CONTACTS		
Informational		
Sales		
Marketing		
FIELD TESTING		
REPORTS		
Weekly		
Quarterly		
Other		

inclusive but to provide the product manager with another start in budgeting his time. This checklist should be developed by each and an appropriate apportionment of time made.

In identifying external contact one should understand that, as indicated in concerns over communication, there is no substitute for personal contact. This applies to the gathering of market information as well as to other functions. This means that the product manager should plan on direct market and customer contacts not only for specific marketing purposes but to obtain the most meaningful first-hand impressions of the situation and to elucidate certain points. Only he knows what he is looking for. When he must depend on others for information, he should tell them precisely what it is he wants and needs to know.

General Management Techniques

Over the years there have evolved several different techniques and approaches to management. Management by directive, by exception, by objective, and by results all have become popular phrases, and each has its own school of advocates and dissenters. Rather than treat these at length here (they will be further considered when we discuss their application in Chapter 5), suffice it to say that the product manager should familiarize himself with these different management philosophies. He is then in a position to discuss them knowledgeably and to choose the one or two best suited for the product management operation in his particular company.

Product management's deep and growing concern with general management theories is a logical outgrowth of interfunctional activities. It reflects the need for the product manager's comprehension and appreciation of total management objectives. The extent of his personal involvement and shift in emphasis occurs as the relative position of the product manager to product group coordinator, to product group manager progresses. As his managerial responsibilities shift, so does his perspective, a point that product managers should bear in mind as they consider evolving trends in product management. But the product manager had best learn to manage himself before he attempts to manage others.

PART TWO

Implementation

5

Techniques
of Product Management

In an era of great change, the problem of techniques is not availability but selection. Like any good craftsman, the product manager needs and uses creative techniques in the execution of his chosen profession. Sometimes simple, sometimes sophisticated, and always necessary, they are the basic operational needs that he requires and must master if he is to be successful.

The product manager, whether new to his job or not, is beset by a deluge of recommendations, claims, counterclaims, and a vast array of procedures designed to aid him. In some cases they actually claim to do his job for him, even do it better. Before he can critically examine any of these methods, mechanical or otherwise, the product manager must know his own needs and see their usefulness in the specifics of his situation. This somewhat negative sounding caution is cited because of the perfectly natural tendency to buy or use gadgets (a) because they are new and pretty, or (b) because the other guy does or does not have them, or (c) just because they are there.

Before buying or trying, the product manager should obtain a basic familiarity with general techniques and the most commonly encountered tools pertinent to his problem.

Only those basic items and areas of most direct and practical benefit will be discussed here. Many specific techniques must be excluded. Space and broad scope are the criteria, not quality or partiality. Each product manager has the benefits of experience, and his favorites may be based on optimum results or mere familiarity. The product manager should never hesitate to cast away the old if the new is found to be more suitable.

In this context, since the needs of each product manager vary tremendously, it is to be expected that all techniques are not applicable to all situations. Coincidentally, there are sometimes no developed practices or machines that meet the needs of a particular problem. The self-reliant product manager must blaze his own path. And with a strong foundation in present methodology, his task will be simplified.

There are many available techniques, apparently not suitable or designed for another purpose, that can be modified or used to meet his particular requirements. Good examples are the use of statistical analysis in specific product situations and adaptation of the Program Evaluation and Review Technique (PERT) to civilian management problems. In any event, let the purists stand aside. The practical manager must not be afraid to alter an old system; in fact, he may implement a new one based on elements from several existing techniques in the evolution of what is most suitable for his purposes.

Elements to Consider

In selecting those that most adequately fulfill a particular product manager's needs, there are several factors to consider:

Objective	What purpose is to be served?
Practicality	Can the tool or technique actually be used?
Alterability	Can it be altered to meet changing needs?
Flexibility	Can it be used for more than one purpose?
Training	Is any extensive training required? Who will operate the machinery if the operator leaves? What is retraining time?
Obsolescence	How long can it be used? How long before replacement?
Reuse	How many times must an action or function be repeated?
Space	Can the necessary equipment be installed in present or future locations?

Cost   What is the cost of equipment and of installation, mainte-
              nance, and operation?

Expansion   Will it meet anticipated as well as existing needs?

Each factor should be given appropriate thought as it relates to particular requirements. Special consideration should be given to future needs, since the realities of business life are such that output requirements are increasing exponentially.

In the area of cost, hidden expenses require further elaboration. The less obvious operational costs, such as additional equipment needs, operators, supplies, and training, are often neglected or insufficiently weighed.

While there can be no doubting the economy of efficient, applicable techniques, one last factor must be considered in their selection—trade-off. This involves assessment of how the function for which the tool is intended can be accomplished by other and possibly more economical means. Do the advantages of the equipment under study outweigh the deterrents? Obviously, when they do, such equipment should be used.

Broadly speaking, we can distinguish between tools and techniques. The former nearly always involve mechanical devices and the latter usually do not. Both are important and contain elements of product management approaches that are essential to development of basic methods. Because each product manager is different and every situation varies, selection and balance are individual judgments. The tools and techniques to be considered are:

Nonmechanical Techniques	*Mechanical Tools*
Personal contact	Electronic data processing
Systems	Model studies
Records and files	Electronic communications
Documentation	Calculators
Planning	Data storage and retrieval
Analysis	Visual aids
Service	
Communication	
Data matrix	
Product-mix concept	
Statistical analysis	

This chapter will deal with techniques. The following chapter will treat the tools.

Nonmechanical techniques are primarily constructed on the foundations of management psychology, sociology, and philosophy. They also involve those guides that have been determined through human relationships. Further, they take into account educational, mathematical, and logical processes with their application in the areas of personal contact as well as data handling, interpretation, and use.

In other words, we are now asking the product manager to be a master of all trades. In this situation he should also implement the teachings of specific behavioral sciences since they have been greatly concerned with organization and the function of the individual in the corporate body. As the product manager relies heavily on people, he must know both how they function and, as much as possible, why they function. This is not mere academic curiosity; it stems from the motivation for management objective accomplishment.

With such a complex derivation, it is apparent that opportunity for creativity in management abounds. Drawing from this vast repository of knowledge, the product manager has the unique opportunity to exercise latitudes in judgment and give free range to his intellectual interests. To put it simply, he applies whatever he can to get results.

In the foregoing tabulation, several techniques were indicated. All of these are important, and their relative positioning was not intended to imply any particular sequential significance. It would not be possible to rank them in importance. What might be a vital technique in one product management situation may be relatively insignificant in another; only the product manager can make this determination. Relative importance also varies with specific objectives and peculiar circumstances.

It is also worth noting that many of these areas have been comprehensively described elsewhere. Therefore, no attempt has been made here to do other than provide a brief statement of principle and discuss possible application to the needs of product management. Several references to details of theory, principle, or practice may be found in the bibliography.

Personal Contact

This technique is listed first because it is probably the most important; it is certainly the most pervasive. It is impossible for the product manager to function without coming into contact with people—unless he manages an undertaking establishment. The product manager's ability in this area is central to his effectiveness and performance.

However, in the context of his personal dealings, we must differentiate between internal and external contacts and the practical implications thereof:

Internal	External
Data gathering	Data gathering
Data disseminating	Data disseminating
Nonspecific—contact call	Sales support
Plannnig	Marketing support
Technical service	Problem solving
Problem solving	Purchasing
Meetings	Contract discussions
Technical programs	Technical programs
	Educational purposes

In any of these instances personal conduct, as well as conduct of the situation, will vary; however, there are a few helpful basics. One is that, regardless of the problem, a face-to-face confrontation is best. There is no substitute for personal contact. Whenever and wherever possible, the product manager should arrange to see those with whom he must deal.

In his personal contacts, the product manager should be:

Courteous. Don't be argumentative unless it is deliberate, and don't lose your temper unless it is deliberate. When provoked, only provoke back intentionally and try not to lose control of yourself. This is tantamount to losing control of the situation, the last thing you want to do. The Spanish have an old proverb, "you catch more flies with sugar than vinegar."

Punctual. People don't like to be kept waiting.

Considerate. People are busy; don't be abrupt, but keep to the subject and conduct your business as expeditiously as possible.

Knowledgeable. Know your subject and, better yet, know what you want. Prepare for your meeting.

Attentive. It is unquestionably true that one must be a good and selective listener in order to be a good product manager.

Neat. Appearance means a lot; he who looks good, rightly or wrongly, is good.

Reasonably aggressive. A delicate balance; but a moderately aggressive, positive attitude kindles respect and mutual enthusiasm.

Positive. An affirmative attitude generates positive results. Negativism and defeatism—well, enough said.

Intentional. Know what you want; know what you are doing, and do it deliberately.

Diplomatic. Hard to define. We all know what it is; practicing it is another thing.

Systems

To say that a great deal has been written on systems is beyond understatement. Yet confusion still exists and probably always will. It should be understood that being systematic is not using a system; nor are systems limited to mental processes. Systems, as they are thought of in the management sciences, are far more comprehensive and encompassing.

We all use systems in our business and personal activities, yet many are reluctant to admit this and to employ the more formal systems of management. Therefore, when one studies systems and becomes convinced that a particular type is ideally suited to his problem, he may encounter unexpected personnel difficulties as well as the usual problems associated with implementing a new technique. Such a situation is akin to introducing product management to a nonproduct management organization. Not insurmountable, but worth prior rumination.

In the next few pages we will treat some of the important systems and determine their potential application in product management. We shall deal only with a general description of the technique, requirements for implementation, and consideration of application, keeping in mind the added possibility of coexistent utilization for multifunctional purposes. However, let us first review the overall nature, purposes, advantages, and disadvantages of the "systems" approach.

Nature and Purpose of Systems

In the complex and volatile environment of our business world, it is imperative to ascertain, describe, and project the impact of interrelated variables on the business situation. This the systems approach endeavors to do, thereby providing management with an information control and integration technique. Moreover, it provides predictability in the real world of business. Therefore, systems have several inherent parts:

Objective: They have a clear purpose.

Input: Provision for data assembly and inclusion.

Integration: Mechanisms for data integration.

Output: Development of analyzed data.

Distribution: Provision for output to reach proper people.

The system usually contains one or more subsystems which are smaller systems performing functions necessary for the total system analysis and interpretation but independently derived as the consequence of the subsystems operation. The results of subsystem output then become input components for the total system.

While there are myriad combinations and permutations of systems development, depending on objectives and specific requirements, systems are built from two major elements: combinations of procedures constructed to meet operational objectives; and combinations of machines and devices to meet similar objectives. Naturally, there are subsequent combinations of the two major techniques.

In any event, the output objective is to provide management with the instrument for integrating technological, personnel, equipment resources, and capital in a realistic, ordered interrelationship to optimize performance, corporate position, and growth.

Systems Methodology

In order to obtain the optimum system, there is a definite methodology to assist in its development and structure. Dealing with complex inputs and outputs, as well as constant and inconstant variables, the system is usually somewhat complex, and these elements should be thoroughly considered. In other words, we have a system to obtain the system.

Problem definition. Be sure that the problem to be solved by the system is clearly stated and clearly understood. Moreover, be sure that the system can indeed solve the problem.

Objective determination. Develop a detailed description of the objectives of the system: what output is to be obtained; the utilization of output data, and the system.

Examination of current practices. Before implementing a new system, be sure all aspects of older ones are completely understood and that the system will perform a function not already covered. Elements of existing practices may become components of the new system.

Identify critical areas. This means those areas of particular complexity, criticalness, or anticipated problems.

Input analysis. Provide for analysis of input data and determination of data to be input.

Model development. Use a system model to test function, objective determination, practicality, and usefulness—all the systems testing and validation.

Testing model. Model utilization for ascertaining objectives in above.

Modification. Possible systems alteration depending upon results of model testing.

Implementation. While this step appears to immediately follow the previous one, this is not quite precise. The cycle should be repeated from the prior four steps until results are completely satisfactory; then implement the system fully from model to total operation.

Data distribution. Provide for distribution of output. This is a most important element because regardless of systems sophistication or perfection, the old communications problem must be faced—the right information in the right hands at the right time. Otherwise we have accomplished nothing.

Once these elements have been considered and the system introduced and functioning, the job is still not complete. We are dealing with the integration of complex *variables.* This is a key factor, for we must have the capability of changing the system since the variables themselves vary—alteration of variables to be considered as opposed to variation in the dimension of the variable. In effect, this means that we are dealing with factors that not only vary themselves in degree but fluctuate in degree of importance at different times and are not fixed in terms of exclusion, inclusion, relevancy, and influence. From a systems standpoint, then, after data distribution we must: constantly evaluate the system; constantly evaluate all inputs; provide for loopback; and revise the system.

From this it is apparent that a system is not a simple managerial device, but is frequently an expensive technique. However, the implementation of a system will provide numerous benefits consistent with the dynamics of change essential to modern effective management. To examine the systems approach in perspective, we must examine the benefits and limitations as areas for critical evaluation. Keep in mind when reviewing both, however, that this is a reasonably young and not yet a precise management science. Like others, product management included, it will be subject to criticism, alteration, examination, and perfection, but it provides otherwise unavailable capabilities.

Limitations	*Benefits*
Failure, usually due to human causes.	Systematic problem solving.
Overcomplexity.	Development of communication base.

Limitations	Benefits
Excessive cost.	Data integration.
Requirement for critical and constant assessment.	Additional decision-making tool for management.
Flexibility.	Permits accurate (or at least more accurate) management by exception.
Alterability.	
Timeliness.	
Predictability capability.	Frees executive time.
Capacity for correction.	Can expedite decision making.
Elimination of human elements can be negative unless properly implemented.	Common data analysis.
	Isolates problems.
	Can be rapid and time saving.
Perspective; the system must be the tool, not the business.	Can cope with, analyze, and integrate far more variables.
	Has some predictability capacity, depending on system and objective.

SYSTEMS APPLICABLE TO PRODUCT MANAGEMENT

After giving some thought to the philosophy, methodology, and implementation of systems, we come to the role of systems in product management. The product manager must be conscious of the systems approach because he may use it in product management. Equally important it should be part of his knowledge of management techniques, since his department may provide data and receive output as a systems element.

In addition, he is naturally concerned with newer management techniques if for no other reason than his needs for total involvement in the context of his interrelative and coordinative activities.

Since our purpose is primarily to consider those systems most applicable to the problems of product managers, we shall deal in further detail only with those that have been successfully used in one or more phases of the product management operation. In so doing, we can only review them to a limited extent, which is done in Table 1. There are many publications that deal with these systems in greater detail.

However, in providing basic comments on deriviation, characteristics, and general examples of application to product management, we have given the product manager the basis for considering the systems approach, and for identifying those systems that might hold the most interest to him in his situation, and warrant further exploration.

(*text continues on page 88*)

TABLE 1. *Systems of interest to product managers.*

Designation	Derivation	Characteristics	Possible Application to Product Management
Gantt chart	Developed by Henry L. Gantt in World War I for military requirements	Essentially a scheduling technique Involves plotting estimated conclusion of component activities rather than actual completion Operates on premise that graphic representation is clear and time is common operational denominator	Product action scheduling Action program summaries Control and review Development program and planning Summary for PERT programs Development of preliminary PERT master planning
Line of balance (LOB)	George E. Fouch of Goodyear Co., 1941. Originally applied to Navy Bureau of Aeronautics in World War II	Analysis and display components and sub-components shown horizontally with their interphases Standard or estimated time assigned for elements	Has limited product management application unless applied to specific industrial or manufacturing situation, hence reference here.

Designation	Derivation	Characteristics	Possible Application to Product Management
		Results indicated in a calendar or time scale as working days to completion	
		Set-back determinations made	
		Three charts required	
		LOB drawn on progress chart indicates performance	
Learning curve	World War II	Plots learning and value resulting from repeated exposure of cost reduction in manufacturing	Limited product management application. Main use in cost projections in reasonably stable, simple situations. Not an important technique.
		It is limited but predictive	
Statistical analysis	Mathematical base	Discussed in detail in this chapter	Has several applications, which are indicated in this chapter.

TABLE 1. *Systems of interest to product managers* (*continued*).

Designation	Derivation	Characteristics	Possible Application to Product Management
Program evaluation and review technique time and cost (PERT time cost)	Admiral W. F. Rabon, naval special projects office, for integrated planning for fleet ballistic missile system in 1958. Expanded to PERT cost in 1961-1962	PERT time Essentially a network programming review technique Reduces results to events that are identified in time and interrelated Has a definite start and conclusion Employs activities to join events PERT cost Determination of realistic cost estimates in original program Control Improvement programs	Now one of the most important techniques available because of control and review facility, critical path identification, and these predictive features: planning, scheduling, fixing duties and responsibilities, problem solving, applications in technical, manufacturing or systems problems, probability determination and decision making. It is primarily suited for use in one-time projects. It is not for multiproject or repeat operation application. Requires expert for best results. Can be used jointly with Gantt charts and critical path method. Enables graphic representation of time and interrelations and dependencies of all required elements, and provides for variations and projections.

Designation	Derivation	Characteristics	Possible Application to Product Management
Critical path method (CPM)	Morgan R. Walker, Engineering Services Division, E. I. du Pont, and James E. Kelly, Remington Rand, 1957	Based on interdependencies of developments A network technique Identifies critical areas Focus attention where necessary	Largely supplanted by PERT, but now used as an element in PERT analysis.
Milestone method	World War II	Separates operation into components Graphs components in time Indicates sequential operations and dependencies Relates to time analysis	Present usage, like Gantt chart, restricted to master scheduling because of limitations.

Records and Files

To overstate the importance of maintaining records of activities, products, specifications, and costs would be impossible. And rarely does the product manager pay enough attention to this vital area. More critically, he may neglect the need for systems and procedures that will enable him to relocate the valuable information that he has obtained and painstakingly recorded.

The key to filing and recording is care and attention. There is no easy out, no quick method, and there is no ready-made, completely satisfactory system. However, the job is far more readily accomplished now than ever before via the use of many available aids, including computers and microfilm. Later we will speak in greater detail of these two aspects in the chapter dealing with product management tools. Here we are concerned with the nonmechanical aspects of records development, records storage, filing, and manual information retrieval.

The complexity of business necessitates increased paperwork, and with it, requirements for documentation. The number of products, wealth of information on each, competition, manufacturing data, planning data, and other factors too numerous to detail here have to be kept, sorted, stored, and still be accessible; accessibility is imperative since we must be able to locate data quickly and accurately.

All of this must be done expeditiously and economically. Fortunately the problem is not insurmountable, provided the product manager applies himself to an analysis of his needs first and the development of data systems—not the full-blown fancy ones expostulated before— but reasonably simple, old-fashioned ones, updated to use modern filing concepts and available copying and updating techniques.

First, the product manager needs certain data and therefore must maintain a number of files on this relevant information. He should consider this information from two viewpoints: what must be maintained permanently and what is temporary.

Second, he should consider two other broad categories: what he needs actively, that is, highly specific and readily accessible information used on a day-to-day basis, such as prices, specifications, manufacturing or shipping schedules, delivery reports, and competitive products; and what he uses only infrequently, that is, information that does not have to be instantaneously retrievable, such as the history of a product, planning data, annual manufacturing schedules, research and development reports.

The precise nature and organization of such categories will obviously vary with the requirements of the individual product manager, but analyzing his records and files accordingly will enable him to place all his data requirements in these larger segments. He can then determine what filing system to use and apply it.

When this is accomplished he can begin to control his data base. Because secretaries hate to file, the product manager must show some personal interest and concern; otherwise, this is one area of the operation that can quickly degenerate.

Consideration of recording and filing, then, takes on significance from the standpoint of the type of data—including the requirements of documentation and reference—and its use; that is, its day-to-day operational activity or whether its reference is short term or long term. The following list typifies the records that product managers should consider.

A. Product sources
B. Product component sources
C. Manufacturing
    1. Processes
    2. Lead times
    3. Processing or manufacturing cycling times
    4. Process units or batch sizes
    5. Optimum cycling
    6. Schedules and scheduling
    7. Capacities
D. Specifications
    1. Product overall
    2. Components
    3. Quality control
        a. Parameters
        b. Performance
        c. Cost
        d. Errors and reject rate
        e. Reprocessing expense
        f. Customer relation problems
E. Costs
    1. Manufacturing
    2. Distribution
    3. Controllable by product if known
    4. Controllable by market if known
    5. Miscellaneous

F. Sales data
   1. By customer
   2. By product
   3. By units
   4. By class of trade
   5. By source of supply
   6. By source of manufacture
   7. Ratio by calls, by trade, and by supply
   8. Prices and pricing
   9. By sales territory
   10. By salesmen
   11. By program
G. Competition
   1. By trade
   2. By product
   3. By activity
H. Performance data—product or process
I. Available literature—internal and external
J. Samples of product—own and competitors'
K. Market data
   1. Past
   2. Present
   3. Future
L. Planning data
   1. Market analysis
   2. Competition analysis
   3. Product data
   4. Research and development data
M. General correspondence
N. Specific correspondence
O. Follow-up or tickler
P. Customer claims or complaints
Q. Trade or organization

Again a word of practical caution: use only those that are really needed. No benefit derives from the establishment of intricate cross-reference filing systems that are never effectively used and that require endless hours of preparation and maintenance. It is far better to be supercritical in the establishment of a recording and filing system than to implement one without sufficient thought.

In this connection all systems should be reviewed periodically to determine whether or not they still serve a purpose. If they don't, product managers must have the courage to risk deleting them; too many systems are retained through inertia. Similarly, files should be established with a predetermined discard time.

For example, cost records can be maintained for two years, then discarded; product data, no disposal without specific product manager authorization; technical reports, five years; and so on. This simple but effective device will ensure automatic control of the size of files, which have an unhappy facility for self-generation at a rate faster than a pair of passionate rabbits.

Planned discards save the product manager's time in two ways: he doesn't have to be consulted on disposal except where he so specifies; and he knows precisely how old his data are and will not have to revert to data discarded earlier.

Considering the product manager's specific needs, his file organization should be based on filling these needs. Our primary orientation is based on the product itself, and therefore the most useful approach may be the master product file—a "dossier" for each product, which is filed either alphabetically, numerically, or by an alphanumeric system. Whatever the filing base, such a file would contain almost all of the above listed records relative to the individual product.

In many instances it is helpful to file duplicates of certain information that has broader application in general files dealing with such topical data. For example, an individual product folder could contain customer complaints with a duplicate in the general topical customer complaints file. The latter gathers trends or indications on overall performance or locates sources of manufacturing, engineering, distribution, or other trouble causing the complaint. The former (by product) is part of total product documentation, indicating performance of the product as well as isolation of individual product processing, manufacturing, and distributing—difficulties that then must be resolved, but only relative to the particular product.

It is also valuable to consider files of the following general types—numerical, alphabetical, or topical, depending upon classification and needs.

Product files (individual file per product)
Product class files (file on common class of products)
Competition files
    By individual product
    By class
    Combined as an element in product file

Market file
Topical
  By source
  By marketing activity
  By process
  By trade
  Relative to application
General correspondence
Specific correspondence
Tickler or follow-up
Activity
Old calendar—particularly useful to file old daily activity calendars
  for use in later report compilation
Technical data

Before leaving this topic, another few words of caution: Information, no matter how well conceived, documented, recorded, or filed, is no good unless it can be relocated. Retrieval requirements must always be taken into account.

Documentation

Having already reviewed records and filing, one may well wonder what documentation is left. This is worth questioning since we have already discussed outside reference sources and what is traditionally called documentation.

We refer to that area of paperwork of great and direct concern to the product manager not only informationally but legally. Since the product manager is expected to react to certain market situations, particularly those involving price, he has a legal requisite for documenting the information that is provided to him. This is all the more important if there is any competitive pricing response.

As this is a particularly sensitive area and one that involves corporate policy, it is beyond our scope to do more than advocate caution and legal counsel. In this instance, the legal advice required pertains to competitive pricing policies and documents to be obtained and retained. Most large companies have their own legal representatives, and smaller ones can obtain the services of appropriate experts. The concern is that we do not act hastily, ill-advisedly, inappropriately, or, of greatest importance, illegally.

Too often we find that this aspect of marketing activity is given little more than superficial treatment; frequently those responsible for pricing decisions are not that familiar with the pertinent legal requirements and restrictions under which they are operating, nor have they taken action to ascertain these and comply with them. Normally the product manager is not responsible for the establishment of competitive prices, but he is involved in an advisory capacity. And he often obtains, complies, and interprets market information germane to the pricing question. This is where we frequently encounter real difficulty. These problems relate not only to obtaining positive verifiable data, but to documenting what is obtained and to the recording, filing, and availability thereof.

We cannot consider all the ramifications inherent in this area, but suffice it to say that when the product manager is involved in this critical matter, he should, along with the chief marketing executive:

Familiarize himself with the overall legal aspects of competitive pricing.

Seek legal advice regarding practices, policies, and records.

Coordinate his activities with the chief marketing executive or responsible corporate management in respect to recordkeeping, practices, and pricing policies.

Establish and require appropriate documentation before taking or recommending action.

Establish files or records in accordance with above.

Maintain liaison with legal advisers on competitive pricing and practices.

Another area of documentation is more general relative to the decision-making or recommendation process. In these instances we find the product manager making product addition, deletion, and modification recommendations based on scanty and often unrecorded or unsubstantiated data. In a sales-oriented organization, it is difficult to document thinking and action, no matter how necessary. However, through painful experience, both the product manager and the company learn of the need to do so before ill-considered or ill-advised action.

There has been a gratifying trend toward recognition of this problem and its rectification. The modern marketing concept alone goes a long way toward attaining total involvement. Second, integrated management is on the ascendancy and will also help. In the interim, the third has been the installation of the product manager whose position calls for his involvement and participation in these areas. As a focal point for such information, his efforts can go a long way in securing the data needed, and he can play a vital part to redirect thinking and action in this vital and sometimes costly area.

Planning

In a later chapter we will deal in considerable detail with the planning concept as it applies to operational, marketing, and product plans as well as their development, promulgation, implementation, and role in the total management operation. We should now pause briefly to consider the more specific requirements of the product manager in the more confined area of his direct product management authorities and responsibilities.

In doing this we can, with no small benefit, refer to the product management hexagram and contemplate constructive product planning in this more limited sphere. Examination illustrates again that one principal element of the job involves planning; this relates to actual planning and planning requirements. But review of the remaining five elements with respect to planning needs reveals generalities that can apply to all planning efforts. These elements may be criticized as too superficial and general. But the details of planning implementation must vary with the requirements of the product manager's situation. They should generate what is most vital—thinking in the planning area; they will also provide a framework for evaluation of the planning process in the context of product management requisites. Once this is accomplished, the product manager will be on his way to implementtaion of specifics.

Let's deal with the problem first, which means admitting its existence; then, the alert manager will determine the elements to be employed through selective assessment and will immerse himself in application.

Analysis

Now that the fabled box of bugs is open, out flies the next management apocalypse, that apodictical requisite, analysis. Theres is no denying that raw data often finds its way into reports or plans without analysis. Or if analyzed, it is sometimes impossible to ascertain conclusions thereof. We can all cite examples of endless data collations that have the semblance and often the ability of proving information; but if these are critically examined, they draw no conclusions and obviously have not been subject to the mental searching, probing, and questioning that are necessary elements in the analytical process.

When using information, it is automatic and axiomatic to determine its accuracy, authenticity, reliability, significance, and portent. This is something that we all do automatically either formally or merely intuitively. The product manager is the recipient of mountains of information, whether it concerns the compilation of an internal report, the formulation of a product strategy, or the development of the annual marketing plan. It is imperative that he cultivate an analytical attitude in self-defense. He must be able to sort from this maze what is meaningful and what he wishes to pursue further.

Once this is done, the analysis of the useful is possible. To accomplish this, the effective manager has many individual techniques. First, he almost subconsciously considers his source; then he regards the pertinence and timeliness of the data, the corroborative information, and the relationship of these data to other known information. This process allows him to seek additional information required for substantiation, or possibly to comprehend the importance of the original. All this seems recondite, and puts information gathering and "the understanding game" into the realm of counterspy. Those familiar with intelligence operations know of the emphasis placed on the analysis and subsequent use of interpreted data.

Since we are practical people, we cannot go to the extremes and lengths of espionage agencies. But we can learn from them to the extent of recognizing the need and employing the following analytical techniques:

Evaluate source.

Assign reliability factor to source.

Evaluate information.

Assign reliability factor to information.

Assign probability factor to information.

Verify information through other sources if possible.

Correlate information to other knowns and probables.

Discard unessentials, unreliables, and improbables.

Assess residue relative to situation.

Interpret essentially verified, probable, or actual information.

Pose probables resulting from above in terms of possible and probable outcomes.

Select one or more of the most probable.

State conclusions or alternative conclusions.

While we cannot be expected to use such detailed procedures in the analysis of all information received, we should cultivate an analytical attitude that will subconsciously assess information and situations in this light. When more cogent considerations and critical evaluations are necessary, the full-blown process should be applied with judgment and common sense. This sequence can be visualized as a staircase, a staircase to conclusive, usable data in which the following elements represent each level of sequential activity commencing on the lowest step and ascending to the highest: 1. Obtain. 2. Assemble. 3. Challenge. 4. Reassemble. 5. Assess. 6. Interpret. 7. Conclude.

Service

Earlier, some thought was given to service; a distinction was made between service that is sold as is and, effectively speaking, is a product itself and service that is offered in support of the product, usually *gratis,* forming a part of the marketing effort.

The first, our real product, has been dealt with, and the needs for recognizing and treating this service as a profitable or nonprofitable product are clearly understood. The product manager and his marketing management must not confuse this issue or lose sight of it. The same principles of product management apply to this product as to any other.

The second, a less substantive service, is of equal concern to the product manager for different reasons. It is less tangible, difficult to assess, and problematic to cost. Yet, it is costly and should reap its return. The other concern is that service is an element of the marketing effort, and can play a decisive role in the success or failure of a product. This implies that proper attention must be given to service in the marketing effort after product release as well as in the planning and preparatory stages. It is rueful, for example, to introduce a new product only to find that planning had not considered the laboratory service-analysis facilities that are essential to successful results. Or a seemingly trivial matter—purchase of equipment—may involve endless waiting for installation and training of operators.

Service falls within the planning and use domains of the product manager, especially in the critical areas of technical support and sales efforts. Customer service, more logically, falls to other hands, although some organizations have the product manager's finger in this pie too.

To provide adequate service, corporations must first ascertain what is expected and necessary, then take into account competitive service practices. It is not unusual to hear of successful competitors with an inferior product. Service or support make the crucial difference. Alert product managers will place due emphasis on this aspect.

Where new products are being introduced, this concern should originate in the initial development provision, and it should be one object of test marketing to ascertain the service levels that will be needed.

The decision of whether or not to supply them must depend on costs and the assessed risk of failure without them. If the answer is yes, adequate preparation and staffing are required and should be provided concomitant with product availability. We then face the need for reassessment in response to the competition and return for our efforts. Service, therefore, is not a one-time determinant but another of those many variables.

Where we have existing products, they should not escape the critical eye of review and redetermination. Service, or the lack thereof, is sometimes a hidden reason for success or failure. When seeking to ascertain the why's and wherefore's of product acceptance or rejection, it is all too easy to miss this one.

Where we have the product or products actually out in the marketplace and are offering service, assessment involves assurance that this is both appropriate and adequate. Having already stressed the dynamics of market and technological change, it is now evident that service requirements also change, and we must alter service offerings to retain or improve market position.

Communication

In an earlier chapter we mentioned communication needs and what the active product manager can do to satisfy them. As was indicated, his interests are simultaneously ultraistic and altruistic. His selfish concern is due to much of his information being dependent upon the efforts of others; and the results of his objectives are contingent upon efficiently communicating them and then obtaining cooperation to effect them. His more philanthropic concerns center around his managerial responsibilities, an appreciation of the need for total involvement, and the requirements of communication in creating the cooperative, informed atmosphere necessary for responsibility and involvement.

Earlier, we examined the total communication activity, summarized as verti-lateral communication, and later dealt with reports and reporting—one of the devices for implementing effective communication. In this section, more specific attention is given to the communication needs of the product manager.

The product manager must know four things: what he needs to know, where to obtain it, what he needs to submit, and to whom. Not all product managers need the same information. However, there are certain basic elements that all product managers should be concerned with; these will be discussed. There are also some classic sources that we can also mention. Many product managers will recognize them immediately.

Before developing any information systems within their own organizations, product managers should pause and reexamine the outline for systems development considered earlier in this chapter. While that dealt more with the requirements for developing a complex system to satisfy a clearly defined objective, the principles expostulated provide a basis for analyzing the communications problem; they also give the manager an outline to follow in reviewing his problem and determining the best means for its solution.

Whether he is a practicing, experienced, grizzled old product manager, or a fuzzy-cheeked neophyte, the manager will find merit in carefully reexamining his data objectives or requirements and then applying every step used in systems development to his particular problem. In effect, he is creating a small system, or sometimes even a large one. In so doing, he should extend this to include outgoing and incoming informational and directive requirements, for communications is a two-way street.

When doing this, the manager should evaluate existing channels for communication, reports, generated data, distribution, and use patterns, for often we find more useless data generated than either imagined or admitted. The reevaluation must involve eliminations as well as additions. We should also consider a distinction between formal, programmed, fixed-interval communications on certain items and informal information dissemination, based on a need-to-be-known criterion.

The exact nature of the systems devised will relate to available equipment. For example, an elaborate form for salesmen to provide market-survey information may be feasible in some companies and not in others. The same company that permitted it once or twice will think very carefully the third or fourth time. This means that practical consideration must be given to the limits of people, time, and the gain achieved for the effort. Only certain types of information can be obtained from sales people.

It is part of the product manager's job to assess these information sources, both actual and potential, and then use those most suitable. However, the most suitable are not always the least expensive. It is sometimes cheaper to hire the expensive outside professional market researcher than to "do it yourself."

Despite these expected variables, we can refer back to some underlying principles of major communication concern. Table 2 outlines the basic requirements.

With much information going back and forth, it is little wonder that planning is necessary and that the unnecessary be discarded. It is also clear that not all of the information is being exchanged at any one time, although it is a continuous process.

Systematization, control, review, and analysis of both input and output are required in every step of the operation in order to avoid duplication of information and effort, unnecessary investigations, unnecessary data gathering, misleading information, dilution of effort, confusion, unnecessary expense, and lost time and lost motion.

Therefore, while much of this information, and even more in given cases, is required, and many of the sources listed are available, they are not always the most appropriate. It is always a good practice to review desirable sources, particularly when working with people who are unaccustomed to seeking that type of information; they should be given complete instructions. Members of the sales staff are often asked to be information gatherers for product managers. This is not their true function. And when they are used, they should be given the appropriate guidance.

It should be remembered that the recipients of product department communications have the same problems in comprehending us as we do them. In any communication situation, whether written, oral, formal, or informal, one should always consider the audience, and gear the presentation accordingly.

Data Matrix

While the thought of using a matrix or grid may not be original, it is very helpful in presenting, organizing, interpreting, and approaching information. The product manager deals with a great mass of data, and there must be, in self-defense, an approach to organizing such information. Systems provide one approach; computer-based systems are even better. Unfortunately, these are not convenient for day-to-day operational use. Even if they were, the question of economy and acceptability would certainly arise. And in all probability we would find that, even if we could afford it, we would not be able to find computer time available to perform the relatively simple organizational and analytical feats we need here.

It is then a question of selection. If the problems are sufficiently large, we may have to use something more advanced than simple matrix analysis, something that is capable of dealing with involved variables and interrelationships. It is surprising how much can be accom-

TABLE 2. *Basic communications requirements*
of product management.

Information to Product Manager		Information from Product Manager	
Type	Sources	Type	Recipient
Market	MIS°	Price	MIS
Share	Market research	List	Finance
Trends	Publications	Competitive	Accounting
Dimensions	Trade sources	Bulk	Customers
Segments	Sales personnel	Other	Sales personnel
Other	Consultants		Management
	Management		
		Cost	MIS
Sales	MIS	Per unit	Management
By unit	Sales pesonnel	Per range	
By area	Management	Other	
Total	Trade sources		
Other	Publications	Quality control	Plant
		Acceptance	Warehouses
Forecasts	MIS	Rejection	Inventory control
By dollars	Market research	Specifications	Order department
By units	Sales personnel	Tolerances	Customers
By location	Management	Other	Management
Other			
		Market analysis	Management
Manufacturing	Manufacturing and		Planning
Schedules	engineering		Market research
Delays	Plant		Sales personnel
Capacity	Budget department		
Other		Forecast	Finance
		Sales	Manufacturing and
Advertising	MIS	Market share	engineering
Budgets	Agency	Manufacturing	Production
Response	Management	Profit	Plant
Other		Market	Planning
			Inventory control
Production	Manufacturing and		Management
Schedules	engineering		
Delays	Plant		
Capacity	Inventory control		
	MIS		

° Management information systems provide reports that contain data on such items as sales, market share, plan figures, budgets, performance analysis, and contribution cost analysis. Such systems are normally computer based, and will be dealt with more fully in the next chapter.

TABLE 2. *Basic communications requirements of product management (continued).*

Information to Product Manager		Information from Product Manager	
Type	Sources	Type	Recipient
Patents and trademarks	Legal	Product data	Customers
Filing recommendations	Patents Publications		Sales personnel Management Manufacturing and engineering Planning Marketing Advertising and promotion
Costs	Manufacturing and engineering Finance Accounting Management Budget department Purchasing	Product selection and emphasis	Marketing Sales personnel Management
Plans and performance	MIS Management	Product control	Marketing Sales personnel Management Customers
Competition	Sales personnel Management Publications Trade associations Personal contacts	Technical data	Manufacturing and engineering Plant Customers Marketing Sales personnel Management
New products	New product development committee Research and development Manufacturing and engineering Management Planning	Specifications Establishment Tolerances Other	Manufacturing and engineering Plant Customers
Objectives	Planning Management	Objectives By product By range By market Overall	Management Line and staff Sales personnel

plished with one or more matrixes used in series. Often such organization is a step to more sophisticated techniques, and grid structures are used in data sorting for later systems applications.

So far we have used the words matrix and grid interchangeably; however, this is really not accurate. A matrix is, by more stringent definition, anything that gives form to an unformed body; to wit: a mass of information organized by chart, graph, or boundary. A grid is a form of matrix analysis in which a box or series of boxes is established, representing arbitrary data; information is then systematically posted in the respective boxes. For our purposes we are more concerned with the concept and shall elaborate further only on grids, since they are more readily comprehended and employed.

Before we can set up a grid we must ascertain our objectives and then define the elements to be analyzed. In most instances we will not be using a grid to determine a conclusion but to identify missing elements needed for analysis or conclusion, or an additional device in decision making, or an organizational tool to structure and interrelate information, or a thinking aid, or a planning aid. The sample illustrated in Figure 10 will save many words of description. Here the object in using the grid is to determine what information is missing relative to products A through F. The left-hand column or parameter represents the products and the top row the factors required for the decision, numbered 1 through 8. Those boxes marked x indicate where information is present and those that are blank, where it is missing.

In examining the grid we can immediately see that an additional application can be made or multiple objectives accomplished. The data relative to the elements posted per product can be meaningful in

FIGURE 10

Product	Factors							
	1	2	3	4	5	6	7	8
A	x	x		x	x		x	x
B	x	x	x	x	x	x	x	x
C		x	x	x	x	x		x
D		x	x		x	x	x	x
E	x		x	x		x		x
F	x			x	x	x	x	x

establishing product-to-product performance data, absolute and comparative analysis, trend indications, and a host of other possibilities depending upon the nature of the input in factors 1–8.

Since the technique is reasonably simple and its applications vary with the dictates of the product management situation, no more need be said except to stress its advantages of speed, economy, adaptability, flexibility, and utility. Its limitations are also equally impressive; it is restricted in the number and degree of combinations and interrelationships that it can handle; it is not capable of predictability, nor does it eliminate or minimize the need for interpretation and decision making. It is a true tool in the sense of a performance aid.

Product-Mix Concept

Once upon a time many, many years ago, a discrete concept of marketing developed that was summarized in the marketing mix. Later, in Chapter 12, which deals with the role of product manager in marketing, the marketing mix is discussed in depth. For the moment it is only necessary to understand that the marketing mix, as a concept, attempted to distill all the variables in the marketing effort into a few control or key elements, indicating that these were under the control and direction of the marketing executive. Via manipulation, he was able to plan, control, and organize his activities to the end results of profitable performance.

While the original concept of the marketing mix more than adequately served its purpose, and the elements contained in it are just as valid today as they were when first promulgated, they are somewhat obsolescent in the sense that marketing has outgrown its original confines. The marketing mix and the marketing concept have been expanded and reevaluated in the light of modern business organization, structure, function, and philosophy. In Chapter 11 this aspect is given due consideration, and the modern marketing concept is fully described. At the same time, the marketing mix is also structured as it relates to this concept, and the function of the product manager is related to the marketing organization—not structurally, which was previously examined, but functionally, in the specific context of the marketing effort.

We will now borrow from the classics and consider a more circumscribed segment of the marketing mix. Let's extend the concept internally within the marketing group to the product management function and postulate the product mix. In so doing, we distinguish between the product management function and the tasks of the product manager; and we focus our attention on those product elements that, through control, planning, organization, and utilization, constitute the basis for the product manager's ability to accomplish his two primary objectives: support of the marketing effort and maintenance or improvement of the company gross profit.

Like the marketing mix, there are central elements in the product mix, paralleling those items in the product management hexagram that are subject to the direct purview of the product manager and constitute the building blocks of the product marketing effort. For the sake of easy comparison, the elements of the marketing mix are also shown.

Product Mix	*Marketing Mix*
Product	Product
Price	Place
Profit	Price
Promotion	Promotion
Integration	

Before expanding on each of these elements and their significance, it is worth noting that several of the elements in the marketing mix, such as product, price, and promotion, are the same. When discussing the marketing mix and considering the elements in detail, it will be apparent that the perspectives of the marketing director and the product manager are similar; both involve the sales and profit of the product, but the specifics of implementing activities in support of these objectives vary, as does the commensurate individual responsibility.

The other significant difference is the inclusion of other elements in the product mix and the very remarkable omission of profit in the marketing mix. This is not accidental; it reflects the statement of the classical marketing mix; it is one of the most significant differences between the old marketing mix and the modern marketing concept. Having examined these similarities and differences, it is a good idea to examine each of the elements in the product mix.

Product

This implies all those elements contained in product as we have already considered them, and encompasses such aspects as quality, quantity, distribution, development, research, modification, packaging, and direction. It means having and managing a salable, marketable item.

The product is central to the company and the product manager. Within this structure there is the added relationship from the managerial and marketing standpoint of having balanced, profitable product lines. Having the product is a positive element; the negative side of this determinant is apparently not having the product.

There are two situations that can and do prevail in not having the product. The first is out and out product omission, based on technical, financial, commercial, or marketing factors. The other is not having the product because it is eliminated as a consequence of product control. While the first case may have its favorable implications, it is more often a real negative—no product and no sales. Good product management should minimize these instances. The second example, however, should never be a negative from the corporate or management perspective since it is the direct result of product management control functions and is used to effect improvements or maintain the marketing effort and profit.

PRICE

This means all aspects of price. It is a correlative of the next factor, profit. To give justice to the old marketing concept, when price was sighted and profit not, profit was understandably implicit in the concept of price; good management would not price without profit. While possibly a valid assumption, it was not one borne out in practice, hence evolution of the separate profit identification and clarified profit responsibility.

PROFIT

This is a new addition to the marketing concept, as distinguished from the mix, and is certainly a critical element in the product mix. Having considered profit and price at great length, it is hardly necessary to repeat all the factors involved in the profit concept and the control activities of the product manager in the profit sphere. What remains to be said is that via profit comes the corporate life blood.

Techniques to improve or control profit have been reviewed also, but if any message bears repetition in product management, it is the need for cultivating an attitude of profit consciousness and profit conscience.

PROMOTION

Often advertising and promotion are either confused with each other or treated synonymously. This is not correct to the extent that advertising is one form of promotion. In this instance we are dealing with all forms of marketing our products—from increasing consumer awareness through advertising and mass mailings, to give-away and prize campaigns, to the simple art of writing intelligent letters to customers in response to their inquiries. All these, though vastly different in practical implementation and cost, are factors of concern in the promotional effort. The product manager most often is involved in advertising and indirectly in promotion.

INTEGRATION

After examining many elements that appear to relate to individual segments or tangible quanta, the introduction of this nebulous factor may seem irrelevant. However, one of the product manager's primary functions is to integrate the operational elements of the company's marketing groups. This function recognizes the total effect of product management and marketing in the corporate environment and reflects another of those distinctions between old and new marketing concepts.

Effective use of the product-mix elements is the product manager's responsibility. They constitute the most powerful influences that the manager has; ultimately, all other tools and techniques are mere instruments for refining his understanding of product, market, process, system, or situation so that each may be optimally implemented to sustain the marketing effort.

Each has its effect on the other, and the selection of components to be affected, increased, or decreased must be predicated on assessment of the situation, corporate capability, and evaluation. Often there are several alternatives to choose from, which is part of the management process. When to increase effort, decrease effort, or abandon it altogether is another.

The summation of all systems information and procedural implementation is the result in the market. A part of the system-flow problem is the assessment of this effort, and modern marketers realize that this need is as important after as before the marketing fact. Two dynamic tensions ensue: information before marketing (product development, market analysis, marketing effort), and information after marketing (sales, market status, market share, forecasting). Each of these has its bearing on the other. Hence the dynamic tension. Each affects, influences, and eventually creates or modifies the other.

The inherent problems in data gathering, selection, and interpretation differ in each case but are of no less consequence. Rapid evaluation and rapid response are becoming increasingly difficult and necessary in contemporary marketing. Management has realized this need, and computers and systems operations are partial approaches to their solution. Too often analysis has come too late, and corrective action long past due is also long past appropriate—another of the many justifications for planning. To be effective, the product mix must be an element in maintaining the tension or shifting the marketing equilibrium. Therefore, the product manager is concerned with practice as well as theory. He must rapidly comprehend the two ends of the balance. He must have the ability, both personal and corporate, to select his product mix quickly and implement it expeditiously. And, lastly, he must know the results of such activity with equal alacrity if he is to achieve his product and marketing objective.

Statistical Analysis

Often left to the realm of statisticians and most commonly associated with population studies, statistical analysis has a definite place in business management. The reasons for approaching data statistically are familiar and involve the same problems in handling and interpreting that we have been concerned with for some time. Statistics provide another means of organizing, analyzing, and further comprehending information. Also, the statistical approach has the advantage of being prognosticative; it can indicate future trends and provide an efficient basis for predicting statistical facts.

That these statistics can be related not only to quantitative data but, by extrapolation, to marketing, indicates their value. The difficulty lies in the sampling and data input, which directly control output both in quantity and quality. Also, the use of statistical methods involves considerable training, expertise, and mathematical ability. But despite these limitations, and despite the cynical attitude reflected in the old saw, "There are liars, damn liars, and statistics," contemporary business has come to realize the applications of this science in its more practical world. And the product manager, while obviously not a professional statistical analyst, should become familiar with the basic precepts and employ those elements that may be of direct value in his management position. When there are problems that he cannot solve himself, he can call on a professional statistical analyst on the company's staff or he can get help from consultants.

Essentially, statistics is the science of ordering, classifying, and manipulating numerical data in an effort to draw conclusions. Though it sounds simple, the problems associated with it are often extremely complex; the statistician works with numbers, and it is essential that they be both accurate and representative. The outcome of his analysis can be only as accurate as the data input, organization, manipulation, and correlations. While some of these are under his control, the first one clearly is not.

DATA INPUT

The information used by the statistician is ultimately reduced to numbers and generally involves two types of numerical representations:

Discrete data. These are numbers resulting from counting, examples of which would be census figures, number of customers, number of sales, and number of products.

Continuous data, or numbers resulting from measurements. Examples would be height, weight, time, percent profit, percent market share, and percent sales by territory.

In either situation, a basic problem is to obtain the representation that is normally accomplished by sampling, since it is rarely possible to count or measure all items to be analyzed. Indeed, that is the object of the analysis: the ability to draw conclusions or inference without having all elements individually quantified.

There are several approaches to sampling, as well as lengthy, mathematical formulas illustrating the advantages and disadvantages of each. Since the object here is general familiarization, we have not included any mathematical formulas in this discussion. For those who are interested, the bibliography contains references to books that deal exclusively with this topic. They all, in effect, state that the sampling must be as accurate, representative, and thorough as possible; and the sampling technique optimal for ascertaining data in one situation may not be in another.

In the final analysis, two basic approaches are used: counting (census) or sampling. Counting does not really mean mere physical head counts, but involves discrete data determination and actual measurement of the characteristics being analyzed. In sampling it may be necessary to do the same, but no effort would be made to count more than a representative group. Since the first is often impractical, it is the second that is more readily used.

Of the various sampling techniques employed, random sampling is the most commonly encountered. As the name implies, this involves taking samples at random and then employing them for the analysis. If random sampling is used, the question of representation arises, and some compensation might have to be included in the analysis. In the context of product management, there is a very definite and important area in which this question arises—quality control. Statistical, analytical principles have been applied in this area, and the difficulties of sampling, sample control, sample representation, and program are quite familiar to all product managers.

In an industrial chemical product for example, how representative of a 10,000-gallon quantity is a four-ounce sample extracted for batch-quality control evaluation? In a consumer product, how accurate is the representation of a 50,000-unit run when tests are conducted on only three units? How many units, or what size sample, should be used? What are the variables? What are the probabilities of error, or of accuracy? How many evaluations should be made; and when should the product be tested as finished sales goods only? Are additional evaluations on precursors, intermediates, components, and elements required? These and many other questions can be approached satisfactorily. This is an important factor in establishing control functions for a new or developmental product.

ORGANIZATION AND MANIPULATION

If we are to avoid mathematical examples, we will have to limit this discussion to mere mention of the requirements for the statistician to organize and manipulate the data, which is done through arithmetical and mathematical techniques. These lead to the output data, which is our basic interest, for this is what the product manager would receive.

While the application of statistical techniques is admittedly difficult, requiring a foundation in mathematics and statistics, there are obvious advantages to be gained.

We cannot delve any further into specific, statistical techniques and their extensions in marketing or product managerial situations. It should be emphasized, however, that the statistical analytical approach is not an obscure tool of theoreticians; it has application in the real world of management problem solving.

6

Tools
of Product Management

In the previous chapter we dealt with those nonmechanical devices and systems that the product manager could employ to assist him in his job. The distinction made at that time was between these manual or intellectual approaches and those that involve some mechanical devices. In this chapter, however, the mechanism involved is essentially incidental, serving as a true tool since ultimately either the data input or the data generated have been subjected to the mind of the manager and still represent an extension of the man. The machine here serves its purpose but does not replace individual judgments, assessments, and, in most cases, requires further decision making. This is particularly true in many computer studies or simulations where multiple solutions are provided. All these require a final interpretation and personal decision.

The advantages to the mechanical techniques, however, are many, and while not all of the following apply in any given case, they do have general veracity and application.

Speed. This usually is a very significant advantage that often offsets the cost of systems developed, the equipment itself, and expense of maintenance and operation.

Efficiency. Machines once adjusted and operational are usually far more efficient.

Accuracy. Once proper programs and systems have been developed, machine accuracy surpasses that of manual transactions; fatigue, human error, and similar problems that lead to inaccuracies are obviated.

Complexity. Certain mechanical devices can compute or integrate data of such a complex nature that while eventually it might be manually accomplished, for practical purposes it could not. Hence we have added a new dimension in capability.

Economy. There are several instances where the economy of mechanical or semimechanical devices far exceeds the cost of manual activities. This can be demonstrated even to the level of carbon copying on typewriters where new duplicating equipment using dry techniques and inexpensive paper makes the cost of copying by machine lower than that of carbon paper and concurrent labor.

There are, of course, disadvantages that should be considered:

Cost. This can be quite high, as those involved in computer installations know. This cost is not just that of the machinery but of trained professional operators and all of the auxiliary equipment and people needed. This requires careful analysis that is often more than justified.

Availability. Scheduling and use of equipment can be a problem— not insurmountable but relative.

Programming delays. Where computers are involved, or in any complex situation that involves multiple stages and systems with mechanical devices, delays can be experienced in developing the system and the program. It is good to recognize this and one must not be dismayed if it takes several years to develop one of the more complex systems and completely debug it.

Unnecessary work generated. There is no doubt that, once available, equipment will be used and the work will expand to employ the machine's time.

Fortunately, there are more advantages quantitatively and qualitatively than disadvantages. And the obvious fact that personnel for conventional methods are becoming increasingly difficult to locate, train, and retrain, makes it apparent that any mechanical technique from highest order of complexity to lowest order of simplicity will eventually work its way more expansively into every company and management situation just to offset this purely human problem.

Training for Mechanical Tools

The product manager cannot expect to do justice to an entity as complex as the computer without knowing something of its operation, function, and theory. There are limitations to every machine, and often, more than one technique can be employed. How can judgment in selection and application be made without some specific knowledge? If this seems an unlikely situation, one should reflect on the misunderstanding of computer applications and the waste of time, money, and availability created by it.

Obviously this book cannot deal with the theory, development, capabilities, and limitations of each mechanical device; nor does the product manager have to become an expert in electronic or photographic techniques for information storage and retrieval. However, it is to his advantage to learn something of them. Fortunately, this can be easily accomplished, for many equipment suppliers are more than willing to be instructors, and there are numerous courses available.

Such training, while it may cost money and time, will more than repay the effort.

Electronic Data Processing

Probably no area of mechanical devices is so familiar to so many as electronic data processing (EDP). Little introduction is required; theory, cost, and availability are now part of every manager's cumulative knowledge and experience. What does require elaboration is the application of computer capability to marketing, product management, and related considerations. Primarily employed in financial activities, the computer, because of its speed, and ability to integrate complex and divergent information, can perform a host of operations far beyond human limitations; it therefore provides marketing with an excellent tool.

However, we must be candid and admit that marketing was relatively slow to realize this. The delay is partially due to the lack of scientific development in management. Computer application in marketing has still not reached its full potential because of a lack of human comprehension and imagination. But the concept does appear to be expanding.

Basically the computer is called upon to do two things: (1) Store, retrieve, integrate, and report information, and (2) Perform calculations based on operations and provide information. Of the two, the second is the more sophisticated and valuable ability, but the former is the one most often used in business operations. Considering the nature of the commercial world, this is not surprising. However, here too, changes are accruing as expanded application of computers in scientific services prevails and as management also expands computer and system employment in forecasting, model studies, and problem solving. The product manager should remember these differences and the opportunities offered to him and to marketing in both instances.

In our discussion, we are not going to make this distinction, since the orientation is toward application in relationship to the product management or marketing effort rather than the computer functions themselves. The information provided will indicate recommendations for reporting or other applications to provide information of an absolute or relative nature to use in decision making.

COMPUTER UTILIZATION

Before requesting any computer service, the product manager should consult all available data in the company and the general principles of systems discussed in the preceding chapter. In this way, the value of the service will be ascertained and its relationship to existing or future requirements simultaneously determined.

Once this is accomplished, we face two situations: the development of an entire series of marketing information, documentation reports, and systems or mere individual reports required to augment existing reporting or systemization. The second is the more common situation since most companies considering application of EDP in marketing already have some in-house capability and familiarity based on other areas of previously existing use. Such existing reporting systems or data bases should naturally be used in the structuring and development of new ones. Where totally integrated reporting systems, combining elements of reporting data from several areas are entailed, this essential is already provided for because systems representatives will take this into account. Whatever the case, the reports listed below are indicative of information required by marketing and product management that can be provided by EDP.

While there are many types of reports and specific formats possible, we shall refer here only to four essential categories of reports and reporting; the format is too variable and depends on individual circumstances and preferences, hence it should be designed internally.

1. Total reporting—all accounts, products, and territories.

2. Exception reporting—major accounts or key products.

3. Trigger reports—a variation of exception reporting, the report is triggered when deviations (sales, profits) exceed established limitations.

4. On request reports—a specific total, expectation, or trigger to be provided only when requested.

More detail on market and product management EDP reporting and services is given in the following longer list:

1. Sales (total, by product, by account, by territory, other).
2. Profit (gross by various categories, net by various categories).
3. Turnover.
4. Expense.
5. Ratios of sales to expense to cost.
6. Major or key account (sales, potential, profit, costs).
7. Market studies (size, location, potential, distribution).
8. Distribution studies (for alteration of marketing tactics; for location of additional warehousing or marketing locations; traffic determinations).
9. Budgets (contents depend on budgets established).
10. Performance review reports (sales to plan, profit to plan, territory to plan, total, other).
11. New product performance (by sales, by profit).
12. Inventory by product and location.
13. Selling prices and competitive prices (by products, by accounts, averages, comparative and absolute profits).
14. Packing and packaging variations (by product, by accounts).
15. Account accommodations (deferred billing, consignments, discounts, other).
16. Service (account, product, ratio of profit to service costs).
17. Delinquencies (shipments, invoices, payments, other).
18. Performance assessments (orders shipped on schedule, delinquencies, transfers, other).
19. Marketing expenses (administrative, travel and entertainment, other).
20. Forecasting reports.
21. Management account reporting systems.

Special technical reports would include:

1. Product development with PERT applications (schedules, status, projections).
2. Competitive product data (by product, by industry, performance and relative position).

3. Product data (specification, tolerances, performance, production records, rejects, cost of reworks, forecasts).
4. Pricing studies (to establish price initially, to determine requirements for price alteration).
5. Technical services (performance, cost, external customer services requiring computer time and application).
6. Analytical integration—advanced application of EDP to analytical techniques and utilization in internal functions and in customer service).

The foregoing list indicates a few principal reports and report elements. Using this as a starting point, one can construct a simple or complex EDP-based information system. Certain major information requirements can be distilled from this restricted tabulation, which, even when selectively developed, still includes a number of activities. Examination of the principal ones may be helpful in that no more involved, complex, or expensive a system should be evolved than is required to meet basic informational needs. These involve data on: sales, profit, market, products, customer, cost, and technical aspects.

These seven building blocks form the primary marketing and product management information elements. From the tabulation we begin to gain some concept of their enlargements and refinements as they would prevail in many marketing situations. The infinity of permutations possible precludes further extension here. However, this introduction should provide a guide to what elements should be considered. Combining this with the discussion on reporting found in the previous chapter, it should be possible to design a new system or improve an existing one.

FORECASTING APPLICATIONS

Before leaving EDP, the tremendous possibilities that computer applications hold for forecasting should be mentioned. We have already considered the importance of forecasting now and its increasing importance in the future. This subject, still in its infancy, has already been vastly improved with several available computer forecasting programs. Their application and complexity prevent detailed review here, but we can say that there are many techniques or specific systems used for the forecasting of individual products, submarkets, total markets, and the economy. These systems can be adapted to particular marketing situations; such modifications depend on information available, information desired, existing computer equipment, and time. All product managers should become thoroughly familiar with such capabilities in their companies.

Scheduling

With a number of time-consuming and complicated report requirements, scheduling becomes extremely important. This can only be resolved in the confines of the company, but when developing such schedules there are a few requirements that should be considered:

Sequential importance. Some reports and their use follow a sequence that relates to the interdependency of the report and its user. One depends on the other. These should be identified and scheduled accordingly.

Application of the report for analysis. When the report is required for analysis of performance against plan, for example, and this is scheduled for a specific date, then the report must be available accordingly.

Business calendar. The schedule should conform with established business calendars that have been internally developed.

Alternatives available.

Priorities.

Exception, trigger, and "on request" reports as opposed to regularly scheduled periodic reports.

Computer Time

There is in every company a real problem with real-time, or instant EDP usage. This may be a play on words, but it certainly states the case. When this occurs, time sharing or complete resort to external computer facilities may be required. Both of these approaches are available. Product managers should remember this since so often tight schedules must be met and internal computer capacity may not suffice at the time. Cost may be a factor, but this is readily determinable.

At this point it is also noteworthy for the product manager who works in a company that does not have its own computers to consider application of EDP to product management by external computer service agencies. These are available, and in many cases, complete service, from programming to duplicating, is available at reasonable cost. The savings in time, effort, and expansion of capability can justify expenses in most cases.

Wherever there is a large volume of data to be stored, sorted, integrated, computed, systematized, or any combination of these elements, then EDP can perform functions that cannot otherwise be practically accomplished. The product manager and the marketing manager are rapidly assimilating computer language and computer technology and finding new ways of employing EDP in the marketing and product management operation. The beginning has only begun.

Model Studies

The use of models for prediction and performance analysis is not a particularly new technique in scientific circles; however, in the field of management, it has only recently been employed. Basically, the procedure involves establishing a set of premises that create the environment for the function under study. By changing the parameters and the input, the model can then predict outcome. This is admittedly a highly inexact and oversimplified explanation, but it should familiarize product managers with the availability of the technique and its possible applications in product or marketing management.

The model itself, if it is relatively simple, can be constructed and manipulated manually. But this severely limits variables, size, and scope. The more common approach is to employ model studies, based on computer systems. In this way, extremely large and complex models can be developed, the most famous of which is the Wharton model of the U.S. economy.

It is beyond our abilities to review construction of any model in detail that involves advanced mathematics and detailed knowledge. The question, however, is how product managers can use models. And the answer has to be equivocal: they can and they cannot. They can, if they are willing to employ modifications of the existing model or spend time and money to develop a new model for their own purpose. This latter is practical but can be extremely costly and difficult because of the model's complexity. It can take years and thousands of dollars to develop a model, and there are no guarantees of accuracy or reliability.

The second phase of the answer is even less encouraging; it is the one that says they should not be used at all, and this is based on the assumption that if a cheap, rapid technique is desired, there simply is no such model available, and the product manager had best employ empathy or "guestimation."

If, however, the problems are so complex and costly, why is this apparently esoteric and slightly out-of-reach technique considered here at all? The whys of this are basically related to dynamics we have already discussed and the needs for future management. While the problems of model development and implementation are here today, they may well be gone tomorrow. The model provides a powerful device by which to test hypothesis and product performance, analyze markets, and determine product reception in markets. It also helps predict the direction and future activity of economy, market, and product. Therefore, despite its expense, the device is less costly than the "develop, market, and see" technique.

The underlying value of model studies for marketing is twofold: one, for projecting specific markets, and economies; two, for determining the response to individual products.

The implementation of models in specific marketing situations is a long and arduous struggle, but the situation is improving. It is practical to study the technique and review individual problems with the ubiquitous computer experts.

Electronic Communication

Communication is the lifeblood of product management. One almost universal technique is through electronic devices. From Mr. Bell's omnipresent black box to very intricate telecommunicators, there seems to be no end to such devices. The message here is the importance of electronic communication and some remarks on its application.

First, electronic communication is a time-saving device. Picking up the telephone and calling 3000 miles may be more expensive than writing a four-page letter, but when examined comparatively, is it really? When considering the two methods, the comparative rather than absolute cost should be evaluated, and with it the intangible assets of time and place. While few firms object to extensive use of telephone, teletype, Telex, or other devices, many do not avail themselves of additional savings in labor and time through the acquisition of such devices like automatic dialing with punched cards for frequently called numbers. This may seem a trifling point, yet it is one that many companies neglect; hence, much managerial time is spent on a function that could be automated for little cost.

Whatever the communications problem, external or internal, there are many approaches that can be taken toward its solution. Awareness of the problem is the first difficulty. Once this has been achieved, there are an almost staggering number of ways to improve communications electronically. We cannot expand on the individual devices or their installation and operation here. It is enough to state that they have an important place in management's hands and should be particularly valuable to those whose central functions involve the speed and accuracy of information gathering and dissemination. Experts in these fields abound, from the "friendly" telephone company to electronics firms that produce tailor-made equipment for specific requirements. A very interesting one that combines electronics, radio transmission, and information storage and retrieval is discussed a few pages hence.

Calculators

Seemingly insignificant, calculators can save incalculable time and effort. Most of the arithmetic functions performed by the product manager are admittedly simple, but these can be extremely time consuming when a large number of items is involved. In the planning, forecasting, costing, and control areas, this is often the case; and simplification, extension, factoring, or submission of given input to several sequential mathematical operations can reduce a seemingly complex and lengthy project into a faster, easier, and less error-riddled performance.

The number and diversity of electronic calculators available makes selection more of a problem than the availability and ability of equipment. While there is virtually no limit to reasonable machine performance, there are basic requirements in every situation. As we said in the earlier part of this chapter, selection and expense are important; but it is wise to recall that a slightly larger investment will provide equipment of much greater capability. When considering such equipment, the user must also be taken into account. Some of the machines are complex and require training for their operation. Where this is the case, the product manager, or those who are to use the machine, should receive same.

Data Storage and Retrieval

There is no more important area of mechanization than the equipment for information storage and retrieval. A vast amount of important documentation is lost because of inadequate filing and recovery procedures. Every office, no matter how small or large, has this problem. The time lost in trying to locate a missing document or, even more devastating, the loss encountered because of the necessity to redo, is imponderable. In the realms of literature searching, patent reference, scientific documentation, and library science, these problems have already attained astronomical proportions; and business is not far behind.

Fortunately, machines have once more come to the rescue, and there are several to solve both simple and complex information storage and retrieval problems. Each of the mechanical means thus far developed has specific limitations and advantages, but there are so many approaches available that a device can be obtained to satisfy almost any requirement. The main limitations are usually the number of documents that can be stored and the time necessary for sorting, locating and displaying them.

Essentially, either a purely mechanical technique, such as punched cards and corresponding indexing, or a microfilm apparatus with complementary coding and indexing is used. The type and preference depends on variables such as sequential information, number of items to be filed, updating requirements, locators, and speed requisites. With each technique systems can be developed that will enable efficient searching and location of an individual document from several thousand, with display in a matter of seconds.

The two major approaches can also be combined to obtain the advantages of both. For example, consider the following devices:

Technique	*Advantage*	*Disadvantage*
Card punch	More information can be stored. Can be less expensive initially and to maintain. Updating relatively rapid and inexpensive. Total in-house capability.	No visual display. Two-step process involves locating the reference and locating the document. Pictures cannot be filed in themselves. Slow.
Microfilm or the later variation, microfiche	Rapid, direct, one-step searches and locations of actual document. Can display document directly. Can reproduce photographs or illustrative material. Can be adapted to color as well as black-and-white images. Can be directly linked to photo reproduction devices for direct generation of copies.	More expensive initially and to maintain. Updating can be problematic. May have to use outside film processing unless more expense for internal equipment is justified. Preparation time is long. Some equipment has severe storage limitation, although two or more units can be employed.

In examining these systems, it becomes apparent that, depending on needs, either one might suffice; but in some situations, both could be useful. For example, in filing product reports, the first system may be more than adequate, and a product file containing all the typical records we have discussed could be developed and then referenced by code. The code reference and an extract of major data could be located on the index cards for immediate retrieval in the card system. Therefore, expense and complexity of microfilm for every document would be obviated. And considering the reference requirements, a little time spent in searching and finding would not be of paramount importance.

When, however, immediate data are required, such as answering pricing questions by telephone, the second, or microfiche-based procedure, would be advantageous. In such a system, the films are filed usually by code, and in one of the newest systems, by binary codes, enabling greatly expanded filing and cross-referencing possibilities. By employing the code, which is keyed into the films, one can display the exact page of information on a console screen within seconds. Employing such a system might involve placing the entire product price listings, after appropriate codification, in the machine with profitability and other pertinent data. Then, when the call is received, simply pressing the right buttons will display all the information needed for the pricing decision.

Though this may sound incredibly easy, it is, nevertheless, true, and exemplifies the possibilities in information retrieval. There is one system that works by remote processing. All of the data inputs are stored in a central computer that has the information under private code. To retrieve information from this service, one subscribes and is then given a code number. Data are submitted in the conventional manner and located in the computer under the proper code. When information is desired, a person using a desk console radios the request to the central storage location, and within seconds the data are retrieved and radioed back to be displayed on the desk console. For now, this technique may be a trifle expensive, but within the next few years, as the problems faced by business greatly mount, such solutions will be practical.

Every product manager is involved, so that data retrieval is worthy of emphasis. The possibilities mentioned above are only a few of many. It is more than worth the effort to carefully review information storage and retrieval requirements now and then, project one's needs into the future, and consider a system, whether augmented by these techniques or not, that will meet these requirements. Time spent now is time saved later. One should always remember that time is money.

Visual Aids

Frequently, obvious visual aids are overlooked or not fully used. There are many occasions when the product manager is asked to make presentations, either within the company for, say, marketing plan presentation and training programs, or outside the firm, for customers or trade associations. In any of these situations, we often find that too much reliance is placed on words and not on the techniques to support them. There are several inexpensive and portable devices that can be rented. Equipment that can make presentation easy, entertaining, and informative is always available. Let us review these briefly.

Projectors. These can be still or movie, sound or silent. The silent slide is most commonly used, and excessive application has made this approach trite and stilted. An animated movie presentation can awaken new interests. It may be a little more time consuming, but it is well worth the effort.

Models. Management people think of sophisticated mathematics when the word model is mentioned, but here we mean the miniature physical representation of the product or equipment used in the process. It can be very effective.

Charts and graphs. Again, these are well-known techniques that can be brightened with simple things like extensive use of color and transparent overlays. Photo and montage techniques are also excellent attention-getters and keepers.

Felt boards. These are very simple. Felt backing is applied to the objects that are to be displayed. When the objects are placed on the felt board, they adhere to it. This is a very rapid and effective technique that can be used in an endless number of constructive ways.

These are only a smattering of the equipment and ideas available. They do reflect, however, a concern for the problem. If presentations are to be effective, they must be well conceived and executed. Often the conception is no serious problem, but the execution is another matter entirely. The effort expended on developing the speech, short or long, deserves attention to aids that can make it more presentable and profitable.

7

Monitoring and Controlling the Product

CENTRAL to the activities of the product manager specifically and the corporation generally are products. It is the product manager's job, redundant as it may seem, to manage them and the corporation's lifeblood to market them profitably. Obviously, then, techniques must be employed to assess not only the sales or marketing performance of a product, but more fundamentally, to relate the product itself to longevity and anticipation.

Without such analysis, management knows nothing of the real status of the product itself. One preeminent difference between success and failure is true knowledge of the product's present and future positions. Response time being what it is, it is more important to have a feel for anticipated position than the current one. Too many companies operating on excellent present performance have not recognized impending product disaster through lack of perspective; they had no clue of the product's eventual position in the market place. Once they did, it was often too late.

To accomplish this vital objective, there are three principal techniques. Fortunately, all are relatively simple in concept, easy to master, reasonably economical to implement, and within the monetary reach of all. More important, they are adaptable, flexible, and completely within the scope of any product manager's activities, thereby providing his company with the ability to answer this pressing question: How is my product doing and how can I ascertain this expeditiously?

The techniques of product monitoring and predicting are: product audit, product life cycle studies, and product control. While in reality the third technique is predicated on the outcome of information developed by the first two and is, perhaps, not really an analytical tool, it is considered here because it is the management instrument by which a company can exercise control over its product and implement specific product strategies or actions to accomplish objectives; it also allows advantageous use of product audit and life cycle data. At the same time, it is a viable factor in furnishing management's answer to the question posed above. It is one active part of the relationship between product information and action.

In any event, it is the responsibility of the product manager to use all three as an everyday part of his assessment of action and reaction product activities. He must obtain command of these techniques and, where they are not being used, study them carefully.

The Product Audit

Though often confused with the product life cycle, let it be understood that the product audit is an independent, self-sustaining, and useful product analysis tool. It consists of elements designed to assess the performance of the product and to project anticipated performance in relation to the market in terms of price, cost, profit, sales, and marketability. It can be applied not only to individual products but collectively to product lines, series of brands, and total product offerings. Market orientation can also be added to the audit by assessments of the product, brand line or all products in specific markets, market segments, or all markets

Consideration must also be given to frequency. All products should be examined at least annually, and critical products semiannually or even more frequently if particularly significant factors are involved. This determination can only be made within the requirements of the particular product management environment.

In considering the product audit, we can draw an analogy to the product life cycle, which is discussed next, in that the premise of the product life cycle derives from conceiving of the product as viable. If this be the case, then the product audit can best be compared to a product physical examination. Just as we frail mortals take our annual physicals, so must the product. Similarly, we have our aches and pains, and so do products. We must know of them to treat or correct them.

When we find a problem, we follow through on it and have more frequent examinations or consultations; hence, when the product has its problem or critial area, we examine it more than annually. Reexamination and follow-up vary with the problem and correction. Regardless of frequency or cycling, the analogy prevails, and we must treat our "patient" accordingly.

Looked at in this light, we are effectively creating a product profile as we perform our product audit, and we should maintain the profile as long as we maintain the product. We are now talking more about forms and format than philosophy and essence. This, too, is important, for as seen before, records must be kept and located. To audit our product periodically we should therefore pay due attention to forms design.

In this book examples of forms have been deliberately avoided because they are individual in nature and should be predicated on the needs and preferences of individual companies. We have concentrated on content and rationale, thereby furnishing the basis for forms design.

Likewise we have considered the elements of product audit and concomitant questions the product manager should pose to himself in the design and execution of the audit, leaving selection of content and means of implementation to him. While the mechanics of filing should be the concern of the product manager, he should strongly consider filing product audit forms in the file on each product. At the same time he should maintain separate audit files, particularly when auditing collectively, that is, for product line and total product audits.

ELEMENTS OF PRODUCT AUDIT

Marketing position. In this area the product manager should determine and record the following factors, which are to be evaluated in the dimensions of past, present, and future:

Sales (actual, planned, projected)
Market size
Market share
Distribution requirements

Profit. All factors relative to profit must be considered. In the relationship of product justification this can only be accurately and realistically assessed on the basis of established profit goals and minimum standards. Where they exist, then positive determination of relative position and performance is possible. Justification of below-standard profit objectives then relate to product management considerations when below-standard performance may be tolerated because of such other factors as: total product line, company image, prestige, competitive reasons, and corrective expectations. Regardless of the explanation, however, the point is that there should be one and that no unprofitable or below-standard profit product should be maintained unless such a justification is determined and documented. In this profit analysis, the product manager should determine and record:

> Gross profit
> Net profit
> Profit continuation plans
> Contribution
> Expectation for improvement or decline
> Justification for retention of below-standard profit performers
> Strategies and actions for improvement where necessary

Cost. Thought must be given to the costing technique employed in the corporation; and the product manager, while having no direct control over accounting procedures, should become thoroughly familiar with the one used in his company. In particular, he should ascertain and fully comprehend those primary factors that influence his costs. This is essential if any meaningful cost reduction or profit improvement is to be contemplated or accomplished. In the preceding, when we discussed profit, it was mentioned that some products are retained that yield below-standard profit based on contribution, capacity utilization, overhead effects, and similar economic considerations. Many of these factors naturally relate to retention of product with unfavorable costs. Overhead control can be especially important for minimizing allocated cost variations and providing stabilization. The extent to which this is or should be done relates to allocations, throughput, plant capacity, capacity utilization, and other varying factors. Hence the need for comprehensive and continued monitoring. Cost items to be determined:

> Manufacturing
> Standardization
> Engineering
> Quality control
> Material

Sales service
Labor
Packaging
Distribution
Advertising
Promotion
Ratio or relationship of cost to volume, distribution to volume, packaging to volume
Opportunities to improve

Price. Elsewhere the use of price as a product strategy is reviewed. We are now concerned with recording and documenting price and pricing policy in the profile according to these guidelines:

List or book price
Competitive
Average
Our own
Competition
Market possibilities: increases, decreases, competitive activity

Value. While the value of a product is an important consideration, it must be clearly understood that this is more perceptual than actual. When Mr. or Mrs. Buyer tells you, or better yet, a friend, that you have a good product and encourages him to buy it, we should realize that in general he has absolutely no basis for such a determination; he often relates only his conceptions. This does not mean that this is unimportant, but rather that it is difficult to control and more difficult to create the actual product value, as well as its image. Recognizing this, the product manager must then consider value from three viewpoints: To us, which includes not only our assessment of the product's value in the market, but in our assortment, to customer, and as perceived by competition.

Quality. This also is a subjective factor, since most consumers have no basis for accurately determining whether or not we are selling a quality product. But, as with value, this is nonetheless quite important, and the product manager must strive to identify those factors considered indicative of quality by the customer and then determine how to exploit them. From an internal standpoint he is directly concerned with specifications and quality control—an important area given further treatment later. Keep in mind that controls cost money, and many products must be saved from the unreasonable costs of overengineering or quality control.

Specifications
Anticipated alterations
Recommended improvements
Recommended alterations
Quality as perceived by customer, by competition, by us

Competition. We now enter another never-never land where it is more perception than reality—we mention this for it is a circumstance to be recognized and avoided if possible. The product manager faces the difficult task of endeavoring to obtain an accurate impression of the competition, meaning a dispassionate assessment of competitors and competitive activity. He further must always consider the competition in two respects: present and future action; and future action from two viewpoints—what they will do anyway and what they will do in response to his actions in the marketplace, always in the additional constraint of competitive ability, capacity and, most enigmatic of all, intention.

Activity
Atmosphere
Action and reaction
Capability
Quality
Marketing effort and capability
Sales effort and capability
Image
Technical efforts and capability
Service efforts and capability
Strategies, tactics, and practices
Short- and long-range intention

Service. From the product manager's point of view service is several things: it is necessary, expected, expensive, and increasingly demanded. At the same time it is a marketing tool and does generate or maintain sales. Hence it is a fact of marketing and selling life.

Service, of course, means different things to different people. In industrial markets it is usually gratuitous support of the product and the customer whether through technical or commercial assistance. In some markets the same factors are involved; in others, especially the consumer segments, service itself is the product (repairs, installations) and must then be conceived of as a product with all the cost, competition, and other factors analyzed. Here we are concerned with service given in support of the product marketing efforts rather than service as the product.

Internal services
External services
Costs
Future trends
Return on investment
Control
Effective utilization
Projected levels of service activity

Relative performance. Products do not exist in a vacuum; they must be analyzed in comparison to our products, our product lines, competition, the market, the consumer. Each of these comparisons should be established relative to:

Sales
Profit
Costs
Distribution
Rationale for continuation of product
Future outlook

From analysis of the factors developed in the product audit, we should, like all good physicians, be able to arrive at a diagnosis, prognosis, and, if necessary, therapeutic regime, or action for improvement. In so doing we determine the exact status of our product in relationship to ourselves, our competitors, and our market (diagnosis); this should lead to prognostic determination regarding the product, improvement, deterioration, continuation, discontinuation, and improvement (prognosis). In those instances, and there will be many, where actions are required to improve or correct problem areas, specific action programs for improvement (therapy) must be developed and implemented.

When to Use Product Audit

As mentioned, the product audit usually occurs annually, with more frequent review of those individual products requiring remedial action.

The technique of product audit, while a very useful tool, can and sometimes does stand alone, and no further analysis is made. However, in more complex operations it is beneficial to use this technique in concert with product life cycle studies for comprehensive management. Also, it should be understood that product audit or life cycle studies are not used only for existing products. While this is their present primary use, they can also be employed in the development of justifications for new products; here, the technique is used as a base for analyzing the product and compiling a projected product audit and life cycle—a very helpful aid in analyzing and determining new product potential.

At this point it might be well to summarize the cans and cannots of product audit. While most of them are self-evident, this recapitulation can help put the technique into perspective:

A product audit cannot
> Correct a problem in and of itself.
> Replace judgment and good product management.
> Answer all questions about all products and markets.
> Be completely objective since some input is subjective.
> Suffice for complete product analysis.

A product audit can
> Provide statement and analysis of past and present performance and expectations of future performance.
> Isolate product and market problem areas.
> Identify key products.
> Identify key markets.
> Identify products to consider deleting or adding.
> Assist in or develop
>> Integrated product management systems
>> Product marketing strategies
>> Planning
>> Problem solving
>> New product development
>> New product recommendations
>> Identification of marketing needs
>> Market analysis
>> Product control and review

Product Life Cycle Studies

Much has been written about product life cycles. Authors, renowned and otherwise, have lifted their voices loud and long in either advocation or condemnation. Generally, there are more advocates than opponents, and the usual criticisms are not of the concept or its relevancy, but rather of interpretation, usage, or negative management attitudes. This is most encouraging since it indicates a wide, if not universal, acceptance of the product life cycle precepts and bodes well for the future of the idea and its use. Not a panacea, not even a pariah, it is multifunctional and indicative of multidimensional trends. Effectively employed and exploited, the product life cycle is a viable instrument, and though long given credence and paid verbal homage, it has been left to lie on the dusty shelf of management relics. Often treated as academic dogma, it has never fully received that ultimate business accolade, usage.

Life cycle studies are based on the premise that products, like those who manage them, are alive; and like their managers, they live in a living world. They, like people, have their early growth period, period of maturity, ultimate decadence, and eventual demise.

It is the implications of these stages and their application to the management of the product that have been somewhat illusive. Furthermore, the concept usually has been applied only to new products. It has also been limited primarily to sales rather than expanded to premarketing product analysis and the evaluation of older products. Also, the obvious and readily negotiated extension into profit-market-cycle analysis correlated to the product has apparently been neglected.

When we discuss the use of product-life-cycle analysis, we should consider its implementation in three major areas:

1. Prognostication of new products.
2. Monitoring existing products.
3. As an element in an integrated product management system.

Further, it should be extended to include:

1. Traditional product-life-cycle analysis.
2. Profit-life-cycle analysis.
3. Market-life-cycle analysis.
4. Integrated product-profit-market-life cycle analysis.
5. Planning implications.
6. Projection base for effect of altering controllable variables in product life; that is, the product and marketing mix via manual or computer model studies.

We must first consider each of these elements in some detail; it must be further understood that the measurement of cycles should not end with what is merely the beginning—namely, putting ink to paper, calibrating, and drawing a curve.

It is the use we make of the resultant information that is germane. The making or breaking of the new product can be vastly affected by careful monitoring of the cycle with accompanying appropriate action. And the life of a mature or declining product can be prolonged or even revived if the implications of cycle analysis and reaction are comprehended and optimized. As the basis for marketing decisions, these integrated cycle analyses, combined with other product management techniques, provide an effective guide. They also enable one to balance between objective and subjective data in the product management decision-making process.

TRADITIONAL PRODUCT LIFE CYCLE

The classic concept of the product life cycle can be examined by referring to an ideal product life cycle, which is represented in Figure 11. All products do not follow this curve; the cycle is a function of market, consumer, time, and effort. As illustrated, we are dealing with four distinct phases or stages in the cycle. Each has its own characteristics, which can be used for effective management.

1. The introductory or development stage is characterized by:
   New products or new market.
   Demand exists or must be created.
   Competition depends on type of product: new product—no or little competition; "me too"—strong competition; improved or modified product—variable competition.
   Product may or may not be proved technically.

FIGURE 11
Profit Life Cycle

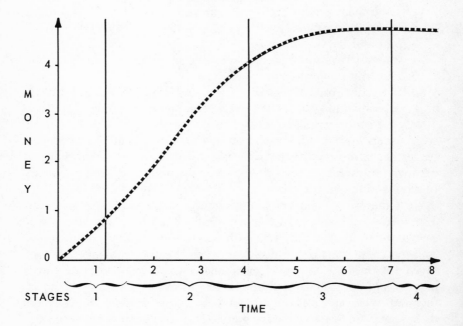

Duration of cycle variable dependent on: market (size, activity, acceptance), pricing, competition, marketing effort, and strategies.

Marketing effort is intense.

2. The ascendancy (or growth) stage is characterized by:

Market, product usage, acceptance, and sales expand.

Profits begin.

Competitive activity accelerates.

New competition enters market.

Marketing activity to be reviewed.

Pricing to be reviewed.

Technical acceptance verified.

Marketing effort remains high.

3. The maturity stage is characterized by:

Growth.

Market, product usage, acceptance, and sales stabilize.

Product modification begins.

Product distribution may alter.

Product packing may alter.

Competitive activity stabilizes.

A holding pattern evolves.

Product future to be reviewed.

Profit squeeze is on.

Marketing effort levels off.

4. The obsolescent stage is characterized by:

Market, product usage, and sales decline.

Marketing effort declines or terminates.

Profit often on decline.

Withdrawal consideration finalized.

Competitive activity usually declines unless competitors step up activity to force others out and preserve market for themselves.

These four clearly discernible phases are encountered with virtually every product. The rate of cycle change and the relative curve shape—rapid inclines or declines—are different in industrial, consumer, and government markets and within segments of these markets. They vary from product to product offered by the same company within essentially the same market. The pragmatic value of the cycle may be doubted by some who sagely say, "With such variations where is the practical value?" This is a valid criticism if the cycle determination were not used for its anticipatory and predictive values, as well as a control and review procedure for development of product actions.

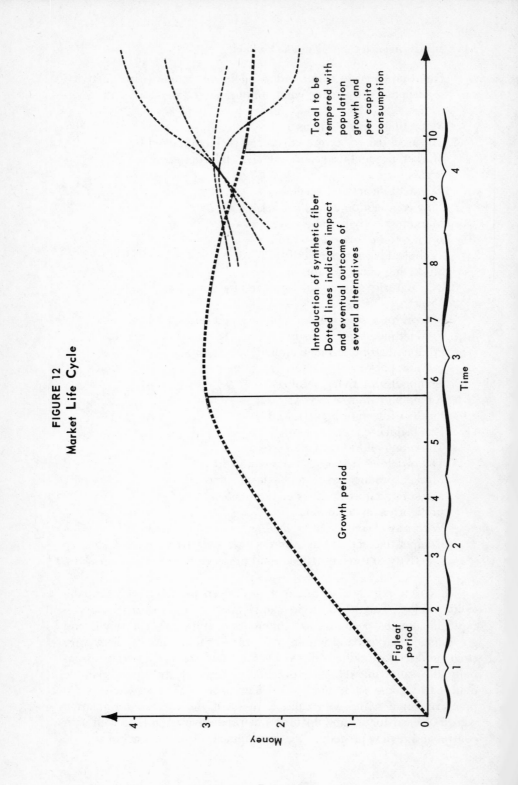

FIGURE 12
Market Life Cycle

LIFE CYCLE APPLIED TO MARKET

The cyclical nature of business is not a revelation. However, it is usually conceived of in more broadly based financial parameters and not extended in application to cycle determination of major or minor market segments within markets. That this is done in some industries is again no revelation. The stages of introduction, growth, maturation, and deterioration encountered with individual products also holds true in the more collective or aggregative totality of the market in which these products are being sold. The determination of these stages in this broader interpretation may be somewhat more difficult but nonetheless possible. And so we can establish market-segment life cycles that would ideally follow a pattern similar to that shown in Figure 12.

Note that in this instance, aside from the decline of specific subsegments, the market does not frequently go into a total decline. It is perpetuated via the introduction of new products and the creation of new submarkets, which thereby effect continuation of the major market segment. A contribution of cycle analysis is the ability to visualize the market in this more refined representation, and then employ it for development of products or strategies within the segment.

This example is, of course, vastly oversimplified, and is merely meant to be indicative of a principle rather than reflect an actual situation. In the real analysis the total natural fiber market would be assessed in relation to the individual natural fiber and those synthetic fibers that threatened its displacement, and then related to natural and synthetic fiber blends with consumption being cross-related to population growth and per capita consumption.

Regardless of the specifics, it can be readily determined that a similar structure of four-phase evolution prevails with equal validity in both the market and the product. The number of markets to be analyzed and the correlative factors to be employed provide infinite permutations that are best left to the discretion of the product manager as they must be pertinent to the product and situation assessed. Again, this relationship can be used for the same purposes as were the cycles developed for individual products.

PROFIT CYCLE ANALYSIS

We will now consider extention of this concept into profit cycle analysis and distribution. While the preceding applications were a direct function of market, consumer, time, and marketing effort, so is the profit—but to a lesser extent. We are measuring a reflection of cost to price and the impact of the cost or sales-price relation, which is a marketing function. More important, we now introduce a third variable: marketing or management philosophy. Before any profit levels can be established, the marketing group must determine acceptable profit and profit strategy, including: (a) high initial profit to recover research, development, distribution and other costs; (b) moderate profit for continued stabilized return; (c) fluctuating price in relation to profit to maintain a given profit ratio; and (d) extremely low initial and continued profit to discourage competition.

The selection of these alternatives is the key to marketing. It separates the art from the science. Analysis of the product and the market cycle will assist the marketing executive in making this decision; it will also help the product manager to make his pricing and marketing proposals.

Once the basic strategy is determined, we can illustrate a typical set of cycles—one for each of the four profit premises, assuming that there is no alteration in strategy for pricing and profit during the cycle. This is admittedly unrealistic, but it indicates the functionality of the cycle.

Use of the cycle is painfully obvious, as illustrated in Figure 13, with a curve predicated on no alteration of pricing or profit strategies. It is exactly in this manner that the cycle provides value. As with product and market-cycle analysis it can provide indications for appropriate activity, such as when to raise or lower selling price or alter acceptable profitability as well as when to consider abandoning the unprofitable product.

INTEGRATION OF CYCLE ANALYSIS

Now that we have examined each of these three cycles in some detail, we can consider their integration. Recognizing that no product exists without some profit, or at least, without some rationalization that amounts to profit, and realizing that it does not sell in a vacuum, we must now be concerned with the interrelationship between product, profit, and market.

While many product and marketing executives will tell you that this can be ascertained subjectively, subconsciously, by empathy, or through intellectual guessing, in the market situation, which is our business environment, we cannot operate solely on such precepts. There-

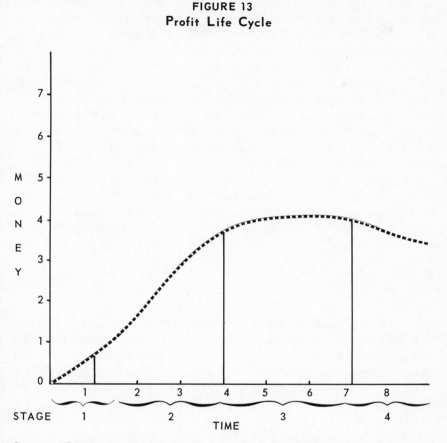

FIGURE 13
Profit Life Cycle

fore, modern management looks to systems, integrated management, and, hopefully, the product manager to employ devices that will assist it in determining the most objective data; this is then melded with the intuitive aspects of decision making.

To accomplish this we can resort to the three analytical cycles we have considered, developing cycles that integrate the market, product, and profit by relatively simple superimposition. By varying the input we can use this technique for further predictive studies or have recourse to even more advanced predictive computer model techniques. Even when using computer models, the cycle analysis technique can be used to advantage in preliminary study for the final model.

It may be helpful to examine a series of integrated cycle analyses and assess their values.

Figure 14 is an example of phases 1 and 2 in a stable market with good potential. The product was off to a good start, but then faltered. Determinations to be made are: why did the product falter, and what possible corrective actions should be taken. The product should then be monitored carefully.

Figure 15 is an example of phases 1 and 2 in a new and accelerated market. It indicates an excellent new market with outstanding potential. The product is off to a good start. Is there anything to be done? Since performance is so exceptionally good there may be a tendency to relax the effort. This tendency should be watched along with the continuing performance of the product.

Figure 16 illustrates an example of phases 3 and 4 of a product in a stable market, but the product itself is in attrition. This product may continue to generate some sales and profit, but both are slackening in a very stable market. Serious consideration should be given to withdrawal.

Uses of Cycle Analysis

Before we can determine the usefulness of these cycles, we must isolate relevant elements in each sector and determine which of these are subject to our influence or control. In so doing, we can visualize those critical factors that affect the product, the market, and the profit. We can also see where improvements can be effected through exercise of options in the areas subject to our influences or direct control.

As with other aspects of marketing management, the combinations of effects and variations that can be built almost defy imagination. However, certain combinations work best in certain situations, and these are usually known to the product manager and his management; thus the field is narrowed to more clearly delineated critical or response areas. But evaluation of these elements in the context of newer markets and marketing situations provides insight into new areas of exploration, and exploitation.

On page 142 are the elements to consider in cycle analysis and use, with indications of: I, factors that can be influenced; C, factors subject to control; and V, variables essentially independent of the market effort and not subject to influence or control.

The relationship to integrated cycles is not shown in the list since it depends on three primary ones. Use of these elements provides management with additional control of the product and profit within the market and predictability of performance within a market. Addition-

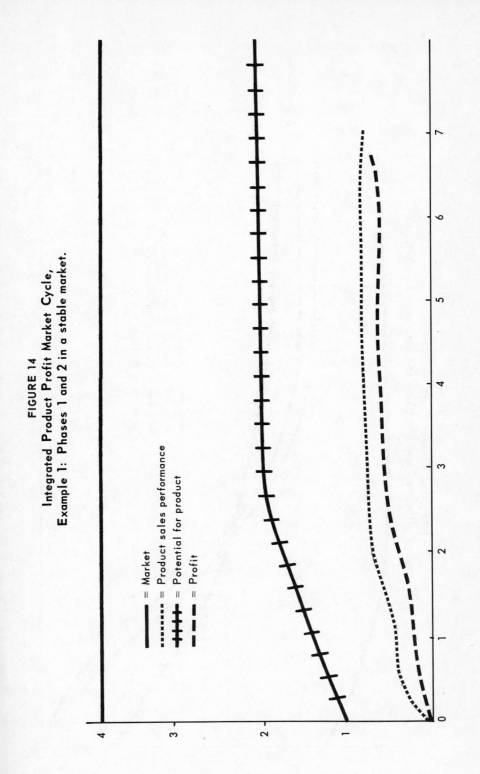

FIGURE 14

Integrated Product Profit Market Cycle,
Example 1: Phases 1 and 2 in a stable market.

= Market

= Product sales performance

= Potential for product

= Profit

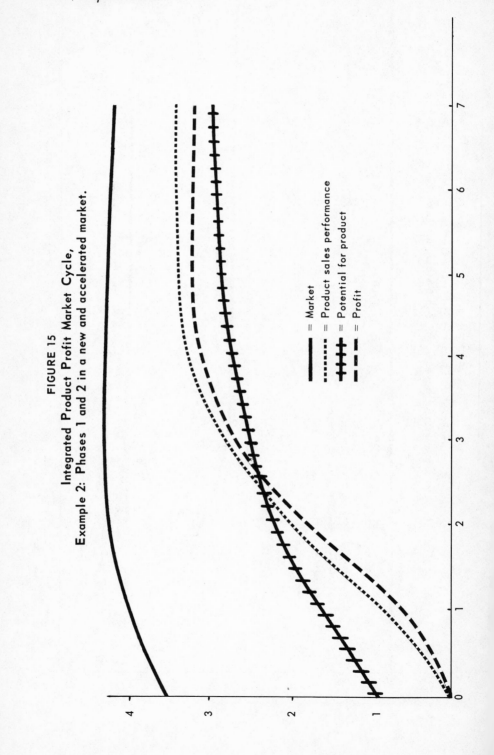

FIGURE 15

Integrated Product Profit Market Cycle,

Example 2: Phases 1 and 2 in a new and accelerated market.

= Market

= Product sales performance

= Potential for product

= Profit

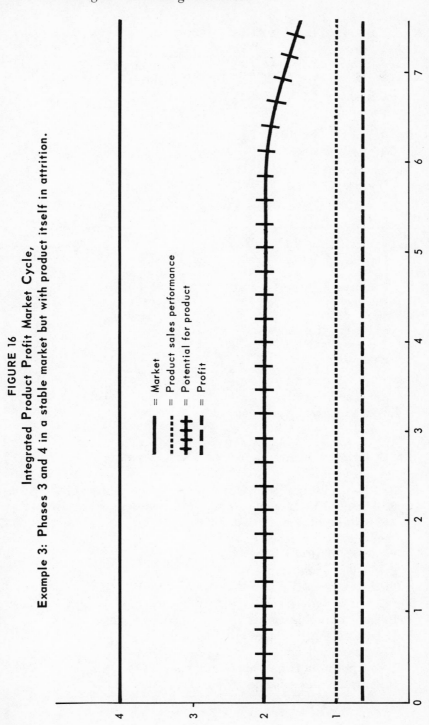

FIGURE 16

Integrated Product Profit Market Cycle,

Example 3: Phases 3 and 4 in a stable market but with product itself in attrition.

Product

Factor	Nature	Factor	Nature
Time	I	Distribution	C
Effort	C	Competition	V
Acceptance	I	Supply	C
Marketing	C	Service	C
Manufacturing	C	Withdrawal	C
Cost	C	Modification	C
Price	C	Packaging	C
Advertising	C	Introduction	C
Production	C		

Market		Profit	
Factor	*Nature*	*Factor*	*Nature*
Time	I	Time	I
Effort	C	Effort	C
Consumer response	V	Amount	C
Duration	V	Improvement	C
Size	V	Deterioration	I
Feasibility of entering	V	Policy	C
Creation	I	Control	C
Elimination	I		

ally, they can be used in determining desirability of entering a market or of trying to create a new one.

USES OF PRODUCT, MARKET, AND PROFIT LIFE CYCLES

It is, hopefully, not redundant to list the principal uses of these concepts. These do not pretend to be either inclusive or exclusive; they merely indicate the major possibilities:

Determination of market entry.

Prediction of new product success.

Prediction of market needs.

Prediction of market trends and developments.

Analysis of performance—product, market, profit.

Isolation of problem areas.

Isolation of key products, markets, profit.

Assistance in planning.

Development of improvement programs.

Information source for decision making.

Product, profit, and market control and review.
Rapid assessment and continuous monitoring.

EXPLOITATION OF CYCLE DETERMINATION AND ANALYSIS

Cycles must be determined, analyzed, and understood before they can be meaningfully used. Too often they have been entrusted to the archives of valued but unused information. Now that we better appreciate their potential and significance, it is inconceivable that this could happen again. Further credence lies in examining a few examples of cycle exploitation and witnessing how it determines performance. Once we have knowledge we can exercise control and provide input to use what we know. Several options are open to us, and these can be well indicated by the cycle and our comprehension of our own situation.

In order to accomplish this, however, we have to approach cycle determination and application systematically. A regimen of preparation and review should be established, which may not be the same for each product, market, or profit situation. Older, more stable products may require only annual assessment, whereas more volatile and newer products must be reviewed semiannually, quarterly, or at other timed intervals. Some practical considerations are staff, availability of data, response time, and information lag time.

However it is essential that repeated analysis be made. Particularly in those instances where corrective action is being taken, or where creative marketing activities have been implemented, the mechanism for determining the results of these efforts is provided. Therefore, the cycle must be frequently reevaluated to assess the results of implemented activities. This will ensure optimum use of the technique and guarantee that effective results of planned actions ensue. As a pragmatic control device, it will enable active determination of success or failure and provide a determinant in continuation, alteration, or discontinuation of activity or product.

Here is something close to the hearts of all who recognize the expenses involved and the desirability of ascertaining what they obtain or do not obtain for their expenditures. There is little point in expending further efforts regardless of their nature, since all ultimately are reducible to monies out, without commensurate return.

To exploit the derived data, five steps should be taken: (1) Analyze performance against plan, time, effort, market, competition, and return; (2) Determine cause; (3) Consider effect of influence and control elements; (4) Vary influence or control elements; and (5) Reassess effect after appropriate time.

Product Control

Product control as used here implies or states that the product manager should manage his product and not the converse. This may seem supercilious since it is axiomatic that the product manager manages—an active process that indicates he is in control. While this may be a philosophical truism, it is not always reflected in the more mundane realities of daily business activity. Often deeply and understandably involved in the day-to-day responsibilities of his position, the product manager becomes blinded to the essentials of control in the more restrictive areas of concern such as the product's number, age, elimination, and consolidation—the more mechanical details of product housekeeping.

Many old dogs lie around in the kennel simply because no one has the time, energy, inclination or, occasionally, courage to relegate them to the domicile of antiquated canines. If we are honest, we must admit this delinquency. Unfortunately, this attitude is costly, for no one can doubt the expense of maintaining marginal, inactive, or just plain moribund products.

Every product, whether successful or inactive, costs money to maintain. Some of these expenses are measurable and some elusive, but they do exist. The first quantifiable ones are derived from overhead and long-lamented expenses associated with just doing business. When a firm is computer-powered, some expenses are higher but, fortunately, more clearly identified. The word is "fortunately" because there is some tendency to discount these expenses as more imaginary than real and to say that "we have to sell something and our people are here anyway," to justify retention. When the computer moves in and fully demonstrates the magnitude of these costs, such archaic philosophy yields to arithmetic.

In concerning ourselves with this aspect, we can list several identifiable cost elements in maintaining obsolete or slow-moving products:

Quantifiable	*Nonquantifiable*
Order processing	Dilution of marketing effort
Internal operations	Dilution of sales effort
Customer billing	Loss of other possibly more
Inventory	profitable sales
Computer records use and	Data capacity utilization
maintenance	Confusion
Operational maintenance	Internal
and use	External
Technical or customer service	Possible misdirection of effort

Quantifiable
Equipment and man-hours
    utilization
Sales or marketing expense

From analysis of the above comes the rationale for eliminating those slow, unhealthy, dead, or dying products hanging like proverbial skeletons in the manager's closet. If we stretch our imaginations even further, we can justify removing some of those low-profit items that we know have little expectation of revival. We must, of course, balance other broader economic considerations, already examined, when considering justification for low-profit items in our review of product audits.

Some of this applies also to slow-moving products, especially when their nature is such that they represent the only use and, hence, payout for selected equipment. Regarded realistically, this is more the exception than the rule, and we are on safer ground when we think in broader terms of removing the obsolete, the slow moving, and the less profitable. The reasons for withdrawal are therefore:

Saving money in areas indicated.
Concentration of marketing effort on those remaining meaningful
    products.
Reduction in inventory.
Reduction in administrative overheads.
Reduction in useless sales efforts.
Improved plant efficiency.
Improved communication, coordination, and focus of efforts.
Improved control.

Now that we comprehend the requirements, large and small, the technique remains to be resolved. There are several different approaches to product withdrawal. Implementation should be related to the philosophy of the company, which reflects attitudes of the market, marketing executive, and product manager. The same approach cannot be successfully employed in every market, and frequently the same technique cannot be used for each product. However, in general, one or more of the following strategies can be used:

PRODUCT ELIMINATION STRATEGIES

Immediate outright withdrawal. The immediate withdrawal of a product, with appropriate notification to existing customers, is particularly useful when only token sales and little or no obsolete product inventory exist.

Phase out. This involves announcement of a product's ultimate withdrawal and provides the customer with notification of the impending withdrawal, giving him an effective date and providing him with the opportunity to purchase in the interim. Usually quantities available for purchase will be limited; otherwise, one may generate more orders than it is possible to fill, and the artificially regenerated interest in the product will only provoke the panicking customer into ordering twenty years' supply. This technique has value both to producer and customer. Where inventories exist, it provides the manufacturer with the opportunity of selling them; it also allows time for internal corporate adjustment, such as shutting off a manufacturing line. The customer's benefits are self-evident.

Limited offering. This means withdrawing the product from any active marketing effort while still allowing customers to purchase it. This is a compromise in that some marketing expenditures are obviously cut, and the only manufacturing outlay is predicated on actual sale. The customer is often notified of the action and advised that his order cycle should take into account manufacturing cycles of the supplier, since little or even no inventories will be maintained, thereby saving additional overhead and reducing the amount of product to be made.

Manufacture on contract only. On an exclusive order basis this can be construed as a variation of the limited offering. But no product is manufactured unless a firm contract is obtained from the customer, and then it is usually produced for only the one or two selected customers who commit themselves to predetermined corporate optimal quantities. This is related to optimum and profitable batch or unit sizes and to production cycles, so the contract should stipulate delivery schedules.

All these approaches, no matter how reasonable to the company, will be, to a greater or lesser extent, considered unfair, unjustified, and reprehensible by the customer. One must be prepared for this reaction and soften the blow. Ways and means to soften the withdrawal reaction syndrome are:

Explain policy and reason to marketing and sales people, and be sure they relate this to customer.

Provide adequate advance notice to customer of whichever technique is to be employed.

Consider recommendation of alternative products—yes, even competitors' products—to customer at time of withdrawal. There is a discernible benefit in maintaining the customer's good will. There was even a day when this was so important that it was an element in purchasing or selling a business. It eventually pays us to keep it, particularly when one considers how much was spent initially to obtain it.

Referral concept. Refer customer to another supplier either for the same or similar product. This can be coupled with increased profit to the withdrawer if, in those instances, we are dealing more with lower profits than with true obsolescence. In some cases, we can consolidate sales to the new supplier without the same profit-consuming expenses of direct marketing. This way we can keep the products, keep sales, increase profit, and not antagonize the customer. This is a most ideal and fortuitous combination of objectives, even if obtainable via a rather tortuous and circuitous route.

Provide technical or customer service in locating replacement product or process.

While all these possibilities should be galloping through the product manager's mind, none of them should be used until the decision has been made to eliminate a product. Before he does so, the product manager, in concert with marketing management, should establish a product retention policy based on what the elimination, selection, or, looked at more optimistically, the product retention analysis provides.

IMPLEMENTATION OF PRODUCT CONTROL

What is involved is the implementation of a product control activity predicated on the establishment of predetermined profit, sales, market share, and goals that can be created based on analysis of existing performance, then correlated to long-range objectives. In practice, this means establishing the following:

Profit minimum or ideal: by product or brand, by product or brand line, by market or market segment, and by overall ideal.

Sales goals related to: profit, manufacturing capability, capacity utilization requirements, market representation, and peripheral market considerations.

Sales goals established according to: product or brand, product or brand line, market or market segment, and total market.

Periodic product review to determine: sales, profit, and expectations.

Decision for retention or discontinuance based on sales, profit goals, and periodic product review.

Elimination through predetermined strategy.

Once done never finished. In other more comprehensive terms, this is a continuous process that must be provided for not as a one-time operation but as a central product management technique. The product manager must make provision for continued reevaluation of the criteria and the performance of his products against these goals. In so doing, it is not unreasonable nor undesirable for him to establish an overall optimum total number of products by line or market. This can be helpful in several respects by creating:

1. A guide for optimum management.
2. Criteria for overhead assessments—operational and functional costs for product line maintenance.
3. A budgeting tool for products—both administrative and manufacturing.
4. A product alarm bell—when near or under, better review and reassess.
5. Careful consideration and justification for new product addition.
6. The necessity for taking lengthy, critical, and often sobering product examination.

8

Product Quality and Pricing

Although quality is both actual and perceptual, there is no denying that we all want it, even if we don't always know quite what it is or how to determine it. Cynical as this may sound, it is often true, particularly in consumer goods; but this is hardly a sound basis for business. Consumer consciousness is ever increasing, and this is fortunate, for the more the customer knows, the more we can, to good marketing advantage, pursue the quality image and capitalize on that built into the product. To keep matters clear, separate consideration must be given to actual, perceived, and experienced quality.

Actual Quality

This entails those quality features or characteristics that are discernible and measurable, if only through intricate, sometimes complex, and costly testing—physical, chemical, or other. In consumer marketing they are often less important, but in industrial and government markets they constitute the bases for sales. In these markets, stringent regulations are often applied, and products must meet or exceed specifications imposed either by the producer himself or the customer. Those who have engaged in government contract business know this very well. Less well known, but equally strict, are the limitations established by quality consumer houses both for themselves and contract-supply producers. In either case the proof of quality exists, and documentation can be provided. Often these characteristics provide the basis for extensive advertising and promotional efforts.

Actual quality stems from manufacture, design, or processing. These elements must be controlled, but they can also be used effectively in the promotional effort. In retaliation to competition, additional quality control or tolerance imposition sometimes is used; this creates a spiral of nonessential costs—a battle of claim and counterclaim raging around relatively insignificant trivia. But we must always keep the commercial aspect in mind and consider what revenue may be derived through such maneuvers. Where our competitors use quality, we must also—or be prepared to use another strategy.

The product manager must be concerned with this question from several points of view:

True manufacturing, engineering, or chemical product quality.
Establishment of specifications.
Establishment of tolerances.
Meeting specifications and tolerances.
Improvement of quality.
Control of quality.
Exploitation of quality.
Quality planning.
Variations in quality depending on market and customer, and their needs.
Technological evolution and its consequences.
Quality costs and their optimization.
Return on quality investment.
Minimum quality specifications for maximum profitability.
Disposal of material that does not meet specification and tolerance.
Response to competition and the competitive quality race.

Each of these represents things familiar to any product manager. Careful monitoring is required to determine the right time for the right action with respect to any; and the full integrative and correlative powers of the product manager are brought to bear in implementing quality control specifications. Under the pressures of delayed shipments or delinquent orders, he and the plant must not succumb to substandard performance. While companies vary, it is often ultimately the product manager who must pass judgment on final material and make the determination to ship or not to ship. His customer and market knowledge rallies to his support, providing the foundation to make this King Solomonlike decision—difficult but essential.

In the overall situation, true quality can be engineered into the product and maintained through appropriate specifications and tolerance adherence. The product manager is responsible for administrating those in force, recommending changes, establishing additional tests, and planning quality for new products. Since quality is costly, he must also consider the delicate balance between the necessary and the unnecessary, and not allow excessive quality control costs to be introduced either for nonessential technical reasons or for questionable marketing ones.

Before we leave this area, two more factors:

1. The product manager usually is responsible for quality complaints, and he should keep this in mind when he establishes quality control measures or tolerances and when compromise acceptance occurs. If he allows shipment of borderline products, he should be ready to defend this to the customer and to management.

2. Special quality products are made for specific customers. But the decision to do so and the premium to be charged are not the product manager's responsibilities alone; often, such decisions are made in concert with the chief marketing executive, although they may be largely dependent on the product manager's recommendations. When considering the possibilities of special manufacture, which entails particular quality control, careful analysis of cost, feasibility, profit, and real expectation of execution are obvious necessities. Less obvious are the problems of disposal if the product is not acceptable to the customer. While the product can usually be sold, there are instances when it cannot. What is more customary is that profit will be adversely affected. This should be accounted for in establishing the initial selling price, and the business should be assured through contract. As usual, forethought pays.

Perceptual Quality

The perception of quality involves subscription more to the determinations of behavioral sciences than to any other school. We owe a great debt to the many comprehensive customer-buying studies and the psychological extrapolations regarding what is and what is thought to be. From these disciplines we have learned much but still have much to learn. No modern marketer would deny the contribution made by these sciences and their application in the marketing effort. Consumer products, in particular, have been subjected to this scrutiny, and it is mainly in the consumer market that the brand manager, especially, has applied the findings. However, it is remiss to think that there is no application outside the consumer segment.

There are areas of profitable application in all marketing situations, although, admittedly, use in some segments is more restrictive than in others. Such simple successful concepts as eye appeal and packaging in essentially nonutilitarian devices have found their way into industrial and government marketing. Many can be justified, at least partially, for their convenience, if not for their attractiveness, while others are predicated purely on aesthetics; and if these help create or perpetuate the quality image they have their marketing value. Green wine bottles, for instance, help domestic wines to emulate their imported competitors.

The appearance of quality is manifestly important in creating the quality image, whether or not we have a quality product. Conversely, it is possible to have a quality product and, because of poor packing, coloration, distribution, or advertising, fail to convey the quality image, thereby losing the benefits of real performance, durability, and reliability.

Two Methods for Achieving Perceptual Quality

It is impossible for us to consider all aspects of quality, but we can roughly establish that the problem is first to identify what provides the quality image to the customer—not an easy task in most instances—and then to divide products into those that possess these characteristics and those that do not. Once these classifications are made, we must decide whether or not to build these quality characteristics in those products that lack them. If so, the mechanisms to be used depend on the product, the market, and the available funds.

There are two courses of action open. The first, to actually improve the product and offer quality which should be marketed in relationship to quality; and the second, to create a quality image without actually improving real but only apparent quality.

The approach taken depends upon the individual situation because what appears to be a quality feature or indicator varies with the product, the market, and even the circumstances of the moment. It is also apparent that this closely relates to price since the ratio between price and quality exists and influences every buyer in every case. Happily, numerous psychological and sociological studies have been conducted to assess customer purchasing patterns, habits, and even those quality features that relate to product selection. Studies of repeat purchases have also been made, for it is one thing to purchase the product once and quite another to buy it two or more times. Concern therefore is with repeat sales, unless one-time sales are regarded as the sole objective. For some (fads and fancies) this is certainly the case, but not usually.

Although factors that determine quality vary with product and industry, there are a few major characteristics that the user, whether he be an industrial consumer or government purchaser, always seeks. Some of these are tangible, measurable, experienced elements, and some more perceptual. The latter should be dealt with first since they are more general than specific. Weight, texture, color, packaging, overall appearance, durability, and advertising or promotion are among the more important. None of these can be applied to every product, or to the same degree in any given situation. The product manager, seeking to promote an existing product, improve an antiquated one, or plan the marketing of a developmental item, should examine each one.

General Characteristics of Perceptual Quality

Weight. We all know the satisfaction of hefting something that has "weight," "body," or "substance"; and we also know the dissatisfaction of examining a product that we think should be heavy and find that it is not. This was of great concern to the plastics industry, which, for many years, had to fight the psychological battle of customer education. Now, lightness in certain products is considered desirable and encouraging—a good example of changing mores and changing market requirements. The point, however, is that there are products that have a "body," whether it be recognized, designed, or essential, and product managers should be prepared to educate the consumer accordingly.

Texture. The sign says "Hands off; if you break it you've bought it"; yet everyone blithely ignores the warning and runs the break-bought risk. It doesn't take much insight to comprehend that people "see" with their hands. Far from discouraging this, some enlightened manufacturers have encouraged it, and due to modern packaging, this is reasonably possible. The feel of many synthetic substances—for example, nylon—was for some time a matter of great concern to the textile industry, for consumer reaction to touching it was quite negative. Eventually, through proper handling, the problem was overcome. In this case we have examples of three different applicable techniques.

The first involved the manufacturer's advocating the use of the product on its technical merits, divorcing it from the natural and turning its unique "feel" to advantage by inculcating in the purchaser the distinctive identification of the fiber by the "feel." Do not be misled into thinking that this was fully satisfactory.

The second approach was to modify the fiber itself and the construction of fabrics made from it to produce textiles having the more accustomed textures of natural fibers. A compromise.

The third was educational, generating an overall awareness, not of the physical difference in the fiber's feel, but in the outstanding properties, including durability, aesthetics, and cost of synthetics in general, all of which led to wider acceptance of the product. Experience had to temper marketing enthusiasm, for initially the fiber was used in all sorts of garments where it had no real business being employed. Despite marketing efforts, the eventual outcome was the consumer's victory, for the textile apparel usages of the fiber are now clearly limited to areas where "feel" is accepted. There is merit in considering this example, for it indicates several approaches to "feel" acceptance and the necessity for planning approaches before the fact.

Color. The positive and negative effects of color have been researched in depth. All of us are acutely aware of the significance and impact of color on sales. But to determine the most suitable color is not easy. For many years people always cited the example of green toothpaste when they wanted to illustrate negative color effects. Toothpaste had to be white. Now we have not only green but striped toothpaste. Also in bygone days, technical or economical limitations often militated against color. This is hardly valid now because the costs of coloring are dropping constantly. This means that a colorful, eye-catching, attractive product is easier for the customer to identify, remember, and repurchase. One should think color.

Packaging. After many years of being a stepchild, particularly in the industrial field, packaging has finally come into its own. However, we must give due credit to consumer marketing areas for having blazed the trail since they have long appreciated the importance of a good package. As the trend stands, no one need elaborate on the necessity of packaging. The many different packaging materials and techniques available make the possibilities limitless and economical. Plastics may be a problem in some fields, but their virtues in the package arena are peerless. In the industrial field, constant packaging innovation is the key.

Product management concerns range from the role of packaging in the general marketing effort—cost of packaging, cost of transfer, unit packaging, production line handling and storage, emptying, economizing, and technical suitability—to the specific consumer response to, say, plastic in place of glass, transparent plastics, palatable containers, collapsible cartons and easy opening containers. The product manager can employ imaginative packaging from these standpoints; he can also advertise his product with words and pictures on containers to revivify slow-moving or dying items.

General appearance. While this results essentially from the combined impact of the foregoing elements, it also involves the necessity for creating a total effect. There is little accomplished by excellent packaging and poor product design, for example, unless there is no concern for repeat sales. It is the total image created by the product in its design, engineering, and functional areas, together with the package and display techniques used in sales and promotion, that provide full perceptual implications. Due care in a harmonious, integrated presentation is therefore necessary.

Durability. Product durability can be measured to some extent and is therefore not a true perceptual factor. But since it was acknowledged during our discussion of real product performance, the conceptual aspect warrants some mention at this time. Product unpredictability leads either to joyous celebration when the customer confronts unexpected longevity or to loud and long lamentations when the product stops functioning after a short breaking-in period. Either situation could have been anticipated, and exploited or avoided, if proper attention had been paid initially to the product's durability. One approach to "creating" durability is through consumer education. Submission to a consumer-testing service and various technical or institutional endorsements are among other advantageous ones.

Advertising and promotion. Quality deserves further treatment, which is given elsewhere in this book, but we cannot do justice to it if we do not concern ourselves with evaluation of advertising and promotional efforts expended in bringing the product to public attention. Later, when we deal more elaborately with advertising, promotion, and the product manager's participation, we will expound on the broad implications involved. The message here is succinct: advertising and promotion must be commensurate with the quality approach and not defeat or contravene it. Psychology teaches us the requirements for constancy and the images associated with certain propaganda media. Mother rarely reads *Playboy,* and so little is accomplished by capitalizing on the sex appeal and prestigious implications by dint of association with a product advertised in *Playboy,* particularly if the product is a geriatric sewing specialty. Technical publications imply technical competency, and medical publications convey an aura of medical authority; certain newspapers reach and appeal to the carriage trade, while others are more public transportation-oriented. It is enough to indicate the need. Product managers will follow the drift.

Experienced Quality

Now that we have discussed these somewhat intangible aspects—intangible since we are dealing with them as manifestations of the consumer's perception—we should proceed to the customer's verifiable factors as these are the outcome of his experience with the product. Like the others, these are perceptual in one sense, but not in another, for they reflect what he has learned while using the product. They may reenforce intial impressions or negate them, thus nullifying the previous marketing effort. This aspect has received considerable consumer-marketing attention; customer-testing is conducted by agencies, internal corporate groups, or facilities established for this sole purpose. This practice should be extended into other areas, particularly that of industrial product management. When sufficient units, profits, and potential are involved and when the product lends itself to such evaluation, alert management will eventually use it.

GENERAL CHARACTERISTICS OF EXPERIENCED QUALITY

Efficiency. Does the product really do the job for which it is intended and do it efficiently? The gadgets and "widgets" are there, but how disappointing it is when they fail to perform, or perform only half well. Surprising as it may seem, this is not just the concern of consumer product managers, but a very real and trying problem in all product areas.

Reusability. Closely related to the durability aspect already discussed, this involves the reuse or continued-use aspects of the product's performance. As in the case of efficiency, there is no frustration equal to that suffered with a product that works once but never again. Built-in obsolescence is a fact of economic life. But unplanned deficiences are an entirely different matter.

Specifications. The use of specifications greatly simplifies the quality picture; but it is necessary to distinguish those that can be understood by the customer from those that, while they have technical and performance significance, are beyond his comprehension. In dealing with basic quality-control elements that concern the product manager from a manufacturing or scientific perspective, we already know that specifications and tolerances must be imposed and enforced. Some of these are then used as elements in the promotion of the product and its quality image.

Labeling. The labeling of a product is most important. It relates to advertising and promotion, and can be used to equal advantage there as in quality determination. Often we do not have a clear understanding of what labeling can do.

Labeling is not, according to the requirements and interpretations of the U.S. departments of commerce or agriculture, restricted to the label on the product; instead it includes all literature, specifications, advertisements, and statements relative to the product; also its uses, properties, applications, and chemistry no matter when or where used and whether or not affixed to the product itself. In this sense, labeling includes diverse paperwork—from elaborate technical literature to rough handwritten statements sent customers in reply to requests for a description of the product or instructions on how to use it. By now, the implications and opportunities implicit in labeling should be evident.

Another more specific aspect of labeling should also concern us, particularly since we are dealing with the image or actuality of quality. This is the product guarantee or assurance of performance labeling practice. All of us have examined, and many of us have purchased, products that carry a written statement promising return of purchase price or replacement of product if it fails to perform as expected, wears out before a prescribed period, or is not resistant to this or that. Clearly, such programs cost money, but they, as perhaps no other labeling device can, convey a quality that is hard to dispute or emulate. Not all products can be so certified, and not all marketing groups can afford the expenditures involved. However, the approach is worth considering when both product, market, and manufacture have the requisites and potentials.

Convenience. Earlier, mention was made of the vast and ever-growing convenience market. While there is a tendency toward relegating it to the consumer segment, this is far from the case. With increasing labor costs the search for simplicity, convenience, ease of handling, using, applying, or even packaging, moving, and storing the product is on. Some quality is automatically attributed to a product that is well conceived, well executed, and convenient to use.

EXPERIENCED QUALITY AND BRAND MANAGEMENT

While these pieces are part of a cohesive quality-product whole, it is apparent that the full implications of all relevant contributory elements cannot be treated here. Too many are concerned with the individual product and local circumstances; but reference to the foregoing overriding and generally applicable factors can be constructive.

Before departing, a word more about brand management. Most brand managers will note that we have failed, thus far, to mention the importance of creating brand identity and consumer consciousness. This has not been overlooked or neglected; it will be treated later, along with advertising and promotion. The quality element is more secondary than primary when equated to the impact of these efforts in product consumer consciousness, development, and maintenance.

Pricing

Having dealt with quality, price is a logical progression. The relation of price to quality is well known—the more it costs, the better it has to be. While this is definitely not true, lamentably it reflects the thinking of many and is the basis of an entire economic outlook. However, there is no question that the price element is a management tool or technique. If this is the responsibility of the product manager, directly or indirectly, as an outgrowth of his role in recommending pricing and price structure, the philosophy is pertinent. Regardless of his function, primary or secondary, he is indisputably involved and should therefore approach pricing with definite profit and marketing goals in mind. As an element in the planning operation, pricing is often neglected and placed more within the realm of day-to-day concerns than in that of short, intermediate, or longe-range planning. Yet profit is as much an element of market planning as gross sales, both of which are related to pricing policies and philosophies.

Whether price controls profit or profit controls price, it is impossible to separate the two, and if either is to be effectively controlled or used, they must both be planned. This requires the use of every available device or system. It is very easy to expound glibly the virtues of price planning and programming, but implementing them is quite another matter. Several possibilities prevail, and planned pricing can be effectively instituted, particularly when the general trend points to planning and formal integrated management.

Today there is far less tendency to price according to the whim of the moment. This is both realistic and necessary. The complexity of modern business and the inert time lag between decision, response, action, and correction do not allow us to rely merely on situational or sporadic pricing.

We also cannot ignore legal restrictions and the large body of law that deals with pricing and marketing activities. As stated before, product managers and marketing managers, along with general management, should familiarize themselves with this legislation and follow closely established guidelines in conformity with these regulations. A summary of major applicable legislation follows.

Sherman Antitrust Act (1890). Prohibits monopolies or any restraint of trade.

Clayton Act (1914). A supplement to the Sherman Act. Also an antimonopoly or restraint-of-trade enactment. Deals more specifically with price discrimination, restrictive contracts, and exclusive dealings.

Federal Trade Commission Act (1914). An agency was established under this act to "police" legislation, including that of the Sherman Antitrust and Clayton acts, and to establish control over "unfair methods of competition." The Federal Trade Commission has pervasive regulatory powers over: discriminatory allowances, pricing manipulation, sales misrepresentation, competitive practices, trade secrets and spying, advertising practices, labeling, deceptive practices, merchandise cornering, lotteries, rigging of markets, and patronage. One of its divisions relates to antitrust activities.

Miller-Tydings Act (1937). Intended to reduce or eliminate price cutting, this act is designed to protect special interests. It is an example of the fair trade laws that exist in one form or another in various states.

Wheeler-Lea Amendment (Amendment to Federal Trade Commission Act) (1938). This amendment was enacted to provide for action against unfair or deceptive practices in commerce without specific regard to injury to competition. This was required because previously, under the Federal Trade Commission Act, there were requirements for proof of effect on competition.

Robinson-Patman Act (1939). A further refinement and, in a way, an extension of the Clayton Act. This act provides that it is unlawful to sell interstate commerce products of similar quantity and quality to different purchasers for different prices. It also has extension into establishment of brokerage fees and commissions for wholesale services and special advertising allowances.

Celler-Kefauver Antimerger Act (1950). Further legislation dealing specifically with merger and merger implications, restrictions, and requirements.

State and local laws. It is impossible to cite any of the state and possible local laws or regulations since these are too numerous and variable. However, they are a considerably important body of laws that must be known and applied.

PRICING PHILOSOPHIES AND STRATEGIES

After examining some commercial and legal implications of pricing, and gaining an appreciation of the requirements for pricing policies, planning, and forecasting, we now confront the arduous task of implementing such activities. In order to do so, we must first realize what price is. It is not merely a number that is printed in a price book or quoted by letter to a customer; it is what we charge and receive in payment for our product.

While these may sound alike, they are not. The latter is far more inclusive and takes into account such elements as freight charges, cash or time discounts, extended payment premiums, and volume payments. Or looking at it even more comprehensively, any element that affects, controls, contributes to, or detracts from the monies received for the product by the company.

Even these elements are only "for the product," which means that we must examine what the product is and be sure that we are receiving payment for *it* and not just for that neatly packaged physical article, service, or machine we sell. While several of these costs are absorbed in general overheads, there are significant occasions when extraordinary outlays—either in equipment, standardization, packaging, or distribution—are encountered, which must be considered in pricing. This means that determination of selling price should take all of these into account, and then become the reflection not only of the exigencies of the market, competition, and value, but of internal, indirect cost— and include all aspects of what is to be paid for and the manner in which payment is to be received.

The cost of money alone dictates careful selection of payment terms. Many large consumer goods houses have discovered that credit extension can be a separate and profitable business unto itself. In those instances where financing has been offered to purchasers, profits have been generated. And in a very real way, an entirely new product has arisen from the objective of increasing or maintaining business as well as meeting competition in the credit market.

This is an extremely complicated and critical subject that alone deserves full treatment. It is not appropriate to consider all its ramifications here; we can only highlight these more obscure aspects of price, pricing policy, and the additional product or profit that can be generated in price and sales relationships.

We have not yet mentioned the balance between price and profit. This is a very important factor. Indeed, the main purpose of business is to generate profit. Pricing policies must, therefore, consider product profit on per-unit, volume, and contributory bases.

Because we have already dealt extensively with profit, profit concepts, type, calculations, and philosophies, it is enough to say here that profit is not only relevant, it is central. Price must also take profit into consideration, and this engenders evaluation of the total price and profit interchange. Therefore, the development of a pricing strategy will reflect the elements of total price conceptualization and the cost elements.

Having advocated pricing strategies predicated on both analysis and planning, we should examine the alternatives and, indeed, they exist even in a relatively competitive market. Despite the specifics of individual situations, and the necessities of flexibility to meet market or competitive countermoves, an underlying pricing policy must prevail. When examined in this light, three basic approaches can be seen.

Price leaders.	Set the price regardless of market, competition, or age of products.
Price followers.	Follow established market or competition trends on old products and take similar structures into consideration on new ones. In an active market with active products, followers await the moves of their competitors, then respond.
Independent.	Do not necessarily lead or follow but take action independently of competition and general market.

Naturally, these are vast oversimplifications. However, it is sometimes beneficial to be oversimplistic in order to gain perspective and critical judgment. When examining the hazy, interwoven intricacies of many corporate pricing activities, it is often difficult to determine that beneath all of it lies some fundamental object that closely parallels one of these three strategies. Admittedly, not all companies may realize this tendency or centricity, but it is there.

Not all divisions of the same company need have the same outlook,

FIGURE 17

High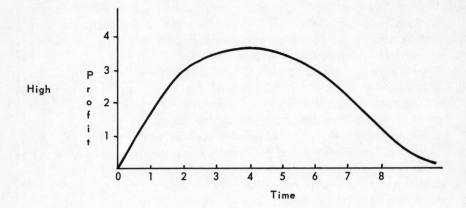

Moderate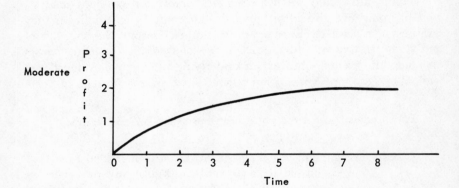

Low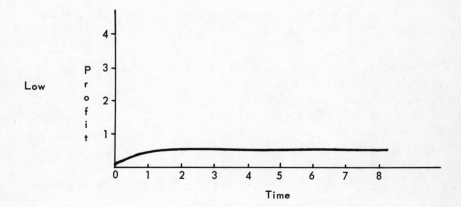

nor must the same approach be taken with all products offered by the same company or division. Dictates of the market, historical position, marketing objective, competition, nature of the product, and the market all contrive to determine the optimum technique for any specific line, brand, or product; they also determine the overall pricing policy.

It is the selection and application of the policy that separates marketing from selling, the successful from the unsuccessful, and business management from business atavism.

The blending of this outlook with that of profitability is essential, and constitutes a vital element in the derivation and implementation of planned pricing. Here again, recourse to simplistics can be helpful. Such analysis reveals three basic profit approaches:

High—lots of money fast.

Moderate—longer-term profit objectives.

Low—plans for long-range profit.

In reviewing these three statements of profit policy, it must be admitted that the element of time is minimized, which in reality cannot be. While looking at profit as a fixed entity, we miss an essential point: profits, as prices, do change. Similarly, to examine them as though they exist at any fixed point without reference to temporal alterations is patently fallacious.

When considering profit, we must extend the profit objective in time, and consider profit objectives as they relate to: profit life cycle, market life cycle, profit cycle, corporate or divisional objectives, and competitive activity. In so doing, it is immediately apparent that three old friends can help us: cycle analyses. And they can be combined with two other significant elements to construct a profit concept that relates to the present as well as the past. Projected against time, profit strategies may look something like the curves shown in Figure 17. The analysis of Figure 17 leads to the development of a price and profit plan that is integral to the attainment of the corporate objective, the marketing objective, and the profit objective.

To explore further how such price and profit objectives can be functionally employed in a product management system, we can resort to Tables 3 and 4, which consider both old and new products, price, profit, market, and competition, as well as that vital parameter, time. The tables relate to price and disregard other commercial or marketing efforts on the product's performance. They do consider identification and selection of competition and products against which to price. The concept applies at any given point in time, but has to be extended in the context of product, market, profit cycles, and corporate goals.

(text continues on page 170)

TABLE 3. *Price strategies.*

Product situation and objective	*For specialty product in noncompetitive market*	*For essentially non-competitive market*	*For competitive market*	*For highly competitive market*	*For expected competition*
NEW PRODUCT					
In new market	High price relative to market potential, quality, function, and performance	High price relative to market potential, quality, function, and performance	Relate to competitive value	Relate to competitive value	Initially high, then lower to meet competitive value
In old market	High price relative to established market value, quality, function, and performance	High price relative to established market value, quality, function and performance	Relate to market and competitive value	Relate to market and competitive value	Alter relative to competitive value
ESTABLISHED PRODUCT					
To maintain market share	Relate price to market value	Relate price to market value and to competitive value	Relate to competitive value	Relate to competitive value	Relate to Competitive value
To increase market share	Lower price relative to market value	Lower price below that of lowest competitor	Lower price below lowest competition	Lower price below lowest competition	Lower price below lowest competition

To decrease market share	Increase price relative to market value	Increase price above that of highest competitor	Increase price above highest competition	Increase price above highest competition	Increase price above highest competition
OLD PRODUCT To maintain market share	Maintain price at level equitable to value	Maintain price relative to competition	Price relative to competition	Price relative to mean or lowest competition	Relate price to mean
To withdraw	Increase price over market value	Price over most expensive competition	Price over most expensive competition	Price over most expensive competition	Price over most expensive competition
To capture residual market	Decrease price below value	Decrease price below lowest competition	Decrease price below lowest competition	Decrease price below lowest competition	Decrease price below lowest competition

TABLE 4. *Profit strategies.*

Product situation and objective	Profit goal	Rationale	Feasibility in:	
			Noncompetitive market	Competitive market
NEW PRODUCT New market	High	Maximize return on investment in minimum time. Projected short life cycle. Anticipated short, high-profit cycle. Market permits. Anticipated competition will drive prices and profits down.	Yes	Not usually unless costs are low enough to permit despite limited maximum price value.
	Moderate	Controlled return. Long-range outlook good. Longer life cycles projected. Little anticipated competition or minimal effect of competitors. Market permits.	Yes	Usually; probably represents a very typical marketing situation.
	Low	Discourage competition from entering market. Capture and retain market. Product really required for other reasons or is a byproduct. Limited by dictates of market. Fixed high cost, but product essential to product mix or marketing effort. Long-range profit improvement feasible.	Yes, but hardly desirable	Yes, if consistent with corporate and marketing objectives.

Old market	High	Maximize return investment in minimum time. Projected short life cycle. Anticipated short, high-profit cycle. Market permits. Anticipated competition will drive prices and profits down. Market situation better known. Pricing becomes more realistic.	Yes, and probable	Questionable unless price is on competitive value level.
ESTABLISHED PRODUCT				
To maintain existing profit	High	Maximize return on investment in minimum time. Projected short life cycle. Anticipated short, high-profit cycle. Market permits. Anticipated competition will drive prices and profits down.	Not usual	Unrealistic, for as competition evolves price erodes and, despite process optimization and know-how, costs creep up and profits fall down.
	Moderate	Controlled return. Long-range outlook good. Longer life cycles projected. Little anticipated competition or minimal effect of competitors. Market permits.	Yes	Yes, provided costs can be maintained at same price and profit ratio.

TABLE 4. *Profit strategies (continued).*

Product situation and objective	Profit goal	Rationale	Feasibility in: Noncompetitive market	Competitive market
	Low	Discourage competition from entering market. Capture and retain market. Product really required for other reasons or is a byproduct. Limited by dictates of market. Fixed high cost, but product essential to product mix or marketing effort. Long-range profit improvement feasible. Product must be essential to effort.	Yes, but raises serious question of retention	Yes, but levels have to be critically monitored. Not an unusual situation as market and competition increase in rate and duration.
To increase existing profit	To high from moderate	To meet new profit goals. To exploit new opportunities. Based on new market or technological evolution.	Questionable; only possible if market price originally very low or profit improved by lowering cost	Unrealistic unless competition also raises price or, through cost reduction, market shifts or competition is removed.
	To moderate from low	Controlled return. Long-range outlook good. Longer life cycles projected. Necessary to remain in market. Product retention required.	Maybe, if market allows	Possible, particularly if achieved via cost reduction or market shift.

To decrease existing profit	From high to moderate or to low	Required because of competition or market development. Response to value position. To increase market share. To extend market, profit, or product life. Expand market potential. Discourage competition.	Yes, but should always be approached cautiously; economics to be critically monitored	Yes, but any advantage against competition may be short lived. Competitive response must be watched carefully and product abandoned when profit drops below acceptable minimum.
OLD PRODUCT	Moderate	Controlled return. Long-range outlook good. Longer life cycles projected. Little anticipated competition or minimal effect of competitors. Market permits.	Yes	Yes; represents a typical situation.
	Low	Discourage competition entering market. Capture and retain market. Product really required for other reasons or is a byproduct. Limited by dictates of market. Fixed high cost, but product essential to product mix or marketing effort. Long-range profit improvement feasible. Test market. Pricing is more realistic.	Yes, but hardly desirable	Yes, undoubtedly.

It is apparent that pricing is reasonably complicated, but it does lend itself to planning and programming as readily as any other phase of marketing. The price strategy, its implementation at given times within the product's life, and its duration in the market is a major element in determining the success or failure of the product.

The remainder of the marketing effort, including sales, advertising, promotion, and distribution, make up the balance. In each of these areas the product manager holds some responsibilities. Later, when dealing with the role of the product manager relative to each, further understanding of his particular duties in these areas will be indicated. Concurrent with these is the relationship he bears to other requisite elements: supply, quality, manufacturing, technical service, customer service, and all those components of a successful marketing concept and marketing effort.

PRICING SUMMARY

To summarize the many elements contained in pricing for profits and achieving a market plan, we can use the following as a guide:

Price philosophy + Profit philosophy + Analysis = Price/Profit/Market plan

Leaders	High	Product
Followers	Moderate	Market
Independent	Low	
	Short range	
	Long range	

These elements operate in the three-dimensional continuum of the overall market, the competition, and time. The derivation of the price, profit, and market plan can never be simple; it is always the distillation of cause, effect, and experience. It is therefore multicausal and multidirectional. Consideration of the following steps in the sequence indicated can be an aid in analyzing these factors and approaching the complexities of deriving the price, profit, and market plan on a per-product or aggregate basis.

1. Determine minimum acceptable profit.
2. Determine sales price to obtain profit.
3. Project general market and specific competitive activity.
4. Project cost increases and decreases.
5. Project economic conditions.
6. Establish price, profit, and market strategy for the short, intermediate, or long range.
7. Project price to cost, to market, and to competition.
8. Review for performance against plan and alteration.

PART THREE

The Product in Corporate Life

9

The Product Continuum

A BOOK about product management without a chapter on the product would be like life without love, empty. For the product does not end with the physical limitations that we normally think of, that item which, once sold, is gone forever. Similarly, the product is in any company central to its activities and touches on all phases of corporate activity. On these very basic circumstances product management developed and marketing received its present stature and structure.

Every product manager is well aware of these ideas; but not every product manager is fully aware of their implications, nor does he necessarily know how to manage his product or products accordingly. Since product management is a young technique, this is to be expected. However, there are certain common denominators that provide insight into the elemental treatment of product management situations. They offer guidance that is applicable to any product, and bring organization, system, and coherence to the problems of managing products.

A continuum is defined as a continuous whole, quantity, or series, and this aptly describes the product as it wends its way through corporate life. From research to market, and even after market back to research, the product seems a never-ending succession of action, reaction, plans, and policies that affect and are affected by the objectives of corporate existence. Since many of these activities have no clear beginnings and ends, but flow into one another, the concept of product within the company is aptly described as a product continuum. This is illustrated in Figure 18.

From a marketing viewpoint, there are three distinct phases in the continuum: premarketing, marketing, postmarketing. These are represented as circular only because each of the phases' components leads to the other and often back to its predecessors.

Often the components lead even further back, since developments in a later stage can require remedies that are developed in earlier component stages. This is particularly true in the premarketing phases where research, development, field testing, and product refinement are the primary concerns. This can be seen in Figure 19, where only the premarketing phases are shown with indications of reverse direction when recourse to earlier components is required—trial and evaluation.

In other phases we have similar situations; thus reversion to other preceding component stages will be required in problem solving, planning, forecasting, and control. And often it will be necessary to revert from one phase to another. Product modifications suggested by market conditions of the postmarketing phase may require implementation in the premarketing phase (research or development) which, once achieved, will be fed back into the stream of the continuum.

The relationships among the phases and their constituent components involve a series of continuous activities, all of which require planning, control, and constant monitoring. The product manager's vital concern with all these activities was illustrated by the product management hexagram. The nature and extent may vary, depending on his special set of corporate responsibilities and the objectives of product management in the given company; but, regardless of degree, he is always an active, concerned, responsible participant.

Awareness of these relationships provides insight into the necessity for careful planning and controlling. Once fed into the continuum, the product starts on a long, expensive, and hopefully profitable journey; but while in transit, various things are happening in the marketplace and the company. Not all will affect the new product, but some will. The problem is how to control the phases and coordinate the

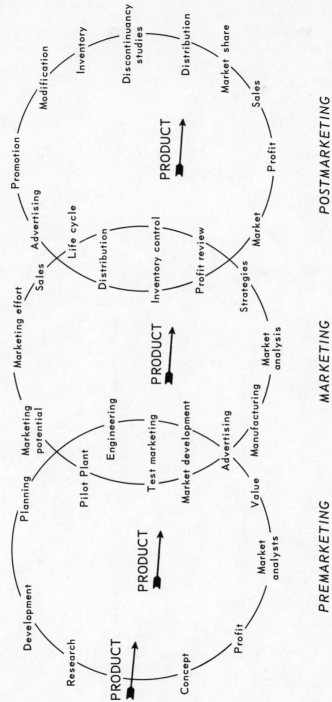

FIGURE 18
The Product Continuum

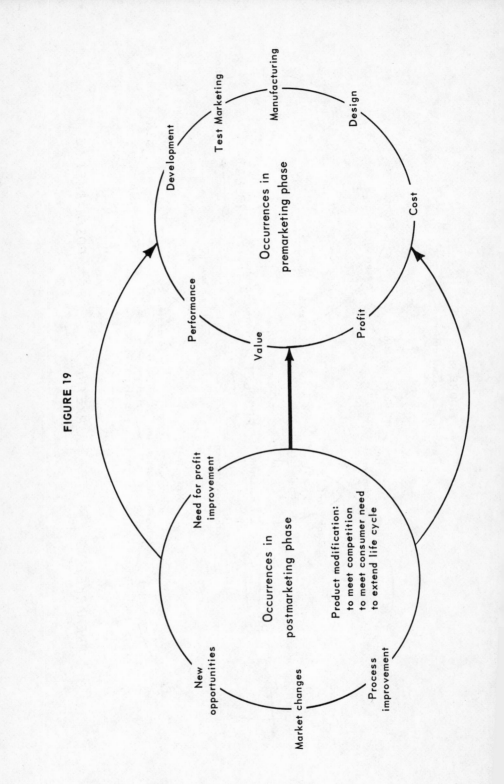

FIGURE 19

activities of each so that time is not wasted, obsolete products continued in research long after the market has been lost, or internal company cost changes implemented to the extent that profits become unacceptable.

These very obvious and superficial questions are only meant to exemplify possibilities. They are a mere indication of innumerable questions, problems, and situations that will arise while the product is in the phases of premarketing, marketing, or even postmarketing. Certainly, the nature and degree of importance of these critical points vary as the product itself changes and its position in the continuum alters. The leading questions that develop from all of this are: Who is going to do the coordination? Who is going to do the monitoring within the continuum? And who is going to monitor the market to provide complete integration of the internal and external influences on the product and the continuum? Ultimately, of course, the answer to all these questions is the product manager.

And so the product manager will find himself flitting back and forth to see that everything flows as smoothly as possible from phase to phase and within phases. While doing this, he will be monitoring the market and the competition, and keeping abreast of internal developments. When there are any indications that the product should be reevaluated in its status in any area or phase, it is his additional responsibility either to effect alterations based on his authority and responsibility, or to call management's attention to such necessities.

When one considers the enormity of the continuum when applied in any moderate-sized active company, the full sweep and scope of product management activity relative to product becomes quite apparent. There are two factors to complicate the concept further: the continuum applies simultaneously to all products in the corporate "bag of goodies," and not all products are at the same stage. What is being monitored here is a vast dynamic in which numerous products are in various stages and degrees of initiation, development, completion, examination, reexamination, attrition, or maturity. Many balls doth the product juggler balance; let not one hit the floor.

The continuum helps management envision the totality of the effort and provides the product manager with perspective on interrelations and interdependencies, a prerequisite in his product and coordinative responsibilities. For others, it provides insight into these same concerns but, more than this, it identifies the relationship of product to company, product to market, and product to internal organization.

While being guided through these phases, the product is being shaped, molded, and influenced by these pressures, and it is important that management recognize this. Last but not least, the continuum clearly defines the direction of product management.

Phase One: Premarketing

The components of this phase are listed as follows:

Concept
Research
Development
Planning
Pilot plant or model product
Test marketing for technical and
    commercial objectives
Market development
Product performance

Product value
Customer assessment
Marketing/market potential
Manufacturing feasibility
Cost
Profit
Yes or no decision making
Marketing planning

In the premarketing phase concern is primarily with research, development, testing (product, market, consumer), and yes or no decision making, commonly called go or no-go decision making. How deep the product manager's immersion depends on the company, but usually, if not in direct charge of new product development and coordination, he is at least indirectly participating. The relationship of product management to research and the input of product ideas varies tremendously from company to company, but the need for directed, market-oriented research is becoming most prevalent. In such situations marketing and product management will play a vital role in the direction of research efforts, in the selection of products for development, and in the establishment of priorities. In those situations where separate market development groups exist, the product manager, while involved as a consultant and coordinator, may not be responsible for the actual testing of individual models of test products. In such cases, the product is transferred to his authority only after it is completely developed. In other instances, he will be involved in these earlier trial periods, directing the experimental marketing and field trial activity himself; he later undertakes the "routine" product management function as well, after the product is transferred from research and development to the normal marketing status. In either situation the requirements for planning, coordination, and screening from the product manager's viewpoint are much the same.

COMMITTEE APPROACH TO PRODUCT DEVELOPMENT

In all larger companies, the decision to proceed with research and development of a new product or even major product modification which involves new research as opposed to formulation or process change will be the responsibility of committees rather than individuals. Variously termed the new product committee, the product development committee, research and development committee, or simply the products committee, this group determines which product projects are to be developed, establishes target dates, and periodically reviews progress as reported by the research, development, market development or product management people. Where such committees are used, their composition depends largely on the nature and complexity of the product and the company. Usually, minimum composition should include representation from:

Management—to approve project and funds.

Marketing—top-level representation for approval of concept, advice on market, and commitment on marketability.

Product management—for coordination, responsibility for development, and informational purposes.

Technical representation—exact representation to vary depending on nature of company and research commitments.

In addition to this basic representation, which would constitute the body of the committee, experts can be called upon for comment, consultation, or assignment of specific responsibilities. Such committees are usually decision-making bodies that rely heavily on recommendations and evaluations that are prepared by product managers, research and development personnel, market analysts, manufacturing people, and engineers, who should be consulted at the start about manufacturing feasibility. Often this rather practical consideration comes too late in the product development effort, and many exciting new products have had to wait for the installation of equipment or the development of process, all because the interphasing of manufacturing and engineering was delayed in the early stages.

OTHER APPROACHES

Many other approaches are encountered in the direction of the research and development effort. They range from the totally non-directed or pure research type to specific product creation based on model or criteria profiles. Selection is determined by the philosophy of the company, and frequently a blend of approaches is used. However, nondirective operations generally exist for pure research groups, for applied research, and specifically organized research teams engaged in a "project" with identified product or process objectives.

It should also be mentioned that the coordination of activity can vary from the committee approach so commonly encountered in one form or another to the "project director" or coordination team. These should be considered further.

Project Approach. In this situation a team is assigned a project either for the development of a product, processing it, or a combination of both. Representation again varies but usually will have research, manufacturing, and marketing as minimal requirements. The team can exist separately or as a subunit of the overall product development committee, working on specific assignments from that body in the latter case and from management direction in the former. In either case requirements for support service, test marketing, field trials, market analysis, and planning will usually be the responsibilities of the product manager, or will be guided by the project director, who will make assignments. The committee will carry the product development project to the point of final approval by the new product committee or management, depending on reporting lines. Once established, it will be turned over to product management.

Team Approach. In this structure a team of experts is assigned research or development objectives either from management, the new product development committee or sometimes as a subunit in the project approach. Representation is selective since teams are normally given very specific goals and frequently operate on only one segment of a total developmental effort. Coordination and evaluation of their activities will depend on the reporting lines established.

PRODUCT CONCEPTION

From what has been said one can see that there is a tendency for the conception of product to emanate from marketing or from indications based on market requirements, needs and directions, correlated and recommended by the marketing group, from which conception derives. If this be the case, the sources for such directions are multitudinous, and everyone in the corporation has his opportunity and obligation to be product research oriented, to bring forth his ideas. Often the product manager will specifically channel all such notions and, in concert with other elements of the marketing group, analyze this input and then, through committee activities, plan further effort. Needed research, imitative recommendations, or product-idea profiles are developed and presented therefrom.

Where nondirective research is involved, overall guidelines are established by management or research directors, and the possible product or process that stems from their efforts is then fed back to marketing for commercial analysis and evaluation. In these cases any contacts with commercial representatives are, of necessity, limited, and information would be brought back from the ivory towers more by informal than formal channels. That some opportunity for contact is needed even here is well understood, and the research scientist is now being brought from behind the bench into the market.

EVALUATING THE PRODUCT CONCEPTION

Let us assume that an idea for a new product has suddenly, like Edison's light, brilliantly illuminated the mind of Mr. X, whoever and wherever he may be in the organization. This concept will be fed to marketing if direction emanates from there, or to research and development in those organizations where these are the conventional routes. The mechanisms for such channels exist in all companies, from the somewhat informal suggestion box to the formal idea disclosure forms that many companies employ in one guise or another.

The question to be posed is: What happens to this idea? The answer is often very unsatisfactory. The problem is that such concepts are frequently presented with insufficient planning and thought. Given only cursory or superficial treatment, many worthwhile ideas are never further developed; and many more worthless ones take up much time, trouble, and money before they are recognized as unmarketable or unprofitable.

Ideas must be carefully prepared before presentation. While such screening is expensive, it is less so than the cost of research and development. With average annual expenses for Ph.D. research chemists and their supporting staffs estimated at between $50–75,000 per annum per Ph.D. and team, the usefulness of good preparation cannot be argued. Dilution of effort and time, and problems with scheduling and priorities are further reasons for care in selection.

The responsibility for such screening will have to lie where management places it; but with increasing frequency it is relegated to marketing and, more directly, to product management. This is a vast change from past eras, where even if preparations were required, inadequate provision existed for thorough analysis and planning.

NEW PRODUCT PLANNING

The word "planning" is something that most people object to. It seems impractical to plan the research of 15 new products for 1971 and 10 for 1972. Yet this is required for effective research, development, and marketing. The difference between planning research and planning specific products is the key. Planning provides for provision of time, money, people, and commitment; it does not stipulate what the specific products will be, but does establish areas for research and indications of need. In this sense research planning is not only possible but essential. Related to this approach is the preceding requirement for systematic selection of product conception and the isolation of those specific projects to be researched. Such projects then become the more precise objects of the planned research effort.

When the impact of these efforts is evaluated in the totality of corporate objectives and the commitment of resources, there is no need to justify further the organizational requirements for systematization, selection, planning, and control. Just as the input needs must be actually met, provision to meet them must also be made. The product manager will be involved in the analytical efforts prior to research recommendation, in the latter selection process and, subsequently, in the cycle that eventually leads to successful marketing. Therefore, all product managers should become thoroughly familiar with the problems of research and research management. It is beyond our scope to treat this in any further depth; however, the bibliography includes references to research and development management. Of more immediate concern are the needs of product managers to appreciate the predecision-making analysis and planning requirements that are in his province and are often elements of his responsibility and control functions.

PRODUCT RESEARCH SELECTION

There are three basic products: the totally new product to fill new needs; the me-too product, a duplication of an existing one; and the modified product, a major modification involving research or a minor modification involving development or manufacturing and engineering.

In addition, there are processes that follow the same three delineations: the new process, a totally new creation, or a new way to do what is already being done; the me-too process, a duplication of an existing process; and the major or minor modified process. These processes may be directed toward the use of existing products, products that have been researched, or those developed as an outgrowth of the system.

Systems are also occasioned by the creation of new products that require new methods of application in order to market them. Such coordinated marketing, if integrated back to research, provides the nucleus for total systems development, and can constitute tremendous competitive advantages. Even where not totally researched, systems selling in itself is an important marketing tool.

Over and above these planned efforts, we should not discount the serendipitous occurrence. Accidental discoveries cannot be planned, but they do occur; and when they do, it becomes research's responsibility to obtain marketing opinion and projection—a reverse justification procedure with analysis and planning occurring after discovery.

Regardless of who is responsible for preparation before selection, and planning after, the requirements are similar and equally important; if there are major causes of new product failure, the blame must be placed on the doorstep of inadequate preselection, screening, and subsequent new product planning. These are often the responsibilities of the product manager, and he must take heed.

All of this is closely related to systematization and planning disciplines. Success or failure depends upon the utmost use of those techniques. No successful effort can be maintained without them.

One point that can bear repeated emphasis is the necessity for early introduction of all required corporate areas in the research and development activity as they lead to eventual marketing. Manufacturing, engineering, and logistics all have their place, yet are often introduced to the problem when it is too late. In an integrated system they are called upon early in the effort to minimize delays and optimize research output. Time in research is long enough, as we all know; from one to several years is not unusual. While this time span may be shortened in some situations, its length is necessary and expected. What is inexcusable, wasteful, and unnecessarily expensive is the delay between perfection in research and the time to actual market. Closer integration through product management can effectively minimize such time differentials and curtail waste of motion, time, and profit.

The events concerned with product research selection, approval, and control can be schematically represented as in Figure 20, and the components of each event are listed below.

FIGURE 20

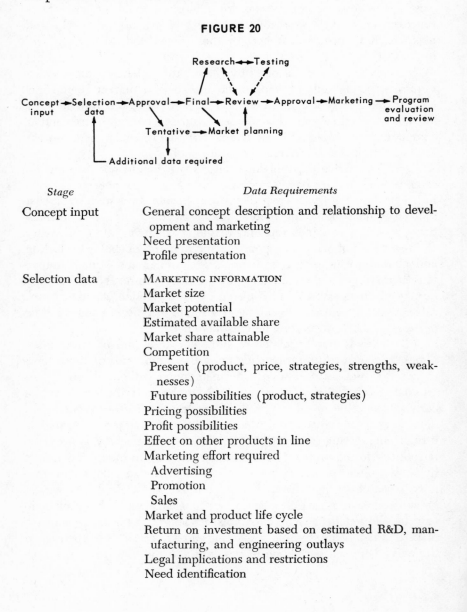

Stage	Data Requirements
Concept input	General concept description and relationship to development and marketing
	Need presentation
	Profile presentation
Selection data	MARKETING INFORMATION
	Market size
	Market potential
	Estimated available share
	Market share attainable
	Competition
	Present (product, price, strategies, strengths, weaknesses)
	Future possibilities (product, strategies)
	Pricing possibilities
	Profit possibilities
	Effect on other products in line
	Marketing effort required
	Advertising
	Promotion
	Sales
	Market and product life cycle
	Return on investment based on estimated R&D, manufacturing, and engineering outlays
	Legal implications and restrictions
	Need identification

Stage	*Data Requirements*

Selection data (continued)	TECHNICAL INFORMATION
	Feasibility
	Other pending research efforts
	Personnel and equipment requirements
	Manufacturing feasibility
	Patent or other legal restrictions
	  Toxicological
	  Governmental environmental control
	  Pure Food and Drug Act
	Confluence with or divergency from existing product research
	Possibilities of extensions
	Hazards in development or handling
	Patent possibilities
	Time and expenditure expectations

Approval	May be possible based on immediate answers to questions presented and satisfied in selection analysis preparation. Usually it will be necessary to provide only tentative approval where obvious advantages exist while requiring further refinement of selection data. Therefore, tentative approval will provide for additional analysis to be fed back through the section process for determinations, rejections, or final approval. In some cases where urgency or optimism dictates, research efforts and marketing studies can be initiated while final approval pends.
Research	Literature search Patent search Developmental studies Process studies Experimentation Sample or model preparation Patent exploration Cost determinations Budgetary considerations Establishment of objectives Establishment of budgets
Testing	Market testing Consumer response Performance assessment Market potential

Stage	Data Requirements
Testing (continued)	Market acceptance Modification determinations Technical performance Product or process improvement
Marketing planning	Cycle determinations Market Product Life Market determinations made in selection studies are refined and quantified Advertising programs Promotion programs Literature preparation Profit analysis and projection Total studies of effect on existing products Phasing in of finance, manufacturing, engineering, logistics, etc. Forecasts Sales price determinations Packaging Response to anticipated events Product control Review procedures Product or process minimum acceptability performance levels Quality control requirements, specifications and tolerances Second and third generation products or process derived from initial product Modification possibilities Initial order size
Review	Assessment of research effort, testing programs and the marketing program. Cost assessment. A constant reevaluation done formally (usually quarterly) at which time the project can be stopped or priority altered.
Approval	Final go or no-go decision based on evaluation of all preceding.
Marketing	Official market release and implementation of marketing or product plan. The product manager's real job begins.

Stage	Data Requirements
Performance evaluation and review	Assessment of performance, technical and commercial. Effectiveness of product and marketing program, profitability and constant monitoring. Now fully within the province of product management and subject to the full scale of product management's evaluations, control and directions.

Phase Two: Marketing

The components of the marketing phase are:

Engineering	Market share determination
Planning	Life cycle determination
Marketing potential	Manufacturing
Distribution	Finance
Inventory control	Quality control
Logistics	Sales
Promotion	Market development
Advertising	Planning
Profit cycle determination	Competition
Profit monitoring	Product control

In this phase, the product has been approved, is in manufacture, and actively marketed as a regular product of the line. There may be occasions to return to the research and development components of Phase One, but this is the exceptional situation. The product in this phase represents the product in introduction, growth, and maturity as related to the life cycle. It is now subject to the full retinue of marketing consideration and all of the vagaries of the market. From the standpoint of the continuum, there is little to be gained from further elaboration, for what is happening to the product and the product manager here is the basic subject of this book.

Phase Three: Postmarketing

The components of the postmarketing phase are:

Marketing success	Competition
Market share	Advertising
Market forecast	Promotion

Market cycle	Distribution
Sales	Profit
Profit cycle	Manufacturing and engineering
Life cycle	Cost reduction
Quality control	Process improvement
Inventory	Continue or discontinue analysis
Logistics	Control
Modification	Planning

This phase is somewhat of a misnomer in that the marketing effort is in some cases continuing and in others totally ceasing. However, it implies dealing with the fully mature or declining product (maturity and attrition phase), as well as the concerns for improvement, profit stabilization, and all of the problems encountered with the older product and the older market. It also implies those alterations in product, distribution, or marketing that are the consequence of the experience of the marketing effort and also the outcome of customer exposure, influence, and effect.

In considering any of these three phases in the continuum, it should be remembered that there are two other elements that temper the entire process—external and internal environmental factors. The dimension of time must also be included. These cannot be explored in any hypothetical case, but in practice they temper the phases considerably.

The practical result of such temporal considerations is their effect on time in phase and its cost. Evaluation and reevaluation of the total continuum are warranted to make improvements in phases and components.

10

The Manager's Direct Control Responsibilities

Everyone in the company is a product expert. This is natural since it is from the successful sale of the product that the company's profit derives. It is appropriate therefore that everyone in the company be familiar with each product and consider it a part of his concern. However, when the veneer is removed, most people know very little about their products. This is not unexpected since real product knowledge is difficult to acquire; to become an expert requires more time than most people have.

The product manager should be the true product expert. As such he has control of informational functions relative to each product and is charged with administrative, functional, and operational duties that will ensure total product knowledge within the company. He then provides the full measure of product expertise. But products and their management change as do the market, the company, and technology. Therefore let no product manager become complacent. There is always more to learn and more to do when it comes to truly managing products.

189

In the discharge of his responsibilities, the product manager will apply tools and techniques in various ways to achieve his ends. A number of his product involvements were mentioned when we described these tools and techniques. There are, however, a group of control or audit functions that specifically relate to the product and which are the direct responsibility of the product manager. These are:

Price determinations, control and audit

Profit determinations, control and audit

Technical determinations

Packaging

Quality control

Competitive assessments

Legal restrictions

Several of these have been discussed to some extent as elements in other situations. However, their full importance relative to the product has not been completely presented. When examining them, one realizes that many of the product manager's own internal functions relate to each other, and that what he gleans in one area of activity is directly applicable to other segments of his responsibilities.

Price Determinations, Control and Audit

In developing information for research recommendations and subsequently the planning operation, the company establishes the price of the product. Earlier we examined the levels of price and the rationale for pricing strategies. The test of these occurs when the product finds its way onto the market and is then actually subjected to market, competitive, and internal pressures. The product manager must be constantly assessing the performance of the product and the effect of price, either his or his competitors, to be assured that maximum sales performance is obtained and maintained. Since price variations consistent with profit objectives are mandatory, alterations are possible and sometimes necessary.

When discussing the strategy of pricing in the chapters on tools and techniques, no mention was made of price tactics—the application of pricing techniques in specific markets and on individual products. For elaboration we can fall back on classical marketing price concepts since they are still valid:

Full-line pricing. Pricing of individual products in the range is predicated on market demand; profitability of each may vary since the market price is a function of the demand element and not based on fixed averages over cost. This operates on the theory that the products involved are related, and their price relationships must be equated to one another and to the market. Product prices in the line vary from high to middle to low, which is highly competitive. Full-line pricing is a tactic commonly employed in the consumer market.

Leader pricing. This must be distinguished from the philosophy of being a price leader; it is really considered to be the items of full-line pricing that are priced at an extremely low and attractive level to induce shopping. It is commonly employed in consumer marketing as the familiar loss leader, the product that loses a little in order to entice customers into the store to buy other higher priced, higher profit items. Sometimes, unknown to the market, manufacturers will accept losing product prices not as a strategy for sales performance but to gain market entry and dollar volume until such time as other performance products supersede them or until they can justify self-manufacture and profit. It is a technique based on long-range profit objectives from the product or segment of market and not on immediate return. This is a dangerous procedure unless very carefully monitored and controlled.

Bait pricing. This is a low, low price but hardly real as there is no intention of actually selling the merchandise. The object is to attract the customer and then convince him to purchase the higher priced, higher quality, profitable item. This is a typical low-quality furniture store procedure.

Price lining. This is the principle of setting a range of prices for given merchandise based on carrying assortments of given quality and price. It prevails in both wholesale and retail operations as well as in almost all phases of business.

Prestige pricing. The price to establish quality is usually far above actual value, real or perceptual. This is not too commonly encountered except in consumer marketing.

Odd-even pricing. This retail technique is presumably based on consumer psychology. Prices that end in certain numbers are supposed to have special consumer appeal. This, of course, would appeal to the numerologists among us. Anyway, it is the typical 98 cents ending approach. If it's $1.98, it is not $2.00.

Psychological pricing. Psychological studies presumably show that purchasing patterns relate to given price structures. At certain levels products will be purchased, assuming similar performance and at least comparable quality. This is the point at which there is no reason for shopping, since comparative values are so close in the consumer's mind. Such pricing also relates to product, market, and income. The larger the income, the greater the effect of psychological pricing, depending on the level of price and product.

In addition to these tactics, there is also the concern expressed in the discussion on pricing techniques of total element inclusion and of the hidden price element: shipping, packaging, and warehousing. When dealing with the mesh of price and product, we must now focus on the specifics and consider the application of the generalities reviewed in techniques and the tactics considered here. The vital concern of the product manager is that the product not be priced too high or too low. And finally, he must not forget to consider the relationships between value and volume and the totality of pricing impact on his individual products and other lines.

VALUE-VOLUME RELATIONSHIPS

There is a relationship, more real than imagined, between price and sales volume and between sales volume, cost of product, and cost of goods sold. This means simply that it is usually possible to reduce cost of goods and cost of sales when volume increases, presuming that the volume is well controlled and directed. Volume sales to few accounts with lower freight charges are obviously more beneficial than an increase in volume based on selling fewer units to many more accounts who are geographically dispersed. Such analysis, while seemingly self-evident, often escapes full consideration, and it is possible by price reduction to improve the dollar volume and the profitability. It is a dangerous technique, in the sense of risk, but if properly analyzed, implemented, and monitored, it can be most rewarding.

This approach should not be restricted to mature products or those that are wasting away on the marketing vine, but should be used also with new products, since the returns may be far greater at the lower than the higher price. Conversely, a higher price may also yield better profits even though gross sales are lower, as unit profit may improve while distribution and selling costs decrease. In this relationship, however, the sensitivity of the cost per unit becomes critical. Do not plan on marketing less product if cost of product doubles whenever sales volume lowers by a few percent. While it must be carefully analyzed, it is still a useful approach.

AUDIT AND CONTROL

It is one thing to establish prices and quite another to keep track of them. With all the elements of price, such as allowances, cash discounting, credit changes, and volume differentials, it remains for the product manager to determine and follow the price per unit, and the price as paid. In addition to this, the manager must record competitors' prices and policies simultaneously, based on continuous monitoring of them and the market. Thus we are faced with a substantial job just in updating, calculating, and maintaining records and analyses of prices, ours and our competitors'. To do this a systematic approach is absolutely essential, and the ubiquitous computer is there and ready to provide an invaluable service.

Once determination of requisite information has been made, programs can be devised to furnish this information totally or on an exception basis. Both approaches are necessary, and the selection of total and exception reports will depend on number of products, markets, detail required, turnaround and response time necessary, availability of computer time, availability of information, and requirements for frequency consistent with the needs of the business.

To accomplish all this there are typical price data required by the product manager that can be considered as a price audit. Virtually all of these possible elements are contained in the following list. Reviewing them will enable the manager to select appropriate audit elements for satisfying particular product management situations. From this choice derives the reporting system and the entire exception reporting schedule. In this selection availability of flash or instantaneous reporting should not be overlooked, since such flash reporting can often eliminate repetitive reporting; it can also provide substantial saving in computer effort and time for report review and analysis on the part of recipients.

Price Audit Data
1. Selling price per product, including all elements such as volume, size, and ranges.
2. Freight and transportation allowances or changes per product and cumulatively.
3. Cash discounts per product and cumulatively.
4. Time-deferment penalties per product and cumulatively.
5. Average selling price per product, line, trade, market, customer, territory, and in total.
6. Exception prices per product, line, trade, market, customer, territory, by volume, by range, and in total.
7. Exception prices as a percentage of sales by product, line, market, customer, territory, volume, range, and in total.
8. Differential pricing by volume, product customer, trade, market, territory, and as a percentage of the total.

9. Selling price trend lines (actual, averages, or projected, predicated on past years, graphed) by product, trade, line, market, competition, industry, comparison of company product lines, and compared to industry competition and market.
10. Competitive prices by product line, and as differentials, policies, strategies, terms, allowances, and discounts.

This information provides the product manager with a panorama of price information. This is necessary for perspective, measuring performance, judging results, and ascertaining position of the product in the market. It is also required as a base for planning and projection. Having this audit information, the product manager can exercise control of price, price reduction or increase, and judgment of other price elements and their contributions or subtractions. The accumulation of this information, therefore, serves not only the passive, historical, or planning aspects of the business, but also aids the formulation of short and long-range price policies, practices, and objectives, as well as the conduct of day-to-day business.

Profit Determination, Audit, and Control

In order to gain an understanding of gross profit, it is necessary to have a familiarity with the elements that constitute the determination of product cost. To do this comprehensively is impossible, as this delves very deeply into accounting procedures, which vary from firm to firm, and even vary in principle on the theoretical side. Since the product manager is not an accountant or cost analyst, it is hardly necessary to try making him one. However, a basic understanding is essential.

From the maze of technical and accounting terms and devices used to determine and express profit, the two of greatest concern to product managers are gross and net profit. Gross profit is that profit obtained from the product before including overhead expenses and direct product costs. Net profit is that resultant final profit that remains after all other costs have been subtracted. It is the final dollars and cents expression of money made by the company. So examined, it appears to be eminently simple. This is deceptive, as complications rapidly enter the analysis: What elements will be included in the cost of goods? Which elements are fixed and which are variable? How will equipment be amortized? What overhead and other burdens will be carried? What valuations are to be placed on what equipment? What about fixed or variable cost systems? Do we use direct or indirect costing in product cost calculations? What will labor charges be? How do we offset costing valuations on under- as opposed to over-capacitated operations? Do we always apply the same rules and regulations, or do we permit costing exceptions?

These questions only hint at the complexities. And in this forest of queries and answers, no one is ever going to completely agree; accountants don't, so how can we expect to? However, being charged with gross profit responsibility, the product manager must be thoroughly familiar with all the specifics of the cost accounting system employed in his company. Not being an accountant, there are occasions when the system employed will appear confusing, and he will have many questions, the answers to which are necessary for his total understanding of the system and the costs he lives with. Since these are so variable, we cannot go into them here, but the product manager should.

The common terms and concepts involved in cost determinations are listed below. They will illustrate the complexity. Happily, all need not be committed to memory or understanding, because only those that apply in the specific product management situations are of real concern to the acting product manager. The others are nice to know but quickly forgotten.

Term	Meaning
Process cost	Cost of manufacturing a product in one or more locations predicated on a given period of time.
Class cost	A job order approach costing out on the basis of a certain product, products, or articles.
Assembly cost	Cost of assembling product.
Standard	Product cost based on standard element determination and fixed assessments estimated before actual manufacture.
Estimated	Similar to standard cost, at least in derivation and computation.
Predetermined	Similar to standard cost, at least in derivation and computation.
Historical cost	Determined after manufacture.
Fixed cost	Predetermined and nonvariable cost necessary in product or process.
Variable	Just as the name implies: variable, sensitive to volume.
Allocated expense	Expense apportioned against product or process.
Prime cost	The sum of direct material and direct labor.

Term	*Meaning*
Conversion	The sum of direct labor and manufacturing expenses.
Cost of goods	Sum of all manufacturing expenses plus allocations.
Cost of goods sold	Strictly speaking, cost of goods plus adjustments for initial and finished goods inventories, but often confused with cost to make and sell.
Cost to make and sell	The same as above plus all expenses in selling and administration.
Daily, weekly, or other frequency	Costs based on time cycles, the frequency of which determines the designation.
General overhead	Includes various and sundry components that differ from company to company.
Average cost	Mathematical average of units in total actual cost.
Average variable cost	This is nothing more than the expression resulting from dividing total variable costs into unit total.
Average fixed cost	The expression resulting from dividing total fixed cost into units. It decreases as quantity increases.
Total fixed cost	Those costs that remain the same regardless of quantity produced, such as rent, executive salaries, or depreciation.
Total variable cost	Those costs that vary relative to units produced and are sensitive to such production costs as packaging, materials, or wages of plant operators.
Total cost	Sum of total fixed and variable costs.
Cost I, II, III	Terms usually found in chemical process industries indicating various costing levels, which include elements from raw material only up to finished goods. Exact elements in all stages vary in each stage.

There are also standby, marginal, differential, opportunity, comparative, future, sunk, out-of-pocket, joint, volume, imputed, replacement, controllable, and uncontrollable costs that we have not discussed, since they would merely add to the confusion.

What has this excursion into terminology taught us? If nothing more, it has expanded our horizons and generated a certain awareness of the complexities of cost and cost analysis. It has explained that to know the cost of product is no simple matter, and that to know the true cost of product is probably impossible. It has also shown us that there can be, and often is, a profit even in cost, although this profit may be indirect and a function of allocations and constructions rather than direct net profit contribution. However submerged, it is nonetheless there. This carries with it the implications of volume and through-put benefits based on capacity utilization as well as internal contributions. The applications vary with the company and its accounting system.

Whether the system is simple or complicated, it is always subject to change, and this imposes the added factor that neither costs nor their means of calculation remain static. Full costing, direct costing, indirect costing, standard costing, variable costing, or whatever, the product manager must stay close to it and to those who compute it. Further, he must understand those elements that enter into calculation of the final cost in order to take utmost advantage of any possibilities for improvement.

Having explored the aspects of product cost, amortization, material, labor, equipment, and manufacturing costs as well as overheads and allocations, we have fairly well covered the cost of product in manufacturing and preparing it for sale. This calculation also includes quality control cost, evaluation expenses, and miscellaneous contributory charges that can be construed as directly relating to cost of product. These additional charges are quite important and bear watching. In low-cost products where any extensive product quality control measures are entailed, it is not surprising to find that such expenses can mount rapidly and account for a substantial percentage of the total cost of product. Coupled with this, packaging, labor, and their cumulative cost often far exceed the value of raw material or product.

From the product manager's seat, this means he should keep a watchful eye on these elements. In other situations where higher material costs are involved, such peripheral costs may constitute a much smaller portion of the total cost. Therefore his attention lies in cost of material and equipment rather than package or control. Knowing the balance assists the product manager in determining routes to investigate product cost control and potential areas for improvements where flagging gross profits are encountered. In this same light, assembly operations, packaging techniques, and handling should also be evaluated as percent of product. And when appropriate, they too should receive due attention for cost control.

Once all this has been accomplished, the product manager can shift attention to the gross profit and his needs in terms of identification and control. To maintain an intimate knowledge of the gross profit of every product and every line, as well as the aggregate profit from all products, is a vital necessity. It is also beneficial to determine profit relative to account, market, industry, and, if possible, competition. The latter is more a matter of "guesstimation," but it can be helpful in assessing competitive pricing (profit) possibilities and limitations.

The solution to these problems can be quick and easy or arduous and seemingly impossible, depending on number of products, accounts, markets, equipment available, and reporting frequency requirements. Where computer operations are possible, the quick, easy route is there and only awaits systems development. Where manual techniques or only quasi-mechanical facilities are available, there is a rocky but not impassable road ahead. In this case informational requirements should be reviewed to provide only that which is absolutely necessary, leaving maximum time for management activities. Where computer capability exists, executive time is not directly consumed; but excess in reporting is wasteful not only of computer time and money but of management time in review and interpretation. In either event the profit audit is essential.

The following section provides the principal elements of the profit audit from which those components applicable in a given situation can be selected. To them should be added the profit cycle analysis previously mentioned, the data for which can be accumulated, extrapolated, and interpreted from the audit data.

ELEMENTS OF PROFIT AUDIT

Like the price audit, the profit audit contains several elements. Each of these is important although it may not be employed in the management situation, depending upon facilities and objectives. The list that follows indicates most of the data relevant to profit from the standpoint of product management requirements. The units by which profit is expressed vary from company to company. Therefore, whether they are expressed in terms of percent gross profit based on sales price, markup, or as gross profit dollars is not indicated.

Frequency of reporting present performance or number of preceding years in historical reports for comparisons of profit is predicated on usage and systems in effect. Similarly, projections employed in planning are also determined by planning cycles and prevailing procedures. The requirements for profit planning are vital and should be the concern of all product managers and general management. There will be more on profit planning later in the chapters on planning; also in the next sections of this chapter on use of profit audit and profit control.

Profit Audit

1. Gross profit per product, per unit, and in unit aggregates sold.
2. Gross profit before allowances per product and cumulative.
3. Gross profit after discounts per product and cumulative.
4. Average gross profit before and after discounts per product, line, trade, market, customer, territory.
5. Gross profit on exception prices per product, line, trade, market, customer territory, volume, in total, and as of list price on same basis as above.
6. Gross profit exception reports based on differential pricings.
7. Gross profit trend lines (actual, average, and projected, predicated on past years, graphed) by product, trade, industry, and intercomparison of various product lines and markets.
8. Gross profit performance against plan (percent deviation against planned profit) by product, line, trade, market, industry, and in total.
9. Value-volume analysis, products ranked by profit contribution by product total, sales territory, region, salesperson, market, and by source.

USE OF THE PROFIT AUDIT

Unfortunately, aside from keeping computer tape drives spinning and systems analysts busy, profit audits serve a secondary role in the management life of many companies, despite the importance attributed to profit. The profit audit can accomplish many things if properly organized and interpreted.

Since we are confining our audit considerations only to gross profit, the responsibility for such organizational interpretation is that of the product manager. The profit audit should therefore be very close to his heart, the one document that he eagerly awaits each reporting cycle and which he drops all else to review and analyze. To do this properly, he should understand the uses of the profit audit.

Identification of profit assets. The audit information can highlight those products generating higher profit and provide an indication of product selection predicated on greatest profit. This, in effect, is the basis for key marketing activities where promotional efforts and sales guidance, related to profit attainment and profit objectives, emanate from the product manager to the marketing groups. Similarly, identification of profitable lines, brands, markets, industries, and segments is feasible depending on the structure of the report and input. In this way profit attainment and marketing direction can be correlated.

In the same way that actual major profit contributors can be identified depending on input, similar analysis of potential major profit contributors can also be obtained. This is useful in determining marketing activities and the selection of products for primary promotional and sales emphasis.

The audit information also provides identification of normal profit contributors and furnishes guidance for increase or decrease of marketing effort where profitability is on a norm and such review is warranted. Usually, such products will continue to receive the usual extent of effort, but occasionally over- or underexpenditures and, consequently, time and effort are involved, and commensurate alteration can be beneficial for savings or added sales profit.

Identification of profit problems. The indication of the low-profit or unprofitable product should immediately wave the mental red flag. The product manager should, upon seeing a product that does not meet established profitability standards, ask himself two questions: Can profit be improved to acceptable or better levels? If it cannot, what justification is there for product retention? There are some marketing justifications even here.

If the answer to the first question is affirmative, he should hastily implement those programs required for improvement, and then use the audit as a monitoring device to determine the effect. When negative, he should still monitor the profit to see that it does not fall even further, and then reconsider action accordingly. Wherever low-profit items are retained, they should be examined for their effect on averages since one extremely low contributor can have an adverse affect on average performance and distort profit appearances dramatically. Therefore, analysis should include this aspect, and justification for retention must encompass total effect and the interrelation to the entire line or total product offering.

Profit control monitoring. Every product range, and preferably every product, should have an established minimum planned profitability. This sounds obvious but, surprisingly, many companies do not have a product line profitability planned even though they do plan profitability as such. Where they do, it is usually left to planning in larger aggregates, such as total market or geographic areas and not down to the level of individual products. It is, however, possible to plan at the product level and even to project planned profits on new products. Some companies that do this have seen the salutary effects that can be derived through such control and planning, particularly where the extension of this policy includes product elimination if profit improvement cannot be forthcoming.

The audit will clearly show the direction of profit ups, downs, or stability by product, by customer, and by market. This is another index of activity requirements and profit return for effort or expenditures.

Performance versus plan is a specific report showing comparisons of actual profit versus planned profit. This is not to be construed as pointing the finger of accusation. It is, rather, a constructive device that can show how accurately planning is being conducted; it also highlights strengths and weaknesses in the planning operation.

The audit over a period of time will illustrate the results of improvement activities. In this way it is an indicator of continuation or discontinuation.

Planning device. The audit itself stems from profit planning and, to be meaningful, must be based on profit objectives. It can in itself assist in the function of succeeding plans through analysis of performance and data provided. In this way the audit itself serves as a control and monitoring device both in the administration of the business and in the creative planning process.

PROFIT CONTROL

In the preceding description of profit audits several control factors were expostulated. Control is the responsibility of the product manager, but it can only be effective if clear profit objectives are established and if he is given the opportunity to analyze (through the audit) profit performance and the authority to implement corrective measures. To establish the profit objective, regardless of the level to which profit planning is enacted, a cycle can be constructed as shown in Figure 21.

Use of this technique allows profits to be planned and monitored, and control functions are automatically implemented that will assure

FIGURE 21
Profit Control Cycle

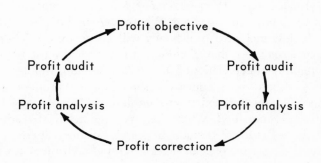

profit review, analysis, and corrective actions. It will also assist in key product and potential key product selection and identification, the emphasis such a product should receive in the marketing process, and be an instrument in the assessment of the success or failure of individual products and the total marketing effort.

The profit control function can be summarized as a planned profit analysis device which, predicated on profit planning, provides marketing with a dynamic instrument for mensuration, control, and direction. To be effective it requires the commitment of all persons to profit objectives and the generation of the profit-conscious atmosphere.

While the product manager is most often charged specifically with gross profit responsibility, he is, by virtue of his overall activity, very involved in many areas that affect net profit as well. He therefore may have no direct say in those elements that influence net profits, but he should know of their existence. Even if he is not directly involved, he is indirectly concerned and has indirect responsibility. These two involvements derive from the scope of activity that has already been described; they will naturally vary with individual circumstances.

Depending on the degree of involvement, the product manager may find that he does have influence on net profits and should be careful in balancing his activities with these possibilities. In the discharge of his duties, he must be fully informed of all elements in net profit calculation. He must also be cognizant of the possible net profit effects of his actions so that he does not inadvertently disturb net profit.

Technical Responsibilities

In many companies there is confusion about the technical responsibilities of the product manager. The record cannot be set completely straight for, like many crooked management paths, the direction taken depends on the leader. If management wants a technically oriented product management, then so be it. Where the emphasis is on planning and analysis, less technical proficiency will be necessary. There is no real right or wrong in either of these extremes; they must be adapted to fit the operational necessities of the business organization.

There is also a third approach, semitechnical product management. This nebulous nomenclature implies the ambiguous state of being neither fish nor fowl. While there is a modicum of truth in that analogy, it is not entirely correct. In a real business situation, unless the product manager devotes all his time and effort to technical rather than administrative planning, he will fall behind in his technical expertise. This means that he will operate further from the performance expectations of product management and closer to the functional operation of a project leader or technical area specialist. There is nothing wrong with either of these positions. Indeed, both are very necessary, and many companies have them as separate staff positions in concert with marketing. However, the product manager cannot be expected to do both well.

Conversely, since the product manager is the center of all product information, he must have some general technical knowledge. A product manager who does not know what his product is, where it is used, why it is used, what its general features are, its advantages and performance characteristics, what systems it can be employed in, or what restrictions are imposed on it is not a product manager but a glorified paper shuffler.

The problem that confronts management and the product manager is the technical-managerial index, how to effect it, and how to maintain it. Here, as in the responsibility-authority quandary, the solution is not totally acceptable to all, nor totally suitable; as an approach, however, it does provide a base for departure and refinement. As we saw variables in the index of responsibility and authority, we also see them here: nature of company and management situation; nature of problems and responsibilities; nature of product and market; and specific needs of the specific situation.

In order to satisfy any technical requirements, the product manager must have either the technical background or the capability to learn. We cannot expect a product manager to provide technical assistance in chemistry and physics if he thinks objects float because water overcomes the effect of gravity.

Therefore, in selecting the product manager, criteria consistent with technical expectations must be imposed. Chemical or engineering graduates are needed where chemistry and engineering are needed. These may seem obvious management requirements, but they are sometimes overlooked. It is usually possible to teach a scientifically trained expert the art of management and the intricacies of the company product, but the company cannot teach him chemistry. Occasionally this can be accomplished through outside educational facilities, but the time is usually not available. Similarly, where the orientation is highly statistical or organizational, experts from business management should be recruited; those with academic backgrounds in these fields should then be selected and given appropriate training in the necessary technical areas.

The technical-managerial index is predicated on the variables and the selection process. It is also variable to the extent that as the needs of the position change, the product manager can be further educated in specific though nonscientific disciplines. And it is wise to use technical consultants whenever necessary.

The company should not try to make the product manager the technical manager unless he is that type of specialist. Another word of warning: the product manager should not make himself the technical manager. Most product managers have a tendency to do this, so we must guard continually against it.

Packaging

To the product manager, the importance of packaging is threefold: commercial, technical, economic. Regardless of the market to be served or the customer who is purchasing, all these factors are significant. Their relative weight in any given product situation varies with the market, budget, profit, and product. In the consumer market, commercial considerations are paramount; in industrial markets, technical factors are more important. Internally these must be measured against the economic factor, or the packaging budget. This occasionally creates problems that result in compromises, which should nev be made if there is a serious question of jeopardizing marketing success. The package is that important and should be so considered. Table 5 shows significant packaging elements in all three categories

According to the table, there are several elements that correspond, and from them a line can be drawn pointing directly to the optimum package for the given situation. But the reason for considering all in such detail is not to illustrate the obvious. Imagination and creativity, which are not shown in the table, must be added by the packaging designer or the product manager. Also, the product manager should give full attention to each element while product research and development are still in process. He should apply all of his marketing knowledge in planning the package and its use in marketing, advertising, promotion, and sales campaigns.

He should also consider the repackaging of existing products where change might be helpful. Many a failing product has been revitalized in a new package. In some consumer markets package importance is so well recognized that the manufacturer has not dared change his package, and still packs and labels as he did from Day One; this same manufacturer might put out a new package containing the same product, thus capitalizing on a new packaging innovation while retaining sales with the old. This is good and valid marketing.

While many may say that packaging is of more importance in consumer markets than in those of industry or government, nothing could be further from the truth. Both these markets are concerned with packaging, and the product manager faces increasingly demanding packaging situations.

Faced with many competitive economic situations, industry especially has come to recognize the importance of the package. Two examples of this should suffice: (1) Continuous processing is on the increase, and metering systems are widespread in many wet-process industries. Packages for liquid products that can be linked directly to metering devices lend themselves to these automated systems and provide a competitive edge for those who supply them. (2) Disposal of waste is a pressing and expensive problem in many localities. Solutions vary from paper bags to drums, cartons, and other containers made of rigid paper or plastic. All of these are receptive to packaging development.

The availability and variety of packaging materials make it possible to solve almost any packaging problem. It is worthwhile to spend money on packaging. Whenever management or the product manager considers it, he should fall back on a variation of that old adage: Do unto others as you would have them do unto you. In packaging terms: Pack it as if you were going to buy it.

There are still two parting thoughts on this subject.

CARRIER REQUIREMENTS

Many carriers have strict regulations over and above legal requirements; and packaging should be checked with transportation representatives before finalization. In corporations that have self-contained traffic departments this is a simple matter and should be accomplished early in the developmental cycle. There is no point in packing the product in fiber drums that may not be accepted for international steamer transport, which is a situation that prevailed at one time. Similarly there are restrictions on dimensions, weights, and contents, as well as certain protections that must be provided, from freezing, for example. These matters should also be cleared with the firm's traffic department or with the proposed carrier.

Freight carries different classifications of charges and rates. A tremendous amount of money is spent by every company on freight costs.

(*text continues on page 215*)

TABLE 5. *Considerations in packaging.*

Factor	Commercial (Consumer oriented)	Technical (Industrially oriented)	Economic (Product manager oriented)
Size	Size of units and assortment of sizes to offer. Good things come in little packages but bigger ones are supposed to be cheaper.	Can be important factor in storage and space savings. Handling problems. Optimum size for processes.	Savings per unit related to units packed. Bulk containers in place of individual units. Transportation savings can be effected in bulk. Can be optimized relative to batch or production capacity.
Shape	The shape does not always have to conform to the product, and several interesting possibilities exist. This is an important psychological factor.	Not as important as in the commercial aspect, but can be important for storage.	Shaped containers can be more expensive. Storage problems can occur or can be improved. With wrapped packaging peculiar shapes can create additional expense.
Contents	Should the product be sold assembled or disassembled. Pressurized units are very popular.	Physical forms very important: in many cases liquids are superior to dry compounds, but are more difficult and costly to package.	Physical forms differ in cost and can be optimized. Pressurized packaging is expensive but in some consumer goods the surcharge more than offsets this and profit per unit is greater. Disassembled products can save internal expense, but they should have clear instructions.

Color	The mecca of consumer psychologists. It is vitally important in consumer packaging where often the package is the product. The question is not alone what color to package in but should there be assortments.	Color application is important as a device for: identification coding locating aesthetic purposes.	Color is usually more expensive than natural packaging. Economics should be developed to determine differential and return. Cost of color is constantly being reduced so more opportunity exists for its use. Effect on sales so critical in some areas it is a must.
Opening	Simple. Rapid. Requiring minimum equipment.	Simple. Rapid. Requiring minimum equipment. Should relate to industrial use.	Easy opening container can be more expensive. Gearing opening to commercial use can be more costly but also can be a competitive advantage; can also command a surcharge.
Closing	Not so important.	A serious problem where all of product is not used when opened. Should be readily possible.	Can be expensive, but can command commensurate price. Can be competitive advantage. Should be consideration relative to product and use patterns and requirements.
Capacity	Important only in that appearance can be problematical, such as the half-full box because of settling during transit. Should be large enough to provide ease of use.	Relate to product requirements. Consider physical phenomena: swelling, shrinkage, transportation.	No special problems provided the preceding are considered.

Table 5. *Considerations in packaging (continued).*

Factor	Commercial (Consumer oriented)	Technical (Industrially oriented)	Economic (Product manager oriented)
Resealing	Not too important except in foods and perishable items.	An important consideration: once opened, if not fully used, can sensitive product be resealed? If bags or less expensive packaging techniques are used, this is a serious matter but can be resolved. A particular problem with toxic or harmful chemicals.	Can be expensive to satisfy this requirement but can mean lost sales not to solve it.
Advertising	A message can be carried on the package and should be. Promotions can be announced. A typical consumer product approach. Relates to brand and product identification. Consider identity factor, such as uniformity of package for products of same manufacturer, or uniformity of logo. The package itself is an advertisement for the product.	Many of the considerations applying in commercial analyses are valid here. Where products go into plants that are highly industrial, logo and product identification important, but extensive, expensive imprints not worth their cost.	If package is considered product advertising, that much of the cost is automatically justified. Costs of advertising on package not so high as at one time—also less than any other form of direct product-for-product and house or image advertising. Can provide competitive advantage. Must be balanced against intangible (sometimes) gains or losses. Difficult to assess value but worth the price since usually not prohibitory.

Should be:	Should be: Aesthetically pleasing / Reasonably durable / Suitable for contents / Suitable for market / Easy to use	A more important factor here than in commercial markets, and must take into account: Shelf life / Technical and chemical requirements of product / Compatibility / Durability under usage / Serviceability / Resistance to stress and strain / Protection for product	Expense can be cheaper than lost product or dissatisfied customer. Expense here should be included in cost of product since it is difficult to surcharge for what is expected of the basic package even if it is more expensive than usual to meet technical requirements.
Cost	Must relate to product market and customer. Can be defrayed via surcharge or included in product. Can be recouped via special packaging at comparable price —a technique that also can be used in marketing to create a demand for prestige-identified products.	Essentially the same considerations as in commercial area except dual lines with same product priced at different levels based on packaging is not practical. Customer will expect a differential when buying in larger quantities based on supposedly lower costs. Often they are but not always, and product managers themselves must not assume larger quantities result in lower cost of their products.	Cost of packaging can be looked upon as a: part of advertising/promotion / cost of product / fixed expense / marketing necessity All depend on perspective; some appeal to the accounts and some to marketers; however, all are correct, and the final application should be predicated on more than classic cost accounting procedures.
Competitiveness	Commercially this is extremely cogent; if their packaging is more attractive or functional, there is a problem.	Same considerations as in commercial area.	Cost has to be balanced against competitive response and situation, but it does put packaging into another marketing perspective.

TABLE 5. *Considerations in packaging (continued).*

Factor	Commercial (Consumer oriented)	Technical (Industrially oriented)	Economic (Product manager oriented)
Instructions	In disassembled products this is important; there is nothing more frustrating than poor instructions in many products. It also assures proper product use and minimizes consumer confusion and potential complaint.	Just as important as in commercial area. With some scientific equipment and products that have known sensitiveness, it can be even more significant.	This costs little or nothing. There is no excuse for instructions either on or in the product. Please do not put instructions on how to open the package inside.
Labeling	There are two aspects to commercial labeling concerns: Identification and instructions, including warnings; these are necessary and should be clear. Labeling programs—relate to guarantees, warranties, and process-related aspects. In such instances the tag or label represents the product and the manufacturer.	Usually concerns product identification to include handling and other precautions as well as toxicological requirements and conformity to Interstate Commerce Commission and other regulations.	Not necessarily expensive per se, but identification of requirements and their related traffic or handling requirements can be. There are regulations that must be complied with, and their expense is naturally unavoidable.
Stability	Shelf life has to be assessed. Durability Appearance Effect on product Psychology to consumer	Very important; must take into consideration same factors as commercial, plus added concern of expense if return or reprocessing are involved.	Same consideration as in storage.

Convenience	A critical factor. People will pay more for it. Assortments or lines should be considered here.	Not a big consideration at one time, it is now increasing in importance. Should relate to in-house usage; relate to batch or process size, storage, handling, emptying, fittings and similar engineering or technical requirements. Can be a competitive edge.	Not necessarily more expensive, and in consumer areas can yield higher profit per unit. In technical area careful economic analysis needed to assure full return, but do not forget competitive aspect: if you sell more you make more even if the cost is slightly higher.
Storage	Not too critical. Consider: shelf life container durability compatibility appearance reusability space	Critical. Consider: shelf life container durability compatibility appearance reusability space warehouse costs handling	Expense can be incurred here, but it is cheaper in the long run to offer a sufficiently protected product than to attempt recovery or to satisfy customer complaints. The time to worry about 20 tons of leaking drums is before, not after.
Recovery	Not critical.	Can be important when reuse is planned to save money or extend life of container.	Can be a source of economy by using, say, reconditioned drums or reconditioning them yourself. Also is a selling point. When returns on refunds are involved, should be examined critically as costs can be excessive and not offset disposables.

TABLE 5. *Considerations in packaging (continued).*

Factor	Commercial (Consumer oriented)	Technical (Industrially oriented)	Economic (Product manager oriented)
Filling	Only important in relation to producing product initially or when the product involves one where transfer of package is involved. Bulk (for home use, that is) containers of one gallon or so, with smaller, refillable, purse-size units have become popular in some cosmetic areas—a reverse approach borrowing from the industrial market, for a change.	Can be most important when handling and use requirements have to be met. Also relates to transfer or reuse applications.	Can be an expensive situation when special designing is required. Must be in balance with objective and estimated return.
Emptying	Not usually considered a problem, but it can be. The product has to be removed and should be readily handled.	Important in processing, and relates to intended use and prevailing mechanical systems and requirements.	Can be expensive if special fittings or engineering required. However, can be worth the investment if position can be gained and maintained.
Handling	Not usually critical.	Important, consider: size weight dimensions shape storage facilities usage and turnover union restrictions	Can be internally significant and takes into account same factors as industrial user. Also can be a source of expense or economy depending on how approached.

Disposability	Has found wide consideration. The disposable age stems not alone from convenience but from expense and contamination and pollution-control requirements.	Equally, if not more, important in technical areas because of costs and disposal problems.	Can be initially expensive to locate, design, and manufacture a disposable package, but once located and perfected, can be more economical than conventional ones.
Return	At one time important; no longer so, since little packaging is done in returnable containers.	Same as commercial consideration.	Not too important since little is packaged this way. Where it is, should be critically examined to be sure it is worth it.
Conversion	This implies that the empty container or package can be converted to another purpose. Glass banks holding foods were popular. It is used occasionally and has consumer appeal often with no real added cost.	Not too important, although some enterprising chemical companies pack in plastic containers that can later be used for personal endeavors. In large units this can be costly.	As a promotional technique can be worth the money. In normal use if the product lends itself, it can be done with little or no expense; when special modification is required, the monetary justification is necessary.
Visual impact	Importance cannot be overestimated. It is the end result of the total effort.	At one time not considered to be too important. Now recognized to have much the same need as in consumer products; less money should be spent.	It is worth any reasonable expense in consumer products, and should not be underestimated in industrial markets.
Quality	Important in total impression; must be commensurate with product.	Same as commercial.	Should be best possible within economic limitations and profit-objective attainment.

TABLE 5. *Considerations in packaging* (*continued*).

Factor	*Commercial* (*Consumer oriented*)	*Technical* (*Industrially oriented*)	*Economic* (*Product manager oriented*)
Wrapping	Important, since many consumer packages have an inner and outer aspect. If wrapped then many of the other factors, such as advertising and labeling, apply.	Not too critical since seldom encountered.	Part of the packaging expense.
Protection	The main object of packaging is either to contain or protect the product. Protection should be considered and balanced with handling, storing, usage, and cost.	Same as commercial.	Should be in balance with costs and profit objectives, but should not be sacrificed since many dollars in claims for return and replacement of damages eat many profit dollars.
Durability	A significant factor since the package, if it is a container, should not wear out before the product is consumed or worn out.	Same as commercial.	Same as consideration in protection.

Where these are not directly transferred to the customer, every effort should be made to control them. This can only be accomplished through close coordination with the traffic department or carrier and the establishment of optimal freight classifications.

Also important to product managers are the rates based on commodity or noncommodity classifications. However, this book is not the place to discuss them since they are quite a study in themselves. The product manager should, however, learn them on his own as they afford many opportunities for profit improvements.

FEDERAL, STATE, AND LOCAL REGULATIONS

There are many regulations concerning the packaged product as it is transported and stored. The federal government's Interstate Commerce Commission controls interstate commerce, regulates traffic, and hence, product packaging. Under this commission there are a number of specific regulations that the package and its labeling must meet before the package can be shipped interstate. Intrastate regulations also apply even though they are under the control of local governments. Familiarity with these regulations is essential, and coordination with traffic department, carriers, or governmental agencies will assure compliance.

Quality Control

In the chapter on techniques of product management, this subject was given rather extensive theoretical treatment. But the product manager must be reminded that an abstraction can apply as a vital constituent in the control of each individual product. In this sense the requirements for control procedures and the tolerances established should reflect practical consideration of the product, the market, the use, and the customer.

The cost of controlling quality must encompass not only tests and valuations but also rejects, reworks, and distress merchandise, not to mention nonrecoverable materials. Each of these situations results in a cost that reflects directly in product cost as an allocation, or indirectly as a variance charged against either the plant or the product. Either way it really amounts to the same thing: money not made. The product manager in this case is affecting not only gross product but net profit. Quality control should then be controlled.

Competitive Assessments

This subject is dealt with extensively in a subsequent chapter, where the nature of competition is discussed on various levels such as company-to-company and product-to-product. The major area of competitive activity centers around specific product-to-product confrontation and the extensions of this approach brand-to-brand, line-to-line, and indirect product competition. The latter is the type of competition where products are similar enough to compete.

Whatever the nature of the competition, direct or indirect, it is ubiquitous. And while competition is both necessary and beneficial, it is frustrating when a competitor gains the advantage, even if it is only temporary. Many hours are spent in devising countermeasures and strategies for longer-range competition; and equally difficult are the harassing immediate decisions that must be made to meet individual competitive situations "on the spot."

Either situation poses significant problems, for there is a balance in action and reaction that is incumbent on all management in order to maintain market stability. Overresponse often creates the well-known negative price spiral that has too often been encountered in too many markets. While price attrition is to be anticipated in mature markets with mature products, overreaction or aggressiveness can precipitate this long before it is naturally due and results in prematurely depressed prices and reduced profits for all competitors. It is not unusual for this to occur in particular markets, and it has been a source of marketing difficulty for years. The only solution to this problem is through intelligent planning and responsible marketing.

In this context it is necessary to recognize competition in all of its positive and negative aspects, and to realize the requirements for planning and responsible actions or reactions. In the formulation of marketing plans, overall or product-oriented, provision for active and reactive competitive strategies is required. The active phase is the generation of the marketer's own competitive activity as a part of his marketing activity, while the reactive represents those maneuvers to be employed in response to competitive pressures. In considering either we should bear in mind that the marketing activity is in itself a competitive activity, and we are not restricted to those limited areas normally considered as competitive.

Ask most competitors what competition is and they will probably say that competition is price. And while price may be the most obvious manifestation of competitive activity, there are others as important. Less obvious and telling influences can be brought to bear, and these, because they are more insidious, defy analysis and identification; these are far more difficult to respond to than overt price-to-price competition. Competitive tactics have shifted from price to such areas as service, allowances, financing, market saturation, and similar strategies. These are described more fully in the following chapter on competition.

The product manager should be fully apprised of competition and its activities at all levels at all times. If he allows himself to become unfamiliar with his competitors' activities, he will become ineffectual and rapidly lose control of his product in the competitive market.

To obtain this knowledge there are many channels of communication open to the product manager:

Trade publications	Trademark reports
Customer contacts	Government publications
Trade associations	Competitive advertising
Salesmen's reports	and promotional activities
Marketing contacts	Newspapers and journals
Personal contacts	Educational institutions
Professional organizations	Seminars and courses
Patent reports	

All of these provide information that sometimes requires a degree of surveillance bordering on the counterspy's diligent ferreting out and piecing together bits of information to determine the whole. But it is worth the effort to keep abreast. Often such information is available in its entirety and only needs analysis and use. Whichever the extreme, it's all useful and all necessary.

Another important point is that competition information received and countermeasures determined are of no use unless they are disseminated to those who need to know. Appropriate data on competitive products should be distributed periodically to sales, technical personnel, and management on a regular schedule and immediately when important situations occur.

Strategies devised to counter competitors should also be distributed; and whenever new products are released, indications of the competitors, their products, comparisons (strengths and weaknesses), and their own strategies and tactics should always be provided if known. When such information is not available, any that is should be given and supplemented later when more data are available or subsequent changes occur. Similarly, on existing products current information should be distributed along with interpretation and relative comparisons. In this way sales and marketing personnel will be constantly informed of the competitors' products, their comparisons, and their own counterofferings and strategic activities.

The product manager should always be willing to discuss competition in all its aspects, and cultivate an attitude of objectivity since there is no place for emotionalism in the assessment of competitors, their actions, and, most especially, his company's reactions.

Product Control

The control of product implies the ability to know what the product is in the way of strengths, weaknesses, and competition; what it is doing in the market; what it is making (profit) or losing (lack of profit); and what it can do potentially or actually. Control also implies the ability to: select products for promotion; direct the product in, during, and after promotion; and add to, subtract from, and balance product and line.

These are all facts of product management life that have been reviewed before, but they take on new significance when considered in their aggregate. This knowledge and these control functions will enable the product manager to direct the product activity and recommend the marketing activity to the marketing director. While it is possible to know all these things, it is not easy and will require use of all the tools and techniques described.

Such information, however, no matter how accurate and detailed, or how well interpreted, is valueless unless specific product policies exist; these provide a basis from which the product direction derives and the marketing activity evolves on an integral base. Examples of product policies that are indicative of the operational requirements fundamental to meaningful product control follow.

Key Product

A key product is based on specific criteria, and contributes to the assortment above a fixed level. The criteria commonly used are gross profit or its near-synonymous criterion, sales volume, or similar considerations. The level chosen for categorization as major or other depends upon the setting of profitability and sales levels (if these be the criteria) and then categorizing those products according to such performance levels as, for example, all products drawing more than $50,000 or returning more than 45 percent gross profit. These determinations can be made only after analyzing the line and then plotting performance.

Basically, this is an application of management by exception; after the key products have been identified, they become the ones to monitor and control because as they go, so goes the business and profit. The object, then, is to identify the major products that constitute the majority of the business—usually 80 percent or more.

POTENTIAL KEY PRODUCT

This is an extension of the key product concept based on identifying those products that, like key products, deserve particular marketing emphasis and monitoring. Unlike the key product, however, the identification is not based on historical activity but on anticipated performance.

In either case the use of the key or potential key product concept can reap rewards. It can be employed on the basis of the total line, or applied on individual lines or product subgroups. In this way the importance of individual lines can be analyzed, their relative performance and "key" position determined, and the individual products contained therein.

This also can be done with markets and market segments, indicating return for effort and efforts to be expended on them, which is of great importance in direction of the marketing effort and then the product effort within the market. Periodic reassessment is required since key products and key markets do shift, particularly if the system is further extended to regional performance within the company.

From a practical standpoint the identification of a national key product or market indicates the entire activity and those at lower levels the specific activity in the individual marketing area. In either situation shifts occur and reanalysis should be made at least annually. Once identified, these "key" elements can be the base of key or exception reports geared to indications of their performance—management by exception.

PROFIT MINIMUMS

It has already been said that many companies do not have product-by-product profit objectives. But they should. When implemented, key analysis becomes possible and clear identification of good, bad, or normal performers ensues. This enables emphasis, deemphasis, or deletion considerations.

SALES MINIMUMS

It is usually easier to get the marketing director to listen to establishing sales minimums rather than profit minimums. However, if properly controlled, they can eventually amount to almost the same thing. Once these minimums are set the same control functions can be applied.

Product Line Size

There are only so many products that can be effectively managed. Too few and the marketing effort cannot be sustained; too many and there is confusion, wasted effort, wasted motion, and lost opportunity. What is the optimum, how critical the number? Who can say, since this is so intimately related to the company, the product assortment, the market, and the management team. But regardless of the difficulties, it is worth the effort to determine the optimum and then to redetermine it since there is nothing fixed in optimum product line size, just as there is nothing fixed in good marketing. One task that should be set for the product manager is a total evaluation of the line and recommendations for optimum size. When this is done the objective should be to bring the line up or down to this level and maintain it there.

Forecasting

In the realm of control activities forecasting may sound a little out of place, but it is not inappropriate since the interrelations of forecasting to key products, potential key products, minimum profits, product selection, and exception management is beyond question. Earlier, in the description of tools and techniques, the mechanisms available for forecasting were discussed in detail. Mention is made here only so that the integration of forecasting consideration requirements is appreciated.

Sourcing

Sourcing is the control and selection of product sources to optimize line and profit. It is often complex since implications outside direct cost comparisons are involved, and such indirect factors as through-put, capacity utilization, contribution factors, intermediate utilization and similar financial, managerial, or technical elements must often be included in the final selection. Added to this are opportunities for contract manufacture, toll processing, licensing, parts fabrications, external assembly, internal manufacturing with external packaging, and so forth. Here we are once more facing a situation where the possible combinations, while not infinite, are certainly numerous and the balances sometimes tenuous.

Wherever multiple sources for product are involved, an optimum sourcing study should be undertaken and reassessment made period-ically to assure lowest cost or attainment of maximum corporate ben-efits. When single sources are used, it is still worth examining to determine whether more economical sources exist, since sourcing com-placency can quickly occur.

Disposal of Obsolete Product

Every product manager, much as he may regret it, finds himself faced with obsolete inventories. Often the results of poor planning or forecasting, obsolescence can also occur because of market changes, unforeseen competition, or competitive advantages; but disregarding cause, the effect is the same, inventory that can no longer be sold or may be slow moving. Whatever the case, provisions must be made to dispose of such material and, depending on the product, this can be critical. Short shelf life, spoilage, or decomposition may occur. In other instances timing may be expensive, and carrying charges are still there gobbling up profits and creating storage and logistics prob-lems. When such situations occur, there are several alternatives:

Mark prices down.

Increase discounts.

Sell to professional odd-lot or obsolete inventory disposal com-panies.

Discard with writeoff.

Modify and sell as new product.

Repackage and sell as new product.

Blend with usable material.

Reprocess into usable product.

Disassemble and reassemble.

The relative costs or economies of such programs must be evaluated, for sometimes it is more costly to attempt product recovery than to eliminate it immediately. Unfortunately, carrying charges being what they are, every day of delay is another day of cost. Because obsolete or slow-moving inventories are always there, ample opportunity for planning exists; but few companies plan for such inevitable disposal situations. Establishment of rework charge criteria or resale minimums helps curtail delays in disposal and provides options for action without jeopardizing profit or creating inadvertent market disturbances. Planning for inventory disposal should occur and policies should be established where they do not exist. If the product manager is not directly responsible for such programs (sometimes he is not), he will be a contributor to policy and decision-making since his product expertise is a definite requisite to intelligent action.

Legal Restrictions

In controlling products we have seen that there are many legal implications related to marketing activities and the product itself. The major laws dealing with these have already been described. It should suffice here to be reminded of their importance in product control.

The Special Product

Occasionally the product manager will be requested to add a product to his range that does not fulfill the normal requirements of sales or profit minimums. The reasons for such products are many; but they always involve some commercial considerations that ostensibly justify the addition. The word "ostensibly" is well chosen, for the usual arguments are that the account will remain 100 percent yours with no competition, or that it rounds out an assortment and increased business will result on other products that are more profitable; the customer will show his appreciation with increased business; systems selling makes the product mandatory; it will only be below acceptable minimums temporarily, for sale volumes will increase in no time, and once they do, sales goals will be met and profit improved. These reasons will be presented to product managers in various guises as inducements toward a favorable decision.

Let us not speak too harshly of them, for occasionally they are true and at least appear to be sensible. What they do not indicate, however, is the disproportionate cost of adding and maintaining the product, cost of withdrawal if it doesn't work out, analysis of success probability, sourcing, and other factors that consume time and money.

Therefore no special product should be added unless carefully analyzed and the risk minimized. The product manager can only do this after securing all available information and then scrupulously weighing it. Where the risk elements are favorable, the special product should be added and then hawked. Followup on such products is extremely important, for if successful they should be removed from special categorization; if not, they should be eliminated after a reasonable period of time.

Special products get special treatment which may involve exception reporting, manual record keeping, and more frequent reporting cycles. All of these are designed to focus attention on the product and minimize handling costs. Either transferring it from a special to a standard product or eliminating it altogether should be the product manager's object, and he should set a definite time for either to be accomplished.

This is the compromise approach that can be used when the sales department clamors for the product, provided that, in time, it is either in or out. If the sales department is made to fully realize the reasons for such action, it will, first, curtail such requests and, second, accept such conditional additions and the requirements imposed when they are adopted.

There are a few instances when it will be necessary to add a product with no real expectation that sales or profit will ever amount to anything significant. The only justification is the account-oriented value in position to be gained. This can be a valid reason and part of a sales strategy. As long as the reason is clear and the impact on average profitability nil, then no major harm is done, provided that such occurrences are kept to an absolute minimum.

Some companies do not subscribe to this lost product theory. When they do not, the very minimum to settle for is the breakeven point, which can be a problem to determine.

There is merit to both schools of thought. The product manager should have a large say in either since profit is his responsibility. Sometimes the individual must be sacrificed for the many; perhaps this has its place in profit and product management.

The New Product

The new product is like a new-born child, frail and sensitive. It must be fed, nurtured, guarded, and protected until it achieves maturity and can stand on its own merits.

What are the elements of new product marketing planning? This is separate and distinct from the planning activity encompassed in marketing or product plans which, being undertaken only annually, cannot cover all contingencies of products introduced within the planning cycle. Many of the elements are similar, however. To see them in perspective, reference can be made to the sections on product planning contained in the three chapters on planning. Here we focus on new product planning as a separate entity—an entity that should be fully explored for each new product in the late stages of research, development, or test marketing. These are the elements in new product marketing planning or bringing the product from birth to early maturity:

Release date.
Initial distribution.
Initial advertising and subsequent campaigns.
Initial promotion and subsequent campaigns.
Minimum profit and time of development.
Minimum sales and time of development.
Assessment of internal and external reactions.
Initial competition.
Price.
Reaction of competition.
Resale or discount policies.
Planned and programmed periodic review.
Distribution.
Modification of marketing activity based on review and analysis.
Packaging.
Marketing objectives: share of market, position, and others.
Initial and immediate inventory requirements and locations.
Product objectives: profit, sales, prestige, competition.
Production requirements and product availability.
Consumer education and brand identification.
Literature requirements.

Each of these elements has specific actions that should be detailed as action programs. Such programs should contain three factors: (1) the action to be performed, (2) the date of performance, and (3) the person responsible for its execution. Subsequent review and analysis will indicate performance against the major elements and evaluation of action plans, their performance, success, or failure.

Development of such detailed new product planning programs and the concurrent necessities for determinations may not guarantee the success of each new product, but will go a long way toward providing it with every chance possible. Where new products fail, it is equally important that the reasons for such failure be clearly identified. Here, once again, we find apathy. Whether such disinterest is real, based on the "what's happened, happened" and "let's move on to better things," schools of thought, or more selfish protectionist motives, is not important. Whatever the cause, the effect remains the same.

Therefore adequate provision should be made for a product postmortem. Let's find out why in a healthy market with a healthy marketing planning activity the new product operation was successful but the product died.

Product Strategies

It is premature to discuss product strategies in any depth since this is another of the planning subjects that will be treated completely in succeeding chapters on planning. However, we cannot do justice to direct product responsibilities without at least mentioning that formal product strategies are an integral part of the product planning and product marketing activity.

A few examples of strategies are provided here only to illustrate the principle. Detailed coverage will be found later.

Profit Strategies	Improvement via process improvement
	Improvement through alternate sources
	Improvement through control of competitive pricing
	Stabilization via introduction of minimum profitability concept
Marketing Strategies	Implementation of minimum sales objectives
	Sales of key products
	Development of systems selling
Product Improvement	Market surveys and need identification
	Use of integrated development activities
New Products	Improved need identification
	Introduction of integrated research, development, and manufacturing approach

These examples are admittedly sketchy but serve to illustrate several techniques and the divergent areas in which strategies can be developed.

In the assessment of strategies several alternatives are usually available. These involve alternatives in strategies with respect to differing areas and variations that are designed to accomplish the same purposes. This means that the product manager will have to work closely with marketing, sales, advertising, and promotion personnel, and any area involved in the product and its successful marketing in order to determine coincidence of effort and to obtain opinion, sanction, and commitment where other functional units are involved in the execution of the strategy. In the chapter on planning we will see the need for such integration before, during, and after planning.

Advertising and Promotion

Many excellent works dealing with this subject exist and should be consulted for specific techniques of advertising and promotion. We are only concerned here with the role of the product manager in his relationship to these activities and those who create them.

In many companies the product manager is directly responsible for such activities and works with internal departments or external agencies who create the advertising campaigns themselves. In this capacity he approves advertising programs and recommends budgets, products to be advertised, approaches to be used—or, by and large, every aspect of the program from start to finish.

With promotional activities that involve giveaways, two-for-one sales, coupon clipping, naming games, contests, or what-have-you, he once more has responsibilities that range from conception to inception to completion. In other situations his responsibility is less direct and primarily advisory; the marketing director will control the advertising activity with the product manager's assistance.

In either case it is usual to find an advertising committee composed of representatives from marketing, sales, product management, and executive management. The responsibilities of each are clear and apparent. In this situation all relevant areas are directly represented, and the outcome of the advertising decisions reflects the consensus of the committee. Since the objective of promotion is to insure product success, it is only logical that such effort should be the result of the best ideas of all concerned.

Considering the expenses involved, budgets must be carefully analyzed to ascertain return on investment. The problem is how to determine advertising success or failure. And solution defies complete resolution.

From our standpoint, regardless of the approach taken, the product manager must be intimately involved in the advertising and promotional effort. At the lowest end of the involvement scale he should select products or processes to be advertised. On the high side he should select the agency, the program, and the degree of effort in both initiation and cancellation parameters.

As with the need for early involvement of manufacturing and engineering in new product development, it is equally important to make advertising and promotional plans early in the new product cycle. Often, as with other factors in the release and marketing of the new product, these elements are reviewed and implemented far too late. Consequently, they may not be fully used or sufficiently thought out. Expenses being what they are, this is wasteful; but even more important is the loss of marketing impetus generated by lack of adequate advertising.

In the integrated approach, advertising and promotion are planned early in the product's development. And if later alterations in specifics are required, based on market conditions or budgets, efficient use of these marketing techniques is that much more assured.

11

Competition
and Competitors

WE live in a competitive world, and this competition extends from our personal into our business environments. Just as the market is becoming increasingly active and complex, so is competition. Management, marketing and general, is vitally concerned with the effects of competition, both negative and positive, as well as the legal implications involved.

With these real and changing concerns, marketing faces a never-ending series of questions regarding the competitor and his activities in any given market: how they exist and operate contemporaneously, and how they are expected to exist and operate in the future. It is necessary to know competition and to anticipate it. The competition's practices of the moment affect marketing practices of the moment, and the expectations of future competitive activity relate to the development of longer range marketing activities and the countermeasures, strategies, and tactics to be employed.

In all these involvements there are varied elements that directly affect the product manager since a major aspect of competitive activity centers around competitive products and the elements of the market/product mix that have already been reviewed. Therefore, the product manager is as close to the competitive scene as anyone in the marketing group. Despite familiarity, it is extremely difficult to accurately assess the competition since most information is second-hand. Perspective is another problem and immediacy of information availability is still another. Having considered these broad concerns, closer examination of the nature, theory, and meaning of competition is extremely helpful. While there is little difficulty in recognizing the existence of competition, few understand its full significance or impact.

The Force of Competition

The existence of competition is undeniable, and its influences are both acknowledged and lamented. There is a tendency, however, to be either overly or underly concerned with this phenomenon, and a resultant complacency or fatalistic negativism may ensue. A more comprehensive understanding of the dynamics of competition, however, leads to a more positive appreciation of these factors:

A. The true significance of competition.
B. Competitive forces.
C. Dynamics of competition.
D. Influence and effects of competition, both direct and indirect.
E. Negative aspects of competition.
F. Positive aspects of competition.

While no one can say he really enjoys competition in business, neither can he deny its value. In some instances it is the very nature of competition to effect creative alterations in the market for the competitive company. Some strategic approaches toward effective use of competition are product imitation or duplicating; the me-too product; the sales and service of parts, equipment, or ancillary products that are used with the competitor's product, capitalizing on his efforts for the market's development and maintenance of the product. Naturally, this is not always the case, and there is little reason for elation in all competitive situations. Price erosion, market saturation, and possible attrition to the point of complete withdrawal of product may occur. This too is in the natural course of business, economic, and social events. Recognizing the force, nature, and structure of competition is a prelude to maximum use of competitive activity, as well as to determination of countercompetitive maneuvers.

Philosophy of Competition

Before one can consider the implementation of competitive tactics, it is essential to reflect on underlying principles from which competition derives. From the urge impelling individuals to excel to the collective efforts of groups to predominate, it is a simple extension to the impulse of corporate dominance. While this partially explains the origin of competition between individuals and provides a foundation for analyzing group competitiveness, there is an added but fundamentally significant consideration in the dynamics of business competition. The needs of economic survival are based on free enterprise, which allows opportunity for the exercise of judgments that will permit the profitable coexistence of many companies active in the same markets.

Implicit in this analysis are the dynamics of the market itself. Since the market is in a state of constant change, competitive activity must also vary. Therefore, competitive factors prevail in varying orders of magnitude, and their influences alter dramatically according to ambient markets and market status. This is well summarized in the supply-and-demand concept. Or better stated, it was well summarized until the recent discoveries of behavioral scientists and the inauguration of creative marketing. While classic supply and demand went a long way to explain economic life, describing the shifts in product and customer, and price and product, it is no longer totally valid because today markets can be created where no real need exists. It can be argued that creating a need or having a real need distills to the same set of supply-and-demand relationships. However, this is not altogether correct, for by guiding needs, demand is also created. Two other factors changing supply and demand balance are education and politics. Both have radically altered the simplistic explanation.

Creative marketing is not as rosy as it may appear since all markets are not subject to such influences, but it does expand our marketing horizons and makes us challenge established marketing thinking and the nature of the marketing-customer-product price relationship as it has for so long been envisioned. What it means is that a new outlook is demanded if effective marketing is to prevail in the modern business environment.

Before we continue, let's review some of the elements that enter into the atmosphere of market and competition.

The Market

As we have seen, the size, posture, and nature of the market varies depending on specific circumstances; it is in a state of constant alteration. The degree of competition therefore in any given situation is variable. In considering both competition and market as coexistent forces in a state of equilibrium, it is immediately apparent that both affect each other and that a change in either results in a change in the other. They are mutually interdependent. In attempting to fully appreciate competition and its effects, the nature and activities of the market must be considered as primary elements. The three traditional market segments once more serve the purpose of providing a basis for examining competitive activities that prevail in these segments. While these are only broad perspectives, they provide insight into the nature of competition on a comparative basis:

CONSUMER MARKETS

It is not necessary to tell any active consumer product manager that this market is one of the most competitive, volatile, and active of the three. The number of firms competing, size, strength, and distribution of any given supplier are of vital importance to his ability to compete in the consumer market. Technical evolution is a determinant, and social change, particularly as it relates to the psychology of customer purchasing habits, is a central concern. Creativity in competition is a reflection of imaginative marketing and is a very important consideration when analyzing or developing competition in this market. Consumer appeal, new products, product modifications, packaging, price, advertising, promotion, and, in more recent years, convenience are all strategies or tactics that have been employed by competitors. In the consumer market we are also concerned with more illusive competitive advantages. Less obvious, like extended consumer credit, they are very effective. With the trend towards credit, competitive activity is bound to increase, and the charge account may well provide the basis for merchant selection. This extends both to the buying public and to intercompany purchases.

INDUSTRIAL MARKET

There are many considerations in the industrial marketplace that parallel those encountered in the consumer area. Distinctions, however, involve the number of competitors, which is often less; but the size of industrial competitors tends to be larger, and elements of peripheral benefits or deficits of bigness brighten or cloud the picture. Sales and purchase reciprocity are implicit. Price, service, distribution, and availability are relevant. Advertising and promotion are important, but their impact is not so great as in consumer marketing. New products, product development, product modification, and customer service are important. At one time the level of such activities was not up to that of the consumer market; however, this is another changing dimension. Recent developments indicate increased activity in such competitive maneuvers, and this will increase in the future as more and more successful consumer marketing techniques find their way into the industrial segment.

GOVERNMENT

Government marketing has usually been thought of as almost sacrosanct. Like banking, it was considered inviolate, stodgy, stagnant, and ponderous. Ponderous it may still be, but government business has come into its marketing own. While traditional approaches remain, the expansion of government business into unconventional areas is fantastic, and opportunities abound. It is still necessary, however, to recognize the traditionalism that prevails in doing business with the government and to know that competition knocks on the same door. The differences from other major market sectors are distinct and provide certain advantages to the competitors. The government, in its contractual relationships, offers protection to the winning contractor so that once the business is obtained for the stipulated contract period, it is his until completed, extended, and rebid. Competition is usually most directly concerned with economics and quality/price of product as delivered. Quality, tolerance, inspections, and rigid control practices are further requirements that can be used to gain competitive edge. Report requirements indicate administrative concerns that may provide another avenue for exploration. While consumer and industrial competitors usually know each other well, government business is by bid and occasions, in theory at least, that competitors do not initially know each other, which means limitation of competitive capability assessments. Entry into government markets is slow and costly so competitors do eventually become known to each other; the general type and special companies that will bid are familiar, which assists in the marketing activity.

Competitive Elements

Having evaluated the nature of competition within the context of its broader significance in relationship to the market, it is germane to consider the principal techniques of competitive activity. The object of competition is of course to obtain, maintain, or improve a position in a given market either initially or over a protracted period. There are several ways in which competitors try to do this. Underlying the implementation of any of these specific tactics, however, is the usually pervasive attitude that constitutes the policy of the company in regard to its competitive activity.

While no company has the same policy all of the time and does not necessarily have the same one for all products in all markets, there is a tendency toward a central attitude governing competition and competitiveness both from the response as well as the action standpoints. This means that companies have an approach that directs their specific activities; they will apply these as the guidelines that govern their activity in the market as they create competition for others and as they respond to competitive situations.

Often these are unwritten and are of that large body of "felt" management that interestingly enough relates directly to the image of company and marketing effort. Often the objective of the company and its competitive guidelines are not those imputed by the competition or the customer either accidentally or deliberately. While it may be intentional to propagate internal policies of one type and create the image of another, this is not often the case. Marketing, therefore, should ascertain what others think they are doing competitively, as this can affect the nature, direction, and degree of competitive activity; the impression may be a far cry from reality. Looked at another way, this can be an advantage since the smoke screen can confuse the competition, and it may be better to be misunderstood than to have a policy so clear that marketing directives and responses are totally predictable. This is a valid objective since, as a competitive counter-measure, the ability to outguess the competition may depend upon the ability to predict his actions and reactions; confusing them therefore helps.

Basic competitive policies of activity can be expressed in three oversimplified terms: high, medium, and low. These are used to describe the level of activity in three dimensions: time, response, and marketing attitude. Naturally, the effort input is a variable functionally dependent on product, market, and circumstance. Having such a fundamentalist approach assists in dispelling the apparent contradictions that occur when examining specific action, reaction practices, and marketing policies as implemented in individual situations.

The nature of competitive activity itself is based on several individual elements that can be looked upon as levels of operational functionality and therefore have two basic active parameters: general, which includes the market, the submarket, and the company itself; and specific, which includes the product, the price, the service, and entertainment.

These seven major categories involve a host of individual tactical possibilities that can be varied in intensity, and in degree of interuse, market, product, and price. People often glibly say the permutations are infinite. They truly are and constitute only one of the many challenges of marketing. Risk is inherent in any application, but the responsibility for minimizing it is that of the marketing group and the product manager, whose knowledge, experience, and judgment are often brought into play in determining the specific activity and levels of intensity on a product price and service level.

To envision the possibilities, examine the list (opposite), which indicates the individual constituent elements that can be applied in exploiting the general and specific strategies as they would be used in given instances. Then consider that the levels of activity in any of the seven major elements or the individual inputs can be varied not only for the total activity, but also on a market or product basis. Once established in any set of conditions, they have to be altered in time, based on market or competitive circumstances as well as on internal matters, including success, failure, profit, available capital, and shifts in the product mix.

Each of these elements has certain characteristics that relate to its implementation. As the product and market differ, so do the techniques by which they are employed. In order to do this effectively, it is necessary to have some greater treatment of their general nature. It is also important to consider the shifts in implementation and emphasis that have occurred in all markets. Since constituent elements were included in the tabulation, we are concerned only with policy and strategy determinations.

MARKET

Competing at a market level means the general activity expended by a company to develop a market or maintain a position in the exist-

Market, submarket, and company
  Advertising
  Promotion
  Image creation
  Public relations
  Public service
  Stature development
  Publicity
  Endowments
  Grants
  Scholarships
  Awards
  Nondirective research

Price
  Credit arrangement
  Cutting
  Volume discounts
  Volume relations
  Erosion
  Instability
  Allowances
  Gratuitous trials
  Repack term manipulation
  Freight charge
    manipulation
  Discounting
    Products
    Payments

Product
  Customer research
  Convenience
  Quality
  Modification
  Distribution
  Special for customer
  Duplication
  Packaging
  Advertising
  Promotion

Service
  Technical
  Financial
  Technological
  Product
  Systems development
  Returns
  Analytical
  Warehousing
  Tie-in sales
  Service allowances
  Convenience
  Speed
  Reliability
  Credits
  R & D
  Consignments

Entertainment
  All levels and forms

ing market place. It usually relates to institutional type advertising and promotion and is not product directed, although it may rely heavily on system or process orientation. Usually this approach is found in industrial and consumer marketing, and the emphasis must be directed toward long-range objectives. As a short-range strategy, it is far too costly and does not yield enough return. Product management and marketing must be concerned because of the many opportunities for tie-in or related efforts on a specific market or product level where they would be more intimately involved from both the standpoints of direction and utilization. The results of competing at this high level are difficult to assess, but equally difficult to combat.

SUBMARKET

Here the approach is similar to the total market situation, but the limits and objectives are more clearly defined since a narrower segment is to be reached. As with total market competition, it is somewhat general in nature unless a concerted effort is made to dominate a market either on short- or long-range goal bases. While limited, the nature of activity, duration, cost and benefits relate directly to the size and identity of the submarket. If large, there is correspondingly more difficulty and expense; but if small, then virtual saturation can capture the submarket. We are once more dealing primarily with consumer and industrial segments when considering this approach. Because it is more specific, product and marketing management can take a more active role in such competitive strategies. Since a relatively small submarket can be affected by such an approach, it is entirely within the realm of reason for marketing management to recommend such activities and then direct the extent, direction, and degree of element imposition. An effective coupling with price and product (and service where necessary) provides a formidable competitive situation, one that an active marketing group can use to initial advantage.

COMPANY

Company-to-company competition is reminiscent of that good old-fashioned approach, direct rivalry. However, while sometimes friendly, it is more usually of the dog-eat-dog variety with the best man emerging financially victorious. Since the prize is the profit, we can well understand the motivation and activity. This basis of confrontation is at an even lower level than the submarket base, and we now find direct market, submarket, and product competition; it is no wonder that this is an important area, one in which product management is highly involved.

Where multimarkets are encountered, the company will find itself in varying levels of competition and in various markets at different times. Flexibility, immediacy of response, and imaginatively planned actions are vital. In competing at this level both image, institution, and product factors take on added significance.

PRODUCT

Product-to-product competition is the product manager's home. Here he will fight many of his competitive battles. This constitutes his single most critical area of competitive activity. Usually, coupled with price and service, the ground roots level of product-to-product competitive activity is the environment in which he and marketing find themselves plying their trades. Planning, forethought, and established strategies must give way to the need for immediacy. Customers will not wait for policies; therefore, quick response is essential for existence in the fiercely competitive situations that are commonly encountered.

In an earlier chapter, thorough consideration was given to the many elements that enter into competition, based on product-to-product confrontation. At one time this was the major arena for competitive battles and probably from the product manager's standpoint, it still is. He is faced daily with questions regarding specific competitive products, and his entire outlook at this level is colored by his assessments of individual competitive products, and in a more agglomerated state, product lines or ranges. Sometimes it is difficult to separate products, particularly where there is an overlap of individual products or a series which, while functionally equal, differ in quality or performance. Competition may be active in only one sector or against one product, but the spillover must also be analyzed. While the product manager may understand that ubiquitous product X goes against his product A only, in the line for product A may be B, C, and D. The impact of the competitive activity on product X can well disturb products B, C, and D, since the consumer is not always so clear in his refinement of delineations as the manager. This is an important fact that should be given all the consideration it deserves. Conversely, this psychological phenomenon can also be used to advantage when developing the company's own marketing strategy, as the same rules hold true for the interpretations and effects on competitors' products as for one's own.

Anticipating product for product competition is exceedingly difficult and requires not only a thorough knowledge of market and product, but also continuous monitoring. Competition moves rapidly. Unless careful controls are devised and pursued, a stable, relatively noncompetitive, position can be completely reversed in a matter of comparative moments, days instead of weeks or months. Later in this chapter, when dealing with response to competition, some ideas for monitoring and control techniques are mentioned. Of course many have already been touched upon in the tools and techniques chapter. Planning is still important and the application of systems is just as valid here as elsewhere.

PRICE

At one time price was the most important single element of competition. This is not to say that it is now unimportant. But price does not have the importance that it once had; this reflects the changing nature of markets, consumers, and marketing. It also reflects some of the attitudes of sophistication in the market and the advanced marketing techniques of the marketers. Price-for-price competition in effect is not sufficient. There are instances where even being slightly outside direct money value equivalency—slightly higher priced or slightly lower dollar-for-dollar product value—the business is still obtained or retained. The reason for this is basically an orientation far beyond that of previous assessments and the recognition that dollars in product alone are not dollars for cost of product or product use alone. Convenience, service (product, technical, customer, delivery), technical and commercial support, total systems availability, engineering assistance, labor and inventory savings—all of these and more are factors offered by the supplier. They are advantages to the consumer that he now analyzes and computes in the cost of product, which he did not consider in the past.

An excellent example in consumer products are frozen foods. Many are good dollar-for-dollar value; but an equal number are not, as they far exceed the relative cost of either fresh or canned counterparts. Yet few foodstuffs have shown such phenomenal growth. The answer cannot be found in economics. We don't have to search far to determine that it is in convenience. The same is equally valid in other consumer market areas, and even in industrial segments. Such factors as storage space for concentrates can be meaningful even though the price of a concentrated chemical may be proportionately higher (as a matter of fact, it is slightly less expensive), but the point remains the same and can be exemplified in dry versus liquid products where two or three times as much storage space is required. Will the charges of warehousing offset the advantages of liquid products (less in plant handling for actual use), or does the difference in product cost offset either? Obviously, answers to these questions cannot be given here, but they typify the tenor of economic analysis now made, rather than the simple straightforward price per unit that was formerly the basis of primary monetary comparison.

Naturally, this price competition discussion has to recognize that this more enlightened outlook does not exist in all markets, nor to the same extent in given markets, or with given consumers, competitors, or specific products. All of this makes it difficult to generalize. It is important to gain perspective for assessing the significance of price in the future. It would appear that the analytical, total economic concept is not only here to stay but is spreading rapidly. This is developing so extensively that it is no more than a matter of time before wider acceptance is given to the validity of such structuring. Competitors will have to shift their base of activity away from price (not entirely —reasonable price equity for comparable quality and performance is still a requisite), but it does signify that less impact will be felt from minor price adjustments than that created through use of other avenues. It is a part of the marketing revolution and evolution.

SERVICE

It is apparent that service is one of the crucial areas of existing competition and seems destined to become the competitive area of the future. This is an expensive proposition and, worse yet, a difficult one to counter once the competitor has gained the advantage. The object of service is to support the product and by so doing the sales and marketing effort.

The exact role of product management in the use of service as a competitive strategy or in its use as a countermeasure depends on the nature of the service and the company. There is no question of the manager's responsibilities when individual product services are required, except where they may be purely technical; but generalized service and financial services would be under the functional control of other departments. However, even in such situations marketing and product management are deeply involved since the service objective relates to the marketing effort.

The product manager who becomes service-oriented will be taking giant steps to assure his continued competitive position. Many examples could be cited, but only one will make it clear.

Assume that a product requires a certain analysis after being used by the purchaser in the formulation of his product. Being ill equipped to handle this himself, the purchaser will take advantage of the seller's offer for analysis, a form of service. Since the analytical technique is only suitable for the seller's product, the seller is assured of his business and the purchaser, "locked in" as it were, until a competitor cannot only develop a product but offer the analytical service as well. The complexities of modern day chemistry, physics, and processing make this difficult. Even if the product could be duplicated, could it be analyzed? And would this be worth the additional cost to the competitor? Either possibility is worth thinking about, and that is exactly what the marketing and product manager should do since the opportunities for service-oriented competition are without limit.

Service is expensive. In cost of product we did consider cost of service as it relates to product. Service in total must be cost analyzed in total. Lest we become too preoccupied with advantages, we had best recognize this disadvantage. This does not negate the approach, for if it is expensive to us, it is equally expensive to our competitors.

ENTERTAINMENT

In some places this is a taboo subject. The implication is if we ignore it, it doesn't exist. But like it or not, it does. Since the basic application of entertainment as a competitive strategy is not within the province of the product manager, except in an advisory sense, it is not worthwhile to delve deeply into this truly marketing directed sector. Salesmen, under the guidelines of general management, must set the objectives and limits of entertainment. Methods and means, moralistic ramifications eliminated, are also for management to direct. Whatever application is made of the technique, either by us or our competitors, we must acknowledge that it has validity.

Like price, entertainment no longer has the importance that it once had in marketing. There has been a definite direction countercurrent to its use. Even where not strictly prohibited limits have been imposed. Entertainment takes many forms—including gifts and gratuities—and a good number of companies have had the experience of being both giver and receiver. Many still do. The choice is there; only the dictates of management and the situation can tell what's to be done. For our purposes the product manager must realize the implications of competition on this basis, both actively and passively, and be alerted to any developments in this area just as in any other. It may, in some instances, provide the missing element to explain lost business; when so, in his contacts, the product manager should provide information and present this side of competitive developments to management for decision.

Shift in Competitive Activity

It is obvious that the nature of competition has changed in direction, effort, and extent. This is not unexpected and should, in fact, be anticipated since the market does not stand still. As it becomes more enlightened, so will competition. As noted before, little has been said about competition in government markets. Most of the activities described and tactics discussed relate to consumer and industrial situations. The major elements in government situations are product and price with a high orientation toward quality, technical service, and support.

The following list shows the most significant of the seven major elements as they are applied in these market segments; it also projects the shifts in emphasis that are now evident and which it can be anticipated will become increasingly important.

Now	Future
Industrial	
Price	Price
Product	Product
Service	Service
Entertainment	
Market	
Company	
Consumer	
Price	Price
Product	Product
Service	Service
Market	Submarket
Submarket	
Company	
Government	
Product	Product
Price	Price
Service	Service

All of this indicates that the nature of competition is changing, and we should be prepared to be part of this change. The one element that repeats itself over and over is service. This word contains as yet untapped marketing potential somewhat like oil exploration: you know the deposit is there but how to precisely strike it is the problem. The important factor to bear in mind is that not only will service increase but the nature of service will also change. Services as yet unimagined will be a part of marketing life: television shopping with automatic home delivery, chargeable medical and dental bills, instantaneously cookable self-contained meals, and automobiles that drive themselves are but a few. And just imagine those that we cannot imagine!

Positive and Negative Influences

The preceding elaboration on the nature of competition illustrates several of the influences competitors have on each other and on the market. Competition, as visualized from the seller's standpoint, has very definite controlling factors that must be given due credence in the marketing activity. From the consumer's view, competition carries benefits in price and quality. Since the customer is ultimately the final reduction of the market to its smallest unit, the customer creates a demand, the satisfaction of which is used as a competitive tactic; but the additional facility of creating consumer demand is not always explored to the fullest.

Whether envisioned as a stultifying entity or as a challenging marketing situation, competition has its negative and positive aspects when evaluated objectively. In order to put matters into better competitive perspective, we can examine a few of these for a fuller appreciation of the competitive effort:

Negative aspects of competition

Limits market share.

Limits market potential.

Affects price.

Affects profit.

Creates market uncertainty.

Creates product uncertainty.

Can be very costly.

Can confuse consumer and affect marketing effort.

Can "copy-cat" product.

Creates price erosion.

Can increase service or support levels.

Can flood and destroy markets.

Positive aspects of competition

Can expand market or markets.

Forces process improvements that can create additional profits.

Forces product modification which can prolong life cycle.

Can be "copy-catted."

Allows for capitalization on initial marketing effort for later entry.

Allows observation of activity; allows decision to enter or not to enter market, learning from mistakes, and exploitation of technology.

Can create new markets, which create new product opportunities.

Allows for free-ride marketing.

The most obvious and positive contribution of competition is that it creates business.

Legal Aspects of Competition

In considering the various aspects of competitive forces, no mention has yet been made of the legalities involved. Management would be wise to evaluate such activities in the light of existing federal and state legislation. Mention has been made repeatedly in this book of the need for legal concern. That message should be taken close to heart in competitive activity. As many unhappy executives know, the time to ascertain one's position is before, not after, investigation and litigation. In our previous tabulation of primary marketing legislation, we have mentioned the relevant laws, which we now repeat for clarity: The Sherman Act of 1890, The Clayton Act and its later Robinson-Patman Act Amendments, The Celler-Kefauver Antimerger Act, and the 1914 Federal Trade Commission Act. As usual, local legislation should also be considered. Legal advice is required, whether circumstances appear good or bad.

The Product Manager and Competition

The product manager's involvement with competition is primarily at the level of product, price, and technically related service, rather than in the market, submarket, or company, although even there he is concerned, as it encompasses the total marketing effort. Here we have another example of coordinated nonprimary responsibilities coupled with direct product-related functions. In the main his worries are going to be:

Competitive activity relative to new products.

Competitive activity relative to existing products.

Introduction of new competitive products and their effects on his.

Competitive objectives, strategies, and tactics.

Development of countermeasures.

Development of his own competitive activities and strategies.

Constant competitive surveillance.

Maintenance of a competitive product line.

Maintenance of a competitive marketing program.

Systems for monitoring competition.

Systems for dissemination of information regarding competition.

Short and long-range countercompetitive plans.

Forecasting of competitive activities.

Analysis of competitive activities.

Advising on overall aspects of competition, competitors, and total competitive activity of the company.

These are varied and involved responsibilities. As usual with product management, the degree of participation in any will be commensurate with the operational guidelines under which he functions. Even if he is only responsible for a few of these areas, it is immediately apparent that this aspect of his job can be very time consuming.

Competition pervades every aspect of his operations; it is for this very reason that it overlaps so many of the basic product management responsibilities as identified in the product management hexagram and must be identified as a separate entity. It is so intimately related to all six functions that it should be considered here as a separate entity that, like a thread, runs through warp and woof of the product management fabric.

To accomplish these objectives, the product manager needs help and in turn gives help. He requires assistance from inside and outside the marketing group and all corporate areas, and even outside of the company (surveys, consultants, and others). Conversely, he is furnishing information to almost the same extent—the major exception being information outside his company. Considering his coordinative responsibilities and his line-cutting, this is no surprise and further buttresses the product management premise.

In relationship to the information that he gives and receives, there are two critical elements: accuracy and reliability. The product manager will often base his actions on the information he receives just as the marketing director bases his plans on information disclosed by the product manager. Therefore it is absolutely essential that all information flowing in either direction be accurate and reliable. In instances where short-range action is required, there is the additional requirement of immediacy; action can only be based on information received. It is incumbent on those obtaining it to transmit same expeditiously. The product manager must reflect this performance and respond with equal alacrity.

WHAT THE PRODUCT MANAGER NEEDS

To meet the requirements of those high-sighted goals, the product manager needs help. While certain information is available to him from personal observation, journals, publications, membership in trade organizations, and his personal contacts, he cannot be in all places at all times. So he must have recourse to internal assistance, marketing, and sales personnel; and in unusual instances, market surveys, trade analyses, and outside consultants.

The extent of his informational requirements is as varied as the product manager's job from company to company. In general his requirements can be summarized as follows:

Status reports on individual competitive products.

Status reports of competitive activities and their success or failure.

Market response to new competitive products.

Samples of new products.

Samples of old products where contentions involving his products arise.

Technical and commercial literature of the competition.

Prices of competitive products, particularly where divergent from normal.

Market and competitive studies.

Competitive development—systems, processes, strategies.

Reports on trials of new or experimental products.

Response of competition to his products.

Response of competition to his prices.

Response of competition to his strategies and tactics.

Competitive advertising and promotion campaigns.

From the assembly of this information the product manager develops an image of the product and of the total product atmosphere. Based on analysis of this information, he develops marketing plans, strategies and tactics, new products, modifications, systems and service development, and to shorten a long story, the maintenance of the competitive product line and the competitive marketing position.

In relationship to these informational requirements, there is one other important need, and that is determination of the success or failure of specific countermeasures. If a customer has been approached by a competitor, received his business, and then been given our counteroffering, it is important to know if we were successful in regaining him, and if not, why not. This is central to the development of future action. While often overlooked, it can furnish significant insights into the useful approach and response.

WHAT TO EXPECT FROM THE PRODUCT MANAGER

One of the main functions of the product manager is the dissemination of information regarding competitors and company position on levels from aggregate performance to product-by-product technical comparisons. This information is used in the formulation of the marketing plan, the product plan, and the more mundane daily routine of running the business: sales and marketing direction and response. The missing element that he contributes goes back to systematic interpretation integration and analysis, all of which was discussed in preceding chapters. The information he receives after this extrapolation is redisbursed in the following:

Answers regarding specific product comparisons.

Price and money value relations.

Competitive summaries, surveys, and reports.

Evaluations of performance against competition.

Competitive strategies and tactics.

Counteroffering to competition and competitive action.

Identification of competitive strengths and weaknesses.

Direction for product, marketing exploitation of competitive weaknesses, and capitalization on company or product strengths.

Technical and technological assessment of competitive products, programs, processes.

Recommendations for product duplication.

Recommendations for new product development.

Recommendations for market entry or withdrawal.

Development of marketing strategies.

Replies to specific competitive product information requests.

Many of these provide the basis for formal periodic reports, whereas others involve response to individual requests. Where formal reports are rendered, formats should be developed and mechanisms established for both internal and external distribution. This has been covered in the discussion on reports and reporting. Where individual requests are involved despite the fact that many are telephonically communicated, written confirmations should be obtained, especially in those cases dealing with pricing or other sensitive areas. In this respect it is worth the trouble to confer with legal advisors regarding the nature of documentation in those instances where it is felt necessary. Since competition is here to stay, we had better learn how to effectively deal with it.

PART FOUR

Relationships

12

The Product Manager's Role in Marketing

I т is easy to say that the product manager has a role in marketing, and from the position of product management in the marketing organization, and the assignment of responsibilities within the marketing effort, this cannot be disputed. But to determine what his exact relationship is, and to fully comprehend the contribution he can make, it is important that the product manager understand the marketing effort and that marketing management understand product management. Equally significant is what product management should not be expected to do.

From this mutual understanding follows a harmonious approach to marketing problems for both product management and marketing management. That there are problems on both sides cannot be denied. Some of these are based on a lack of mutual comprehension which derives from the youth of both areas and the previous lack of defined effort and responsibility. In this regard, the marketing group has the advantage. It is older than product management and has had some time to mature, centralize, and consolidate. Product management has yet to do so. Hopefully, the clarification that is coming will assist in rectifying this deficiency; and while the product management operation will undergo further alteration as it is molded by experience, the present state of its development should provide marketing and general management with a deeper knowledge of its assets, limitations, and problems. This can pay great dividends in facilitating its application since management will better realize what product managers can do, what they cannot do, and what they and marketing need in order to accomplish their marketing objectives.

Full understanding of the marketing function is often lacking in product managers. This is essential to the working relationship that must be effected. This means that any effective product manager, who is working in an organization that has a marketing group, whether he reports to the chief marketing executive or not, has a personal responsibility to educate himself in the techniques of marketing in general and his firm's marketing effort in specific. Where he reports to marketing, the same functional consideration is also manifest, but added to it is the more mundane criterion of his own survival. In such situations, and they are the more common ones, he cannot lose sight of the necessity for satisfying his reporting superiors.

Whatever the motivation, it is incumbent on the product manager to learn about marketing. Most product managers may feel that they already understand marketing; but while a few may, many do not. This is not a deprecatory observation, but a statement of fact derived from several cogent observations.

Source of product managers. Many are not recruited from the range of active marketing personnel and have therefore no practical marketing experience. While often selected from sales, they have little marketing experience despite their sales expertise. Included in this problem is the fact that many, though graduate students, have not had formal marketing education.

Changes in the marketing concept. We have already seen that the marketing concept has undergone many significant changes in recent times. One of these is the introduction of product management itself. These alterations have made it difficult for those not directly involved to keep pace with them and to fully apprehend their importance and application.

Time. An excuse often used, it does have some veracity, particularly when contemplated in a comparative sense. Since the mandates of technical requirements are especially pressing, the product manager often has to make a choice of whether to give marketing an emphasis on his scientific knowledge, or to explore further the commercial aspects as they relate to his managerial, control, and planning functions.

Alterations in management concepts and emphasis. A problem somewhat akin to that of changes in the marketing concept and ideas of product managers themselves, this involves the difficulties in maintaining current contact with overall management trends that have their effect on both.

Whatever causes are involved, it is essential that the product manager and marketing people take the time and trouble to learn what they can expect of each other and what the responsibilities and objectives of each are. This is advisable particularly since many of them disagree; the salesman or manager who wants to retain the low volume unprofitable product and the product manager who doesn't, for instance. Both should understand each other's problems.

While this book cannot be a discourse on marketing, the following sketchy but rather broad coverage of fundamentals should be of value in familiarizing product managers with marketing. Marketing or general management personnel are not so easily let off; they will have to read the rest of the book to gain the same perspective of product management.

The Marketing Mix

Recent developments and the ever changing nature of the market have resulted in a reassessment of marketing's position in the organizational structure and in the business hierarchy. The new approach has given due recognition to the vital function of marketing in the effective achievement of business objectives within the dynamics of the contemporary market. It has been the result of new awareness of the accelerated pace of market change and the need of modern business to remain fully competitive within this dynamic structure.

Traditionally, marketing has been defined as those business activities required in transferring ownership of goods and related activities required for their physical distribution. This has been expanded to include those functions involved in directing the flow of goods and service between the manufacturer and the consumer. This extends the limits of the previous premise, expanding its boundaries slightly to encompass a larger scope of activities. In order to effect this responsibility, marketing has been concerned with two major functions: (1) Planning and organizing and (2) Controlling activities. Both are directed toward accomplishment of marketing objectives.

To accomplish this the marketing executive may use the classic marketing mix, which was tabulated in our previous review of tools and techniques, where it was found to consist of product, place, price, and promotion. This was the instrument, representing anticipated and planned outcome of the marketing effort, by which marketing tried to achieve its goals.

Marketing Activities

Related to this structure, marketing has been responsible for eight central functions: marketing information, selling, finance, standardization, risk, storage, buying, and transportation. Each of these has its own coexistent objectives that must be correlated to the objectives of the total marketing effort, which is the responsibility of the chief marketing executive, and which must vary in direction as related to a given market sector.

The marketing group has had to consider the nature of the marketing effort and the use of the marketing mix in relationship to the discharge of responsibilities in each of these eight areas and to their effective implementation in different markets. For simplicity's sake, and as an outcome of experience, the market is considered to consist of the three primary areas we have already reviewed: consumer, industrial, government.

As we have seen, this development was the outcome of a need to segment the total marketing activity and then determine those operational techniques that are more rewarding in a particular market.

Up to this point we have been dealing with historical foundations, for the modern marketing concept evolved from these beginnings. The difference is that while this approach was satisfactory in its time, the revolution in business has made it necessary to expand the marketing concept.

The Changing Marketing Concept

In order to grasp the differences between classical marketing theory and the modern concept, note first those elements that we have all come to recognize as important but which are not identified with the traditional concept: profit, flexibility, planning, product management, market or market equilibrium, market research, and the relationship of marketing to other functional areas.

Each of these elements has been given thorough treatment in other sections of this book both in the product management relationship and on a broader base as they relate to management evolution. All of them have been instrumental in alteration of the conventional concepts of marketing.

What has resulted from these new factors is the development of a modern marketing concept that includes all these elements and places a host of new responsibilities in the marketing group. Marketing under the modern concept is therefore responsible for an area that constitutes a very substantial expansion of the narrow parameters previously promulgated in marketing definitions. The requirements of marketing, as visualized in the marketing concept, require these more pervasive influences. This imposes a great responsibility on marketing since the direction it takes will effectively create the direction of the entire business effort. With clear profit responsibility (net and gross), it also places an additional burden for success onto the marketing group.

Of these manifold new duties, product management has a finite participation and carries its share of the marketing burden. Several segments are clearly within the direct responsibility of the product manager, product, and price. But equally important, he becomes the proxy of executive marketing management in others. The requirements of integrated management can only be achieved through planning and correlation of effort. This is the province of the product manager in his coordinative and planning responsibilities.

This new marketing perspective charges the chief marketing executive, those participating in the marketing effort, and the product manager with its execution. Before we leave this subject and proceed to the specifics of the product manager's role here, we should recapitulate the elements of the modern marketing concept. These include the following, with emphasis on integrative requirements and the function of product management in working in those areas not directly under the control of the marketing executive, namely, manufacturing, finance, research, administration:

Profit	Marketing information
Flexibility	Selling
Planning	Finance (within marketing
Relation to other	control)
functional areas	Standardization
Product management	Risk
Market and marketing	Storage
equilibrium	Buying
Market research	Transportation

It is apparent that concentration has shifted to the market, gearing the product and marketing effort to it. The second significant change is the element of coordination and the need for total mobilization. The third and most important profit responsibility is this new spirit of total integration and market cognizance which constitutes the essence of the marketing concept spirit, which imbues the company with direction and permeates every aspect of the organization, giving it coordination, meaning, and cohesiveness.

Marketing management must be sensitive to the external needs of the market and to the internal needs of the marketing organization. It is the harmonious balance of these sometimes conflicting requirements, tempered with complete use of the vast technical and functional resources available to them that will insure success of the marketing concept.

It is beyond question that all of the individual elements represent very real concern. Many are quantifiable and measurable; others less finite are more difficult to assess. Success or failure is not easily determined. Regardless of the determination of achievement in particular areas, the impact of the total effort is clearly discernible in corporate profit, corporate sales, and corporate position. The achievement of the company's objectives is, to a large measure, the result of implementing the marketing concept.

Role of the Product Manager

The participation of the product manager in many of these segments has been described in some detail. There are, however, several additional elements which have not been reviewed because they involve not a direct responsibility but the cooperation of the product manager; they exemplify additional areas of his integrative and supportive functions. In order to be comprehensive, however, it is worthwhile to risk being repetitious and reconsider those aspects; if nothing else, they differ in perspective when seen from the standpoint of the product manager's responsibilities as a part of the total marketing effort.

The list below indicates the scope, general nature, and direction of the product manager's role as he participates to an appropriate extent in each of these areas:

Marketing	Prognostication
Policy	Market response
Programs	Development
Analysis	Price

Distribution	Marketing effort
Product	Customer contact
Integration	Advertising
Purchasing	Promotion
Research	Distribution
Forecasting	Feedback
Marketing costs	Literature
Profits	Sales

When examining each of these in more detail, it should be remembered that while some of the examples cited appear to be within the jurisdiction of other areas, for example, when stating a role in marketing policy relative to account solicitation, it would seem that this is more the responsibility of the sales manager than the product manager. The product manager's participation is advisory. The ultimate decision in this area is left to sales management or the chief marketing executive. Similarly, in advertising the program to be followed must be implemented by the advertising manager, and the final responsibility for its technical accomplishment is his.

The product manager may be totally, or at least partially, responsible for products to be advertised, advertising programs, product accuracy, and a host of particulars plus a general overall sanctioning. This brings us back to the need for coordination and integration of function, the modern marketing concept in action.

So envisioned, the product manager is not "taking over" but recommending, consulting, being consulted, and coordinating in selected areas; in others, where he is clearly responsible, he is providing the decision-making contribution, based on the authority/responsibility index, that is his prerogative. We will now examine specifics.

MARKETING POLICIES

The final determination and establishment of marketing policies is the responsibility of the chief marketing executive. However, he will usually take into account the best recommendations of his staff. In this situation the product manager is called upon to provide his analysis of marketing development and policy suggestions related to products. Such advice and direction would involve:

Products to emphasize.

Markets or market segments to exploit.

Products to eliminate totally, to reduce, or on which to discontinue or accentuate marketing effort.

Distribution efforts.

Specific product actions at specified accounts.

Marketing presentations and product seminars both within and outside the company.

Response to competition, including price, service, promotion, packaging, and delivery.

Product modification geared to satisfaction of particular market or marketing needs.

Market analysis.

Assessment of new product needs.

Marketing activity on new and old products.

Pricing strategies.

Profit strategies.

Resale to outside distributors.

Self-manufactured or products purchased.

Discounts.

Each of these items is important in itself but must also be considered in the added light of combined effort and effect, such as new product possibilities in new markets, or the balance of a new product's potential profit contribution against the possible profit curtailment of existing products that might be rendered obsolescent by the new. Since these are areas that require the specialized knowledge of the product manager, they are segments of the marketing policy determination in which he can furnish information that assists in the final determination. From the establishment of these policies flows the overall direction of his specific functions. The operational and functional guidelines that derive from the marketing policy are the basis for further action in many specific sectors that come under the direct purview of product management. For example, once his recommendations on a prospective advertising effort on a product are sanctioned by the marketing director, it becomes his direct responsibility to work with internal or external promotion facilities to develop the total program. This is a typical example of the dualistic nature of the product manager's contribution.

It has already been intimated that marketing management relies heavily on its related operational and functional areas, as well as on the suggestions of other self-contained units—sales, in particular. To accomplish this integration is often difficult, and to be effective, it must rely on channels of direct communication to the marketing manager so that these ideas can be freely discussed. While the mechanisms used to achieve this requirement differ, it is not uncommon; it is, in fact, an outgrowth of the line, staff, and committee organizational approach to set up a marketing committee which, under the direction of the marketing chief, is charged with the responsibility for developing, setting, and effecting the marketing policy. On such a committee, regardless of its specific title, will be found representation from advertising and promotion, sales and product management, and, if need be, executive management. In this manner the principal responsible elements of the marketing group have direct contact and are provided with the opportunity for exchanging views toward their requirements for policy determination. Essentially, in a decision-making body the number of attendees should be restricted with the proviso that required representatives in other involved areas can be called upon for opinion, guidance, and commitment as necessary for total integration and attainment of purpose. In such a situation the perspectives of all major elements can be brought forth, and policy feasibility can be predetermined by those directly responsible for its execution.

MARKETING PROGRAMS

The difference between policy and program is the difference between what and how things are to be done. Often the marketing committee will generate the details of the marketing program. Frequently it will delegate the development of program particulars to those most responsible for execution, and sanction only the final product before actual implementation. Regardless of the approach, it is the marketing committee that will set the program.

To accomplish this, it is important to examine what is required against what is to be gained. Added to this must be the pragmatic factors of expense, capability, extention of effort, personnel, resources, and feasibility. Often this is an extremely difficult set of requirements to account for. It places a decision burden on the committee and the chief of marketing. When the choice between several realistic alternatives arises, the difficulty is much more complex; it is simplified if obvious limitations, restrictions, or more positive potentialities prevail. Since the full assessment of all of these considerations requires expertise, there is a need for consultation with specialists.

Hence we find recourse to the committee and justification for its existence. In such instances the product manager is usually called upon to comment on the following areas:

Product availability   Will the new product be ready in time?
                                   Will production capacity keep pace with sales?

Will supply of intermediate or precursory elements be available at the proper time and in quantity?

Is planned expansion sufficient to provide required quantities?

Advertising	Direction and effort.
	Particular product or product line to be advertised.
	Institutional versus individual product ads.
	Service or technological emphasis.
	Oneshot or series.

Marketing training and familiarization	Who is to participate?
	Who to organize?
	When to schedule?
	Where to have?
	What products to stress?

Profits: where to improve	Can cost of manufacturing be lowered?
	Should product substitution be considered?
	What alternatives are available?
	Can outside manufacturing facilities be employed?
	What are comparative costs of self-manufacturing versus toll or contractual manufacturing?
	Possible improvements via alteration of distribution or warehousing facilities and channels.
	Packaging modifications and possibilities of consumer acceptance.

Technical responsibilities	Customer contact
	Product specifications and product
	Timing and effect
	Requirements for equipment, training, or use in a specific marketing program.

Product liability	Who to handle
	How to direct effort
	Degree and extent of commitment
	Authorization for settlement
	Legal aspects
	Balance of dollars spent to company interest

By no means are these indicative of all relationships that prevail in the administration of marketing programs associated with the marketing effort. In many cases the product manager will be able to do little more than follow the directives of appropriate management representation (sales, manufacturing, finance) as they are required for execution of those actions necessary to attainment of the marketing objective. In other instances he will be given authority for the execution of the program in total or in part. Whichever the case, his contribution is essential to the successful completion of the program.

MARKET ANALYSIS

In order to make a contribution toward determining policy or program, the product manager must base his position on the analysis he makes of the product as it relates to market. There is little point in advocating the best of product if there is no market, actual, imagined, or potential, and no serious consideration can be given to market unless there is product or product possibility. The recognition of product potential is important in determining product need.

While many larger marketing organizations have their own market research specialists, the product manager must often fill the gap for short-range data gathering, analysis, interpretation, and use. Even in the longer-range analytical situation there are many occasions when he will assist the full-time analysts or call upon their services. It is, however, more in the range of day-to-day management problems, as well as in the analysis required for short-range planning and operation that the product manager will find himself deeply involved.

Such questions have to be answered unequivocally:

Will the product or market continue?

Should marketing efforts be continued, increased or decreased?

What new product prospects are potentially available in the market?

What are the applications of existing products?

Are there legal implications or restrictions?

What are the competitive aspects based on known facts?

What are the commercial possibilities?

What shortages are in the offing?

Based on given circumstances what is the best product approach?

These and other questions, some of which border directly on marketing policy, are predicated on market analysis. Often the product manager will, by virtue of his comprehensive knowledge, be in prime position to make a determination that considers the many phases of market, company, and product. This is his unique contribution.

PROGNOSTICATION

In the broadly titled concept of prognostication we must differentiate among projections concerning the market, the product, the
economic and social scenes, and the company itself. We must also consider the individual product element projections that comprise the
total corporate, economic, and business atmosphere. Many of these
constituents are already involved in the creation of the firm's marketing effort, the establishment of its objectives, and the generation of its
strategies. However, there are the more frequently encountered situations in which the crystal ball must be consulted in lieu of the
product manager. In such situations we are concerned with whether
or not consumer purchasing habits will continue in the same direction
long enough to sell existing stock, or long enough for an enterprising
company to ride the wagon of profits. Often such decisions are far
more critical than they may appear, particularly to the smaller company where survival may be the prize.

In such cases, where long-range planning and the compensation of
many products helps smooth out the creative performance, the product
manager will find himself squarely in the middle of many conundrums;
he and the marketing group must try to chart a stable, profitable
course in these stormy seas. Many of the elements required in the
development of marketing strategies are involved. In this situation we
find another perspective. The predictions required are more in the
day-to-day sustenance of the marketing effort than in long-range determinations.

An integrated manufacturing unit poses the following question:
Do we continue to produce at the rate of 10,000 units per day in the
face of high inventories and static sales? All the long, short, or inter-
mediate-range planning that man has developed cannot answer this
question, and it falls upon marketing to render a judgment. In these
situations the product manager will find himself out on a limb. Similarly, in package innovation, will the style continue? Will plastic containers be well received? Should they be continued after initial poor
response? Should a product showing poor quality be stopped? Or must
we continue to produce based on consumer need, predicated on the
probabilities of successful resolutions? These examples, frightening as
they are, and perceived in all their full-blown economic implications,
are by no means atypical.

They do not include the full range of questions that involve prediction. Fortunately, the product manager does have several tools that
can help dispel some of the fog. In the never-ending need for mar-

keting sensitivity, however, there can be no substitute for personal contact, knowledge, and that intangible "feel" for the market's direction.

MARKET RESPONSE

This is a further refinement of prognostication involving specific requirements of market response. There are several approaches to be considered. Are we concerned with response to the product, a market within a market, a price, an activity, policy, the market by competition, or to pertinent legislation? The answer to all these questions is yes. But their application varies in magnitude and priority at different times. In determining such, the product manager will often be called upon for help. It is important to discuss each of these questions individually.

Response to product. There are two separate products involved: ours and the competition's. When we are interested in determining market response to our product, it is apparent that the product manager is the foremost authority in the company. In the section on tools and techniques, extensive coverage was given to the means available. If, however, the more subtle aspects of true consumer response: product apprehension, conception, utilization, or satisfaction are involved, recourse to specialized surveys may be necessary, the techniques of which are commonly known. This is a lesson that must be learned, because numbers alone are deceptive. In either case, the product manager is at his functional best when facing such questions. Of equal concern is how well the competitor's product is doing. Governmental, industrial, and private institutions publish many usable figures that can give good insight into general market size and activity. Not so accurate are the estimates of sales, marketing, and consultation specialists, or those derived through surveys on individual products.

Personal assessment is also possible. However, in too many instances this provides no more than supportive data for quantitative estimates that are, to a large measure, subjectively determined. It is vital that every product manager, market analyst, and marketing manager realize that this is both necessary and dangerous. All have had the over- and underestimating experience, and it must be guarded against and tempered. The more factual the information, the more realistic the estimates become. With time, experience, and added information resolution also evolves. In giving this problem full thought, it must be acknowledged that starting with at least some estimates is better than having none, with the reservation that they are recognized for what they are and constant reassessment provided for. Unless this is done, there is a tendency for the guess to become fact. It is surprising how hard some of these factual guesses die after they have been around long enough.

The full assessment of the market's response to any given product, whether ours or our competitor's, is complex, time-consuming, and expensive. It should therefore be subjected to the same careful scrutiny as any other management objective and receive only that attention that is significant to the company. While it may be ideal to "know" each product, it is hardly practical to think this possible with every product unless dealing in an exceptionally limited market. Although an overall idea of product performance is essential, full, in-depth knowledge should be restricted to meaningful products. Part of marketing management is the acceptance of this precept, then the all-important and critical skill judgment, the selection of products to be fully investigated, monitored, and subjected to all the available scrutiny and control possible. As with many other selection, emphasis, and control problems, we have recourse to exception principles and the implementation of "key" programs.

Response to a market within a market. When a new product is marketed, an entirely new market is seldom created, but a new submarket may arise, a market within a market, as it were. Occasionally this is very specialized, allowing for little competition by virtue of the short life span projected. On the other more positive side, there is likely to be sufficient opportunity for entry depending on the technical problems and the market's response to the product. In this area of specialized concern, the manager should maintain contact with the marketplace in order to furnish data regarding these new situations. It is not beyond probability to consider products other than those made by the company at present, depending on capacity. The introduction of new products in markets of opportunity is very much under the sphere of product management.

Similarly, it is sometimes possible to modify existing products in form, size, packaging, or even marketing presentation. Where many products or submarkets exist, the market research group may be called upon to render judgment; and in conditions involving long-range outlooks, this is very appropriate. The product manager has an obligation to call attention to these possibilities and request that consideration be given. The range of problems in analyzing such markets can extend anywhere from simple decision making to complex studies requiring years of effort. Whichever the case, no new market or sub-market opportunities should be missed.

While this market analysis takes place, product management should certainly try to determine the competition's response to the market's development. Where an open field exists the possibilities of entry and profit are concomitantly good; but where it is strongly suspected that major competition will also develop, an entirely new set of conditions prevail. On occasion this can best be determined through the contacts of marketing people, and the product manager is in an excellent position to make such overtures. Even the negative determinations of competition are important because they may provide clues to hidden problems.

In these new market situations it is also important to think in terms of possible extension outside the original segment and possibilities for product entry into one of the submarkets.

Back to our example of nylon: there was hardly any market opportunity for manufacturers of black pigments to color nylon when it was originally employed for textile fiber production. Later, as this textile fiber submarket expanded, it was extended into nylon tire-cord production. The black pigment manufacturers could readily take advantage of this market potential. However, the physical form of the pigment, as previously marketed, had to be modified for the nylon cord. Those who had anticipated this development and worked on it early enough had an advantage. Such a technique could be dynamically applied, as when the producer of one product may work closely with the producer of another to extend the use range of the product by applying the second company's process. Both firms prosper. The occasions for such effort abound; it requires only creativity and the willingness to take a risk—an accepted element in marketing management.

Response to price. There are two main price response situations that concern the marketing group: The reaction of the market to competitive prices and the response to their own price changes. As the years go by and costs increase, many products also reflect these increases; in others manufacturing improvements, reductions in cost of materials, packaging, or distribution offset such increase and allow for steady stable pricing, or in some industries, price reductions. This latter is particularly the case in commodity chemicals where increased competition generates pressures that force product cost improvements and price attrition.

Regardless of cause, it is the response in the marketplace that concerns marketing management. When a price is increased by competition, what will be the effect on total market? Will the entire market rise? Can such prices be maintained? What reaction will ensue from market and in given instances from government? These factors must be weighed either before or after responding to the dynamics of the market. In those cases where reductions are involved, the impact on the company's individual products or its needs to respond must be evaluated. Referring back to pricing philosophy techniques, many of the questions are dependent on the company's overall pricing policy in regard to specific product and market. In any of these situations the product manager will have to make a decision in regard to action. Elements in the decision will include: market situation, market response, accounts, present market share, competition, expected loss or gain in share, price, profit, and expectations of stability in the pricing situation. These factors contain subjective and objective elements. It is up to product management to quantitatively identify them and then project dollars and cents positions; it must also consider the economic outcome and project into this the commercial implications.

Decisions in this price arena are not easy. However, a decision must be made and often within a short time. Once a price alteration occurs in the market, the product manager must assess its significance and immediately start analysis and determination of countermaneuver. There is no time to be lost in very active competitive marketing. There are several sources of information, and assistance is usually available; but ultimately the product manager, depending on his pricing authority, must recommend to his management the position to be taken. Once this is done, the mechanism for implementation must also be there. The product manager should assure himself that such systems exist so that the price decision is expeditiously made known to the sales force and all others who need to know. There is nothing worse than altering a price and then not telling those involved, including the customer, who is often neglected. Things like this are bound to happen unless adequate notification procedures are established in advance.

Once created, they may not be under the administrative control of the product manager, but he should periodically review them and be certain of their accuracy, currency, and effectiveness. His responsibility does not end until everyone, both inside and outside the company, has been advised.

When the decision has been made and everyone notified, the matter still does not end. The concern now is price durability. The product manager finds himself studying this response and closely monitoring the market price situation. He and marketing must be prepared to respond to both the price situation and the actions of competition. Additional price changes may be necessary, and a sensitive surveillance must be maintained. How long this critical examination period lasts depends on the product, the market, and the competition. Often the problem is not only the action in the general market, but that in individual major accounts or submarkets. This is where the assistance of sales management is invaluable. If ever close liaison must be maintained, it is when price changes are involved and the marketing group must determine price status or activity at specific accounts. The time to cultivate this is all the time, not just when we want something. It is to the best interests of all that the sales department realize the importance of immediate feedback and analysis. It is not sufficient to know that such and such a thing happened. One must also understand what it implies, what is the intention, what is the duration, and what significance is attached to the development. And what is the customer's reaction and intention? Just because a competitor quotes a lower price does not mean he is going to get the business. Yet this is nearly always implied. And though usually the case, it can be simply the old bluffing game. Before reacting, it is best to find out.

A word of caution regarding legal restrictions and implications: Earlier, we reviewed in some detail the major legislation concerning pricing and competition. There is no point in repeating it, but it is worthwhile to restate its existence and emphasize the need to constantly be on guard. Become thoroughly familiar with these laws, review them, and seek legal assistance if the slightest doubt exists. In fact, it is worth talking to lawyers every once in a while, merely to be apprised of any significant court decisions.

Response to activity. Activity is an all-encompassing word and covers a multitude of entities. The ones that are of concern here are: advertising and promotion, commercial strategies, service and allied programs, distribution trends, packaging innovations, systems selling, and process and equipment relations, plus similar marketing-related functions that do not fall within other circumscribed managerial delineations. These activities are very important in that they can tip the scales in favor of the competitor or establish trends in marketing that may represent the market of the future. For example, the packaging of beverages in cans was initially a radical departure from the traditional bottle. This resulted not only in virtually every manufacturer ultimately packaging his beverages in cans but in a revolution of the remaining bottles themselves, one-way, no-deposit. This alteration also effected distribution and handling; with the elimination of deposits, one-way trafficking of bottles imposed a new set of conditions. Even more important was the internal impact on processing and bottle requirements. All in all, a large, involved, and dramatic situation occurred in only a few years.

Small and seemingly insignificant activities can have far-reaching impact on the marketing group and the entire corporation affecting inventory, manufacturing, purchasing, sales—in short, every phase of the business. A good and profitable example of commercial strategies predicated on change is the development of consumer credit. The concept of deficit finance, so long advocated and practiced by the government, has now entered almost every household, and, by extension, every business. Many companies selling directly to the consumer have had to establish some form of retail installment credit-buying policy, and many found a source of additional revenue in extending their own credit, often making more on money-lending than on the product itself. Whether this is the most profitable case is not the significant point. It is the revolution in the marketplace that one must carefully examine.

Watching the market and the product, the product manager frequently has first-hand knowledge of such developments. It is apparent that in those instances where activities are generated as a direct consequence of competitive activity or consumer demand that he would already have intimate knowledge of such developments.

More and more, management has recognized the advantages in diversification; and the growth of giant conglomerates reflects this recognition. Equally important are the possibilities in systems selling and correlated sales that integrate product, process, and equipment. Where service, know-how, and reliability are added to this package, an extended combination is provided that is hard to beat. This approach cannot always be made alone. It requires the cultivation of a combined effort: one company's products, another's equipment, and perhaps a third's service. However, considering the complex nature of multimarketing and the impossibilities of one company being all things to all customers, it is practical and desirable.

The prospects that exist can only be used to advantage if they are known and explored. Part of product management's function lies in the identification of these possibilities and recommended action for application.

Response to policy. The policies of the marketing group have far-reaching impact. When marketing decides to establish a certain container size of given dimensions, weight, and labeling, there are several internal arrangements to be made, details to be carried out, and the customer's reaction to be determined. It is the product manager's job not only to attend after the fact but also to make suggestions regarding initiation of such action.

In the example cited he would probably have been instrumental in obtaining management consideration of the policy to begin with and then attended to plant notification; he would have worked with them on package specifications and with the designers on style, color, configuration, and labeling; he would also have attended to the required notifications both inside and outside the company; and he would have explained the rationale for the new policy and reduced packaging costs with profit improvement. After that he would follow through by assessing the success of the policy from all standpoints: Have we really saved any money? Have customers accepted the new package? Did it create any additional sales? Has it had a negative impact? And much more could be cited that falls within his province.

In other marketing areas, less clearly identified with the product or product-related factors (such as sales to distributors), the product manager will assist in analyzing the possibilities and advising the policy to be established; later, he will aid in the administration of the program.

Responses by competition and to competition. It is quite apparent that the product manager is directly responsible for determining the competition's responses to the activities, policies, and products of the marketing group. Naturally, the responsibility does not stop here, nor is it exclusively his. All segments of the business are concerned with the marketing activities of competitors. However, it is the product manager's function to coordinate even those aspects outside his direct purview, and present to management the total situation encompassing the assessments made by each contributory area.

In so doing he is also required to assess these developments in the light of possible countermeasures. This is a dramatic example of product management's full scope in the area of competition. His cycle never ends; one action leads to reaction and then more action. The pace of these activities depends on market stability. Even in so-called stable markets, it is realized that if competition prevails action and reaction time is critical. A vital function that the product manager can perform is the required coordination between sales and marketing management, or marketing and manufacturing management, or whatever areas require it for immediate decisions on policy, product supply, or specialized service. The time saved is the customer saved.

Response to pertinent legislation. We have already evaluated the impact of legislation on competitive activity, pricing, and related activities. There are, however, equally important laws that influence

total marketing activity: antimonopoly, restraint of trade, unfair practices, antispecific practices. There are a host of laws dealing with the
product itself, all of which must be given due regard in the marketing
effort. While the product manager is not a lawyer, nor can he ever
replace expert legal advice, he, like the chief marketing executive,
must have a sound knowledge of the general restrictions implicit in
these laws.

Product management has direct responsibility when it comes to
legislation that applies to the products themselves. The most generally known of these is the 1938 Food, Drug, and Cosmetics Act, which
is administrated by the Food and Drug Administration. Many others
exist, from laws regulating the percent of fats in milk to the additives
or preservatives in food. Similar laws covering product labeling, purity,
and claims also exist and must be known to the marketing group. If
the product manager is to be fully effective, he must be knowledgeable in this critical area. Recourse to legal counsel is sometimes necessary, especially when new products are being launched or when new
legislation is involved. All are aware of the stringent government
controls on antipollution and the tremendous efforts being expended
to develop and market biodegradable products, nonpollutants, and
effluent control systems for liquid solids and gaseous contaminants.
These developments are restrictive and involve expenditures for control. However, they are also opportunities for new product, process,
or control development. Many companies are working frantically on
antipollution devices, and many have been rocketed into successful
positions by virtue of these new needs. Even in those instances where
no direct benefits can be obtained via new products or process, or by
establishing a new antipollution business, some return can be derived
by using conformance as part of a public-image advertising campaign
such as that employed by major electric companies.

Earlier in the chapter on product, there was a summary of pertinent legislation in these areas; therefore it is not repeated here. But
we should not consider these developments as only negative, expensive, and prohibitory. They are that, but with a creative approach
they can be used to marketing advantage as the progenitors of a whole
new generation of products and processes.

DEVELOPMENT

The development activities involved here relate to the cultivation
of new markets or products. As the coordinator of new products and

their initiation, the product manager is often responsible for developing the initial marketing campaign, including advertising, promotion, new markets, and the overall products effort. He has the most intimate knowledge of the product and plays a very active role in introducing it first to the sales force and later to the customer.

In this then we have two aspects of his relationship: the first, to release the product, and the second, to aid in its commercial introduction and success. There is a third that relates to test marketing where he is actively working to determine the possibility of the product and to assess its technical performance or market acceptance. The concept of test marketing to ascertain customer response is well known and often employed in the consumer marketing field. Working closely with existing personnel or market consultant specialists, the object is to determine the market's response to the product, and most especially, the reaction of the buying public.

In industrial marketing the technique is not so widely employed and involves more verification of technical performance than true consumer response. The need for the product and its potential are usually clearly established long before the test market, but assurance of performance is required. There are many technical and scientfic reasons for this which were examined more extensively in the chapter on product. The other object of these trials is to determine the needs for product modification before full-scale marketing. With consumer and industrial products, the requirements for careful analysis are just as valid. In these instances product management works closely with sales or development personnel, and the outcome of these efforts decides the fate of the product with respect to market.

The involvement of the product manager ranges from experimental to service functions. His objective, regardless at which end of the scale, is still the same: rendering assistance in the introduction, screening, and selection of successful, profitable products.

PRICE

Pricing theory has already been extensively covered. It is apparent that the product manager's price responsibilities greatly depend on the attitudes and position of management. In some instances the product manager is given full control over pricing, including competitive response; in others his role is merely advisory. In those latter situations he recommends the price of product from new to old and the price to be established in a competitive situation. Whichever the case, the product manager is fully involved in the price of his product, even in those more inclusive aspects of price that were also reviewed.

In his pricing capacity there is some occasion to run headlong into difficulty with other segments of the marketing group. Having gross profit responsibility, however, he must have some clear-cut price authority or the profit responsibility cannot be discharged. From a practical point of view it is imperative that the product manager, the marketing group, and the sales force, from active salesmen to management, fully understand the extent and limits of his authority and responsibility. Only in this way can the best interests of the marketing effort be served and much unnecessary haggling and ill will avoided.

DISTRIBUTION

The traditional definition of marketing includes responsibility for distribution. However, with the growth of corporations it should be clarified that, while a marketing function and under the ultimate jurisdiction of the marketing chief, it is seldom found that any active investigation of distribution routes, techniques, or programs is directly undertaken by marketing. Marketing is involved in the decision process and in arbitration during instances of controversy. We must also distinguish between distribution channels involving internal functions and those involving the external marketing effort. In the latter case the marketing group undertakes more direct participation but will call upon the service of logistics or data processing to render assistance in terms of surveys and system analysis for optimization.

Where distribution is used as a competitive tactic, it is purely within the purview of the marketing group and results from initiation there. Assessment of the matter by the product manager and sales management is solicited and considered.

PRODUCT

At this point there is hardly any need to elaborate on the responsibilities of the product manager for product. Strictly within the confines of the marketing group he:

Determines and analyzes competition.

Introduces new products.

Recommends or establishes price.

Controls product activities.

Controls quality.
Controls packaging.
Insures supply.
Provides technical information and assists in service.
Advises on products strategy.
Develops product marketing plans.
Identifies major products for marketing emphasis.
Assists in marketing effort.
Controls gross profit.
Serves the marketing group by providing requisite product data.
Coordinates or contributes to marketing plan.
Provides source of product or product management education.
Monitors market.
Is responsible for product forecasting.
Coordinates test marketing efforts.

INTEGRATION

The marketing effort is comprised of several functions: advertising, promotion, sales, product management, product development, and distribution. All of these are equally important in developing and selling profitable products on the one side and maintaining a profitable internal operation on the other. This balance is sometimes forgotten. To keep the team playing as a team is one of the integrative functions of the product manager. This is a part of his total coordinative responsibility. We will specifically identify the need for this integration within the market area. The sales manager cannot plan to sell the product that the product manager loses money on; and product management cannot program major sales activity on a competitive product that sells only to three significant accounts, which cannot be realistically considered as potential customers to the company. Advertising should not be conducted on marginal products, and a promotional effort that involves a give-away tie-in cannot be introduced if sufficient units to permit double stocks are not within the realm of manufacturing capacity. In each of these cases it is the product manager who must braid the strands and make the rope that all pull together.

PURCHASING

Although many companies have their own separate corporate or divisional purchasing departments, the product manager is often involved in several capacities. These associations relate to the marketing effort as they are directed toward product availability in order to assure salable supplies.

In this regard the product manager is involved in determining the quality and suitability of the product, locating alternate sources of supply, advising on optimum cost and its acceptability and coordinating contracts or special licenses. Packaging, negotiating product specifications, scheduling, projecting and forecasting are also part of the purchasing activity.

RESEARCH

Usually not considered a direct marketing concern, the need for marketing involvement in research is being recognized by more and more companies. "Need-research," a rather new term, aptly describes the orientation of the research effort, based on need identification, which is obtained from the marketing group. The product manager often is the focus of this coordination, and represents the marketing group in bringing forth this need identification to the research group. He makes his evaluations through constant contact with the research and marketing groups on one side and the technical and scientific services on the other. Even in those instances where need-research is not applied to marketing, product managers are just as vitally involved. They are at least consulted in the evaluation of resultant "product" and of products that are developed. This transition from pure, undirected, or only poorly integrated research to need identification, product profiling, and total marketing involvement reflects the modern marketing concept on the theoretical scale. The simple fact is that it works well and is profitable. The future relationship of marketing to research will undoubtedly reflect a continuation of marketing orientation: research directions, research program selections, and priorities.

FORECASTING

Forecasting in the marketing area is vital. From the assessment of the total market to accurately predicting the sales of an individual account or single product, the product manager and the marketing director are concerned and rightly so. Every phase of the company is involved in the product from financial planning to manufacturing and engineering, and from warehouse to laboratory facilities for quality testing. The larger the company, the more involved the need, and the more critical it becomes. Profit planning, while a responsibility of the marketing group, is in one sense not an active marketing consideration or at least active only insofar as it affects product selection and the limits imposed on advertising, promotion, and sales effort. But passive or active, it is a most fundamental business consideration.

Many hours are spent on forecasting, and millions of dollars are committed to manual and electronic techniques used to improve this necessary but difficult informational need. It is crucial for sales management to appreciate this need and render its assistance to inventory control, logistics, and product management, or, in other words, everyone who may be involved in the determination of forecasts. Improvement of forecasts improves all aspects of marketing from image to profit. Therefore its importance to the line salesman is of immediate consequence.

MARKETING COSTS

The product manager is not responsible for marketing costs. His cost responsibilities are limited to the product and relate to his control of gross profit. There is, however, one pragmatic marketing cost in which he is involved, particularly in those instances where·product groups exist. The cost of the group becomes an item of marketing expense and the product manager may have a direct responsibility for controlling his departmental costs. Operating under a budget, the costs of the group are under his purview, and to this limited extent he has some direct marketing cost involvement.

Over and above this is the general consideration of internal costs and the product manager's inherent management responsibility to determine where excessive costs exist and to recommend appropriate action for improvement. Here he is acting within the scope of his integrative functions. In this role he is constantly exposed to costs and cost relationships; he therefore has unparalleled opportunity for first-hand knowledge. While not directly charged with this responsibility, he is always indirectly concerned.

PROFITS

The marketing director is responsible for the profits of the marketing activity; supporting him in this overall responsibility is the product manager, who has control over product gross profit. Through his efforts the sustained or improved gross profit is fixed at his level of authority and responsibility.

Earlier, this premise was explained in relation to the total sphere of product management activity. It was then indicated that the product manager must monitor products and markets in order to effectively exercise control through judgment and fact. There is no point in repeating all of the individual elements that go into the structuring of gross profit, its direction, and control. It is only important to realize that this responsibility is centered in the product manager, that he has a very cogent reason for concern over pricing policy, and must plan the market activity not only on a product-to-product and product-line basis but on gross profit of the business. Management must provide the backing necessary to make this responsibility meaningful; it must also provide support when marketing and profit objectives are not properly attuned.

MARKETING EFFORT

When discussing marketing policies and programs, the more direct aspects of the marketing effort should be included. These consist of customer contact, advertising, promotion, distribution, feedback, literature preparation and distribution, sales and customer service, technical service, customer complaints and claims, and innumerable other factors. In the preceding description of total product management activities, the emphasis was on the passive phases of planning, policy-making, and program conceptualizing, rather than those of implementation. However, the product manager is just as active in getting things done as he is in theorizing about them.

Where many individual product managers are involved, they actively assist in their specific market segments. This means that the extent of active, personal participation will vary with market, product, and requirements of the situation. Customer contact, for example, may be frequent and close with new or highly technical products, which he will help to introduce. Other more stable or mature products will seldom require his personal intervention except as problem solver in the event of customer complaint. In this area, if the claim or complaint centers around the product itself, the product manager takes simultaneous action in several areas. Where financial restitution is involved, company policy determines extent of his authority for settlement. One approach, commonly encountered, is his authorization to make settlement if product replacement is required, but not if additional direct cash settlements are involved. Another is to allow settlement to a fixed sum, above which management approval is required.

In the areas of advertising and promotion he is basically involved since he often recommends and then directs the activity. In the full-scale advertising and promotional programs typical of the consumer industry, this may well occupy a major portion of the brand manager's time; in industrial and government marketing sectors it is of less significance and is correspondingly less time-consuming. The product manager's effort in these activities is obviously variable.

Despite the variation in involvement and the specifics of the situation, as they prevail from company to company, the product manager has a commitment to the active side of the marketing effort. He is there to render service, to perform as staff member to the marketing chief, and to extend this assistance to other management echelons. At the same time, he exercises line authority essential to fulfilling those duties that are his responsibility and vital ingredients in the marketing effort.

In citing these examples no one should be left with the impression that they are more than representative of the scope and nature of the product manager's contribution to marketing. It was stated before that much confusion exists with respect to the nature and extent of the product manager's responsibilities. One of the most vital functions that he can perform for himself and marketing is to clarify this role as it exists in his own company. We can only sketch in the broad background and indicate typical associations and participation. If the marketing effort is to be successful, it is essential that all understand themselves and each other. Knowing who does what and how they do it will enable more effective use of people and resources, foster smoother performance and pave the way for that close, personally coordinated response that is absolutely necessary to profitable marketing.

13

The Product Manager's Role in Sales

THE degree and extent of the product manager's involvement in the many diverse areas vary tremendously from company to company. While this has been said several times before in this book, it is probably nowhere so variable as in the sales relationship. Companies seem to have a very protective attitude toward their salesmen, and while regretting their seeming lack of marketing knowledge, they often place them in veritable isolation where marketing or management people are allowed no access. Even in those instances where the ban is lifted, the contact often has to be through intermediaries rather than direct. Possibly this is necessary and some of it rationalized on the basis that the salesman is a complex person who has a difficult and trying mission. After all is said and done, the final execution of marketing lies in the hands of the salesman. It is he who must face the gripes and grumbles of the unhappy customer; and it is he who must constantly strive to best the competition, deliver his goods, and win for his customer those just desserts in product, service, and satisfaction which, when added together, mean getting or not getting the business.

True as this may be, we also must admit that the salesman makes his livelihood by selling and has a fiduciary interest that may cloud his objectivity, especially when paid on a commission or incentive basis. The selling effort should be kept as uncomplicated as possible; this is the responsibility of marketing management to sales management and of sales management to the selling staff, and vice versa.

The sales force, from management to line salesmen, has a responsibility to the company. An old sales philosophy that many have heard and occasionally still hear is the "my-boss-is-my-customer" law. Some sales people not only say this, they believe it. Time has come full cycle. True, the customer is an important element in the business; after all we must have him to have sales. But we cannot distort the corporate position to allow consumer tyranny, which occurs in some industries or companies. No contemporary sales management purports that its boss is its customer.

What this leads to is the requirement that things, people, and companies have to be put into perspective. From there we can structure the selling effort, giving it the full measure of importance it requires. At the same time we would be recognizing all of the problems and providing the assistance, personnel, product, and service that both the salesman and his customer, who is our customer too, need. But we must emphasize that his primary obligation is to the company. If in satisfying his customer, the salesman gets sales, this is to the best interests of the company and to his, but it must be understood by sales and marketing that a balance exists. The modern marketing concept provides for this and fully incorporates this idea into its development of current sales approaches and objectives. Once the full impact of this philosophy permeates management and sales, it will be realized that it benefits them, the company, and the customer.

These facts, once established, lead the way to restructured thinking as it relates to direct contact between sales and marketing groups. There is a need for contact through sales or marketing management, but there is also a need for direct contact between the product manager and the line salesmen. As a consequence of usual attitudes, two extremes commonly prevail: either the salesman is totally accessible or totally inaccessible. The mean between these limits is what is necessary. Eventually this does come about where the product management system is introduced, since one of the product manager's values is his ability to aid the marketing effort by helping the sales activity.

This poses some significant problems and requires close contact with sales management and advertising departments. The effect created is based on an integrated marketing effort taking into account the objectives of all areas. This can only be accomplished through mutually established objectives. How to do this is further discussed in the chapter dealing with planning; the time and place to accomplish mutuality of objectives is in the development of the annual marketing plan. Where such planning does not occur, the mechanism for such determination is either through meetings of the marketing group with responsible representation from sales, advertising, promotion and product management, or periodic personal contact between these individuals. Even where formal meetings are scheduled and marketing committees convene, they should be supported by such personal contact in the periods between formal meetings.

Whichever the case, the outcome and intention is the same. Product managers are the logical choice to implement such coordinative activities. The requisites for personal contact, even to the line and sales level, are what are often obscure, especially where the product management approach is new or untried. As the details of his sales participation and relationships are unfolded, such a basic question should be answered.

The degree to which the product manager is allowed to participate is necessarily related to the structure of the organization as well as product, market, number of products, number of accounts, and number of employees. There are cases where the product manager will have to play a much more intimate role in sales than in others; in some instances he will truly perform a sales function, although this obviously defeats the purpose of having a product manager. His relationship to the sales group and salesmen should be supportive in some cases, directional in others. Both of these can be realistically accomplished only if the necessary personal contact is permitted. This contact has to be based on the operational necessities of individual situations and not subject to rigid predetermination. Only the mechanisms and channels should concern us, as actual working structures will have to be geared to the specific corporate situation.

Relationship to Sales Management

Implementation of any product manager sales contact must start at the top. The sales manager and the product manager must relate to each other, and both must develop mutual trust, for there are many occasions where someone's feet will be stepped on. This is unavoidable; in the sales and management situations of the moment where answers must be had and customers satisfied immediately, it is unreal to think that opportunities for consultation always exist. When the customer is waiting on one phone and the sales representative on the other, the regional sales manager asks the product manager for a decision; and without time to confer with the general sales manager, he gets it. If the proper relationship does not exist, friction begins.

Conversely, when the sales manager calling on an account, alone or with the account representative, faces a critical question in regard to packing the product in 50 rather than 30-gallon drums, he may have to answer yes or no on the spot, without the benefit of product management opinion or direction. Having the rapport advocated, no serious difficulty will ensue, somehow the problem will be worked out. But if not, sparks will fly. Good management recognizes this problem and provides for it beforehand through the cultivation of contact and the development of this coordinative effort.

In practice this is not easy to come by. It requires a sincere effort on the part of all involved and can only grow with time, experience, and the opportunity to observe others in action. When the mold is properly cast, the outcome will be a marketing team with mutual trust; this eventually opens all channels of communication and generates the active marketing spirit.

Marketing Sales Objectives

It was mentioned earlier that through the implementation of a marketing planning committee, which may exist even where formal marketing plans are developed, commonly acceptable objectives should be developed; these become the overall operational guidelines for the marketing activity.

In this way the divergent objectives of the individually responsible elements can be mutually considered and compromises made. The ultimate statements of objectives then lead to the further refinements of strategies and tactics, the how's of implementation; and it is necessary that these be mutually accepted. Once done, there is a clear basis for proceeding, and the responsibilities, as well as the authorities of the product manager and the sales manager, are understood by both, particularly as they involve the active and passive selling situation.

Overriding all of this is the commitment of general management to the objectives, strategies, and tactics of both and the resolution of any conflicts that cannot be rectified in the marketing planning activity. Rarely does this problem occur, for as the requirements of both become better known to each other, workable solutions are found.

Having confidence in each other and operating under guidelines that have been preselected and mutually supported, the product manager is then in a position to provide specific services to the sales group. He also is responsible for providing direction in certain specific areas. Two hats are being worn, and it is important that they be understood in the relationship between product and sales management.

PRODUCT MANAGEMENT SERVICES

Type	*Examples*
Product information company product	Price
	Availability
	Specifications
	Tolerances
	Packaging
	Physical Forms
	Characteristics
	Properties
	Uses
	Advantages
	Disadvantages
	Status:
	Active
	Inactive
	Being considered for elimination
	Special emphasis
	Little interest
Literature	Internal for information
	External for customer
Technical assistance	Product application systems
	Packing variations
	Performance in particular mixtures or blends
	Process application
Support calls	Visits to selected accounts for:
	Technical assistance
	Product support
	Prestige purposes
	Trouble shooting

Type	Examples
Internal coordination	Followup on product work requests Assistance in obtaining specific product information Analytical evaluation
Product modification	Adjust pH for particular application New physical form Combination of products for one package system Alteration in color
Special customer service	Individual account specifications Increased tolerances Particular products or packages
Educational	Internal to salesmen on product and product strategy External: New or old products Market Processes or technology
Product ideas	Product concept from Sales Customers Identification of market needs
Product requests	Duplication of specific competition products Development of specific products for needs Development of systems and procedures Purchasing of products for line augmentation
Advertising schedules	Dates of individual ads Subjects of ad and ad themes Correlation of sales calls to ad
Promotion schedules	Dates of promotion efforts Subjects and themes of promotions Correlation of sales calls to promotional effort
Customer claims and complaints	Product performance Product quality Contamination Replacement or replenishment Monetary settlements

PRODUCT MANAGEMENT DIRECTION

Type	*Examples*
Price	List Bulk Contract Competitive
Product emphasis	Selected product for major emphasis
Product deletion	Selection and elimination of slow-moving or inactive products
Test marketing	Product selection Assistance in account selection Scheduling Establishing objective of test Personal attendance where necessary Availability of product Evaluation of results Recommendation for further action
Market emphasis	Major markets to be approached Submarkets activities Market identification and selection Selection of products for promotion in selected markets
Products for individual accounts	Addition of specific products for one or more selected accounts Followup on success of such products Withdrawal where expectations are not met
Product	Packaging Availability Specifications Tolerances Minimum profit acceptability Volume requirements Key or major identification New product promotion
Product mix	Balance of elements Number of products Relationships of products and lines with total
Allocations	Selection of accounts (with sales management) for conservation

Type	*Examples*
Purchase	Product or service where needed for assortment completion or marketing reasons
Advertising	Nature and theme Specific products Schedules Budgets (in some instances) Liaison with agency or responsible personnel
Promotion	Nature and theme Specific products Schedules Budgets (in some instances) Liaison with promotion agency or responsible personnel

Distinctions Between Sales Management and Salesmen Contacts

From the preceding it is apparent that two levels of product management contact exist. One is with and throughout management; the other is directly with the salesman. The first, while the more desirable and common, cannot completely displace or replace the latter.

In the chart provided, which elaborates on the service and directional function of product managers in the sales effort, there are elements that relate to contact on both levels. Which applies can only be created in the atmosphere of company requirements. In principle, however, these alternatives exist and should be utilized when possible. Where contact at the management level is involved, the implications, applications, and relations are clear. However, in the direct contact between salesmen and product manager, we have yet to clarify certain aspects that require lucid comprehension by both parties.

Contact with Salesmen

First and foremost, the product manager is not a salesman and never will be. He is, however, able to provide the service and directions that have been tabulated. Both sales manager and salesman must understand his role; and they should not try to use him to do their selling for them, nor should the product manager usurp this responsibility. This often involves delicate balancing, particularly when making a combined call; it can only be effective if both parties recognize their individual roles in the call and their relationships to each other and to the customer. Detailed planning of each individual account call is indispensable to successful use of the product manager in direct selling. For instance, when a product manager calls on an account for an exploratory, product-oriented discussion, he plays the dominant role. Discussion with the salesman should elicit:

Nature of account.

Existing Business.

Potential.

Relationship between account, salesman, and company.

Problems and past performance.

General prevailing atmosphere—receptive, hesitant, antagonistic.

Personalities of those who will be met.

Status of competition and competitive products.

Purpose of call.

Objective of call.

Advantages to be stressed.

Details of items to be discussed and approach to be taken.

Extent of any commitment to be made.

Customer's expectations.

What the customer has been led to expect.

Assured presence of responsible and interested customer representatives.

From these preliminary discussions an agenda should be prepared and adhered to. After the call, follow-up is necessary. This sounds self-evident, but more harm than good is done if commitments are not met. Sometimes they are the responsibility of the product manager, sometimes the responsibility of the salesman, but always necessary. Using this example much can be learned, as it indicates what product managers can do; but more, it illustrates what is necessary for success-ful contacts.

Having looked at matters from the product manager's side, we must now examine them from the salesman's. There are important contacts for whom the salesman is centrally responsible with the prod-uct manager merely providing support. Such an instance might involve a packaging question where the customer wants deliveries in tank wagons. The salesman requests a call with the product manager to discuss details, size of wagon, scheduling, metering or emptying fa-cilities, and storage capacity. In such a case the salesman advises the product manager of what is expected from him; but the salesman must satisfy these requirements. At the account it is the salesman who carries the bulk of the discussion and the preponderant responsibility for its outcome. As usual, followup is imperative.

After examining this overriding balance between sales management, salesman, and the actual use of a product manager in a given set of situations, there is still another major factor that should be cleared up. The word "direction" in the previous listing means direction and not directing. It is important that both the sales manager and the product manager understand this so that neither oversteps his bounds or feels unnecessary encroachment on the other's prerogatives. If the attitudes discussed before prevail, it is hardly likely this will happen, but even in the friendliest of families problems arise. It is far better to appreciate the possibilities and guard against them than to be dismayed when they occur or, worse yet, have unspoken animosities develop. Sometimes these occur through a salesmen's unintentional misunderstanding of the product manager's responsibilities. He can inadvertently create a situation merely through his lack of familiarity with product management involvement and objectives. This can be forestalled by the sales manager's clearly explaining these relationships; and later the product manager should follow suit. Not a major issue, it is one that deserves some forethought to prevent it from becoming just that.

The product manager is exercising his rights when he singles out products or markets, and then directs attention to them as well as to the emphasis to be placed on them. It is not his responsibility to tell salesmen how to sell, who to sell to, when to sell, or, in short, how to do their jobs. Sales techniques, strategies, calls, territories, approaches, and just plain selling are the responsibilities of the sales manager and the salesman. If the product manager is asked to assist in these areas, he is willing to do so; but otherwise his direction is limited to the product or marketing aspects, not the specifics of selling. Again, the problem never arises if appropriate rapport has been cultivated between product and sales management. It is up to them not to let it happen.

Two-Way Communication

Having considered what the product manager can do for the sales force, it is now worth considering what the sales force can do for the product manager. As the product manager is not a salesman, it is equally true that the salesman is not a product manager or a market researcher. But since he is in close contact with the customer and the market, he is often called upon to perform some of the functions of both.

Marketing, in general, and product management, in specific, thrive on current information to determine reaction to product, price, marketing activity, competitive status and activity, advertising, promotion, general strategies, and the outcome of the total marketing effort. The salesman is the person most frequently called upon to obtain this information. This is both fortunate and unfortunate. The positive aspects are that he is there, that it costs essentially nothing in terms of direct outlay, and that it involves him in broader aspects of marketing and management. On the negative side, anything that takes the salesman's time away from selling defeats his essential purpose and dilutes his effort.

Companies have approached this very real problem in several ways. One restricts the number of times salesmen can be called upon for survey information, the other allows for such information gathering but only if endorsed by sales management. Others completely forbid the use of salesmen in such areas, but these can obtain the information through private agencies or internal market research. Whatever the technique, there must be some arrangement for securing this vital data. While it might be most desirable for the product manager to obtain it himself, this is highly impractical unless dealing with few products in a relatively small market. In average circumstances the number of products, accounts, and other pressing duties do not permit even superficial consideration of this approach. Eyes and ears are needed, but they must be directed by a mind.

This last statement should not be interpreted as a slur on the abilities of the sales person; but it does acknowledge his limitations in an unfamiliar field. After all, he is not a professional market analyst. And indiscriminate data gathering can be both costly and useless. Equally important is the issue of discretion and the need for confidential, sensible approaches, particularly when surveying potential for new products or engaging in testmarketing.

In any of these instances it is the responsibility of those requesting the information to identify what they want and to point out any sensitivity. In such instances selection of accounts may also be germane since the product manager, in combination with sales management, can determine where the most reliable information can be obtained. The most common involvements of salesman in marketing information are market surveys, product surveys, assessment of the market potential, forecasting (product, sales, market, competitive position), competition, and the market reaction to the product, the process, advertising, and other activity.

These concerns can be specific or can encompass a total market. Often the information will be required on a routine basis, and at other times only on specific request. Some of it is useful in determining daily action or in decision making on an account-by-account product involvement; other information is needed for the development of the annual marketing or product plan. Whatever the need, it should be clearly indicated to the salesman in order that he may realize what is wanted of him, why it is wanted, and when it is wanted.

To do this management should make the necessary commitment through established policy, instructions, or forms. While we all want to shy away from the latter as much as possible, they do serve a purpose; and when a purpose is served, they should be used. They can save much confusion and assure procurement of all required information. In implementing any of these techniques, be brief, to the point, and painfully clear. Complex statements, no matter how intriguing, must be assiduously avoided, and there should be no innuendos. The place for these, if there is a place, is elsewhere. The salesman's and the manager's time are too valuable to waste; they should be able to understand exactly what is required and have the channels and mechanisms to provide it.

To demonstrate more precisely some of the information that product management needs for its own uses or in coordinative activities with the marketing group, Table 6 summarizes what salesmen can reasonably be expected to obtain.

TABLE 6. *Information from sales force.*

Nature	Requirement	Frequency
Product		
Company		
Performance	Day-to-day	
Acceptance	management	
Need for		Constant or
improvement		on request
modification	Planning	
Potential		

TABLE 6. *Information from sales force (continued).*

Nature	Requirement	Frequency

Competitors
  Performance
  Acceptance
  Position
  Effect on our product
  Advantages and
    disadvantages
  Newly released
    (with price, sample,
    response, etc.)
  Policies and strategies
	Day-to-day
	management
	and planning
		Constant or
		on request

Markets
  Size
  Duration
  Potential
  Activity
  Opportunities
  Competition
  Strategies
  Reactions
  Trends
	Planning and
	marketing
	response
	determination
		Primarily on request,
		but major
		developments
		should be reported
		immediately

Forecasts
  Sales to customer
  Sales by product to
    customer
  Product requirements
  Increase and decrease
  Potential
	Planning and
	control
		On request, but
		major changes to
		be reported
		immediately

Test Marketing
  Commercial objectives
  Commercial
    determinations
  Technical objectives
  Performance
  Customer response
  Product or market
    potential
	Planning, control,
	strategy, or policy
	determination
		On request

Once the general objectives of these informational requirements are made known, the degree and extent of direction is mitigated. Experience teaches. Soon realizing the advantages to the salesman himself, his reliability improves to the point where he will compare and cooperate. Response engenders response; when working with the product manager, the sales force sees the concrete demonstration of his contribution. In addition, they see his contribution to product supply, price, and the marketing effort, not to mention new products and market response; there should be no difficulty in enlisting the aid of sales management, marketing management, or that key element, the salesman. The two-way street must be open and marketing traffic freely flowing.

PART FIVE

Planning

14

Planning: An Overview

PLANNING as an idea is not new to anyone. Every day in every way we all, to a larger or smaller extent, plan our activities. Yet in business when the word "planning" is mentioned, there is a reluctance among many to admit its need, and an attitude of resistance. Considering man's innate need to plan, this is an interesting reaction, but not one that is too difficult to analyze. And analyze it we must, for planning is vital.

As the business enterprise faces increased internal complexity and external involvement, the need for organization, systematization, integration, and defined courses of action leading to predetermined ends, becomes an increasingly necessary activity. This in essence is the heart of the planning premise. For planning is nothing more than setting to paper the distillation of business analysis and the means to be used in attaining these goals within a given time. Examined in this simple way, no one seriously argues the need for planning. But the questions of necessity, justification, reduction to formula, denial of individuality, and personal decision-making must be dealt with. It is these psychological matters that are at the forefront of problems in planning acceptance; these also impose unexpected planning impediments. They are factors of vital concern to the product manager because of his deep interests in the planning area.

Business was relatively slow to accept the need for overall planning. Only in more recent years have the terms, plans, planning, the marketing plan, integrated management plan, and the accompanying vocabulary: objectives, strategies, goals, action programs, and a host of other terms, become commonplace. Now, even those who do not formally plan, speak the planning jargon and appreciate the need. So the first problem of which we spoke, recognition and implementation by business, has to a major extent been overcome. In some instances there has even been overreaction, and some companies have tended to overplan. This too is a natural occurrence. Dealing with a new concept, its applications must find their level, and this can only develop with time and usage. As the company becomes more familiar with the benefits of planning within its own organizational requirements, modifications ensue; eventually the depth of planning is adjusted to reflect the real needs of the company. This peripheral problem is only worth mentioning for those companies who are thinking about planning for the first time. The other problem mentioned, however, that of personal action and reaction is not so readily solved.

Since planning ultimately calls upon people to perform, they must be considered vital elements in the planning process; yet little attention has been given this requirement. Basic analysis of the plan and the planning premise have centered on the assets derived; these are exceedingly significant and justify the time, expense, and effort required in the development and execution of the plan.

In those companies that are new to planning, as well as those that have employed the planning premise for some time, there is a reluctance to fully accept the need for planning at the individual level. So a selling job must be done. The personnel responsible for the planning operation must be sold on its merits to the company. Many firms in introducing planning, do not do this. The entire rationale of planning requirements should be reviewed. And if proper indoctrination is provided, much of the personnel difficulty can be obviated. Often this educational process will fall directly on the shoulders of the product manager and he, as part of his planning responsibility, will have to take heed of these requirements. This will make the planning more efficient. Included in such an approach must be thorough training of individuals in all details of mechanical techniques and in the theory, management perspectives, and applications of the plan.

In this context should be included the reassurance that reduction of mental images to paper does not jeopardize individual creativity. Many feel that the plan, once generated, is an inviolate mandate that controls them and reduces business operations to a series of formulas and preconditioned actions. This concept encompasses all of the serious, self-imposed restrictions that are diametrically opposed to the real meaning of planning. The needs for individuality and creativity have at no time been more necessary. The marketing effort has repeatedly emphasized its requirements in these areas and can only flourish with such talents as well as the ability to function in dynamic situations where predeterminations are impossible.

The "plan" in reality is a viable instrument of management, providing guidelines and stating commitments. But inherent in this concept is the capacity for change. If the plan is static, it defeats its own purposes. This is not to say that plans should be indiscriminately altered, but allowance for valid changes must exist. This provides for the creativity and ability of the individual (1) in respect to creation of the plan; (2) in the implementation of the plan; (3) in the application of the plan; and (4) in any necessary modification of the plan.

The purpose of planning is to provide a concise statement of corporate direction and techniques by which it is to be accomplished, all in the framework of time and place limitations. Having this requisite clearly in mind and recognizing personal needs in the planning process, we can proceed to a deeper analysis of planning and its execution.

What Is a Plan?

Precise description of what a plan is would be difficult. However, both the product manager and management require a working definition. This will aid mutual understanding.

A plan is a statement of company policy and intention, providing a summary of direction and ultimate accomplishment, predicated on a series of objectives, analysis, strategies, and specific actions oriented by integration of intercorporate facilities relating to and encompassing financial, commercial and technical capabilities intercoordinated and confined within predetermined temporal parameters.

This definition should be applied in developing all plans, whether full-blown, integrated management plans or mere subsections, as well as individual unit plans created for limited departmental application. There is every reason to extend planning down from the ethereal heavens of upper management to the lowlier operational areas. Management, subscribing to integrated planning, often overlooks the application of the planning technique to short range requirements of departmental organization. The planning premise, however, is worth the effort even in these smaller-scale operations.

Pros and Cons of Planning

Many may be convinced of the benefits of planning; others are not. It is essential that we review the arguments of both so that users of planning may visualize all ramifications. Here again, the product manager's mission is clear. Where benefits are involved, there is little problem. Examination of some of the difficulties, however, may lead to their solution or mitigation, and this is something to be truly desired.

Pros	*Cons*
Forces business analysis.	Expensive.
Provides total involvement.	Time consuming.
Provides for integration of effort.	Too structured.
Fixes authority.	Relatively inflexible.
Fixes responsibility.	Limits personal activity.
Focuses attention on the meaningful.	Limits personal identification.
Provides for control and review.	Leads to regimentation.
Comparative and absolute performance assessment possible.	Does not reflect true position at any given time.
Encompasses quantifiable and unquantifiable elements.	Must be subject to constant review and adjustment.
Provides for formal sanction of strategies, goals, and activities.	Cannot encompass all activities.
Forces assignment of priorities.	Is highly confidential, must be restricted.
Provides for budgetary approvals.	Difficult to determine marketing or profit return on planning investment.
Enables clear consideration and statement of total corporate activity.	Requires extensive manpower commitment.
Excellent mechanism for disseminating information relevant to management and intention of company.	
Delineates activities and accomplishments in time.	
Forces establishment of set goals.	

The expense incurred in planning bears additional comment only because, while it is appreciated that time means money, there are two dimensions to the expense of planning. The first and most obvious are the salaries and administrative charges involved when people are assigned to compiling the plan. With these are included the cost of additional services, consultants, printing costs, and distribution costs. The second, and more difficult to assess, is the cost of time away from other efforts. It is one thing when the product manager is planning, for it is clearly one of his functions. Therefore this is not time spent away from other duties; but the time a salesman is requested to contribute is time away from sales and not truly a part of his routine. This cost must also be assessed. Two budgets will have to be established, the first predicated on outright measurable expense, and the second, on estimated costs based on possibilities of return for other effort.

The sum of these is the cost of planning and it must be applied against the return. Since the return is even more difficult to determine, it is hardly practical to attempt a direct monetary comparison. What is meant here is a practical weighing of cost versus need. On this basis, there is no question of need, only of relative expenditure and the maintenance of reasonable cost. The meaning of "reasonable" must be determined in the planning situation since the complexities, detail of plan, and concomitant cost are judgments effectively rendered only in the context of same and the requirements of the company.

Before leaving the cost question, one other factor should be mentioned, and that is accuracy in planning. Refinement and increased accuracy only come with time and experience. Later, when discussing quantitative objectives the question of limit and degree of expected accuracy will be discussed more fully. Mention will be made of the obvious correlation between accuracy, its increase, and the time and expenditure necessary to achieve it. The more accurate and refined the plan, the more expensive it becomes. There's a practical "tolerance" which must be established within the company. While yet imprecisely determined, it is safe to say that increased cost for increased accuracy beyond a certain point follows a geometric rather than linear progression. This must also be taken into account in the total cost of planning, and a definite budget should be established wherever planning is undertaken. Just as any major financial commitment should receive budgetary consideration, so should planning.

From the list of pros it would seem that the cons are not only numerically outnumbered but completely crushed by virtue of even superficial review. The need for planning emerges clear and self-justified. From this, even the whys of planning are concisely answered. Planning provides:

An organized approach to conduct and management of the business.

Budgetary control.

Integration of all activities within the company.

Quantifiable and nonquantifiable goals plus a clear statement of company intention with the means by which to achieve it.

Control and review basis.

Functional and operational guides.

Assessment of performance of: the company, the execution of effort, and the performance of personnel and departments.

Types of Plans

Just as people differ, so do plans. Basically we can distinguish between the following categories and types of plans:

Type of plan	Description
Informal	A plan not rigidly constructed. Used for limited time and for fulfillment of specific but confined objectives.
Formal	A full-scale example of the planning effort. It involves predetermined structure and involves long, short, or intermediate periods. For optimal implementation planning in this situation is predicated on cycles in which various phases are incorporated in fixed sequences and predetermined points in time.
Long range	Plans of longer outlook—usually considered to be of five or more years' projection. The five-year planning cycle is probably the most common fixed period of long-range planning.
Intermediate range	Usually considered to be two or three years' duration.
Short range	The most common of all formal plans. It is commonly structured on a one-year basis.
Integrated management	This is a totally integrated management plan which includes all business elements: financial, marketing, manufacturing, research, and development. It can be of short, intermediate, or long range.

Commonly it is based on both the long and short-range approaches: a one-year and five-year plan.

Marketing plan — A commonly encountered plan that is basically a marketing document. It contains all elements of marketing concern and therefore includes certain limited consideration of nonmarketing aspects (research, development, manufacturing) as they relate to accomplishments of marketing goals. Again, it can be based on one- or five-year cycles. This plan often exists as the only formal planning document in smaller companies or becomes an element in integrated plans.

Product plan — Such plans involve elements of formal planning applied on the level of products, brands, lines, and even individual products within lines. It is usually found as an element of the marketing plan and by extension the integrated management plan. It will be based on either one or five-year cycles or both, depending on the organization and planning schedule of the marketing group.

Technical or scientific plan — This is a self-sustaining plan for scientific development including research.

Manufacturing plan — The same as the technical plan but reflecting manufacturing concerns and responsibilities.

Operational plan — Consideration logistics plus personal, capital, and administrative planning concerns; again, self-sustaining or an element of the integrated plan.

Not all companies subscribe to all these planning operations. The most common, and the one from which business planning truly evolved, is the marketing plan. In further discussion of planning in the next two chapters, we will deal in detail with only two of these types. They are, of course, the ones of most direct concern to product and marketing management. The marketing plan and the product plan, both from one and five-year implementation.

Who Plans?

A question often asked by those not involved in planning is: Who does it all? The answer varies from company to company and to large measure depends on the nature and extent of the planning operation.

But it is not remiss to reply that regardless of scope, at one time or another where a company employs planning, everyone in the company plans.

The planning function is either placed in individual hands or in those of a committee. In some instances a combination approach is employed where a basic committee coordinates the planning activities of individuals operating within the planning operation. In those instances where a committee is not involved, some individual is responsible for such integration.

In many cases the delegation of planning responsibility derives from pragmatics. And the same individual may find himself responsible for all planning or only phases, depending on personnel and budgets. As time and fortune change, this will also. Eventually where plans become complicated enough, staff planning specialists will be added. They will perform the coordinative function and be responsible for final format, writing, and organization of the plan, if not for its specific content. This latter still remains the responsibility of those charged with execution of functions contained within the plan.

Taking our two examples and assuming for the moment no planning specialists, it is not infrequent that we find the product manager as the planning coordinator. The reason for this is apparent. Since the marketing plan entails inclusion of other nonmarketing directed activities, who is better qualified than the product manager who is already in liaison with these areas and whose responsibility coordination is. Acting as integrator, he often has the responsibility of pulling together all those elements necessary to compile and execute the marketing plan. In so doing he acts in close cooperation with the marketing chief and plans the plan (dealt with in detail in the next section). The product segment is clearly within his province even in those instances where he does not hold complete coordinative responsibility.

When the marketing plan is under the direction of the marketing group and the product manager, it develops the plan according to its own best assessments. This can mean assignment of planning responsibilities within the marketing group with assembly and coordination by the product manager and the chief of marketing; or it can mean the formation of a marketing planning committee. As this committee would have total marketing representation, it develops the planning schedule and then makes individual responsibility assignments. Where done individually, it must be the task of the product manager and marketing director. Where accomplished by the committee, it is finalized by the committee in principle and set to paper by those to whom this duty is delegated. Often in the committee approach, agreement in principle is obtained by presentation to the committee, thereby enabling mutual acceptance and commitment. Written finalization can also be completed by those individuals who have generated their segments of the plan: product plan, product manager; sales plan, sales management. When we consider the elements of the marketing plan, this concept will be reviewed more specifically.

For our purposes here, it is apparent that everyone is generally involved in the planning process. Often such responsibility rests with the product manager who, working intimately with all responsible elements, develops the planning cycle and ultimately the plan, which is then approved by management and implemented. To accomplish this we must first consider the planning of planning, or planning cycles.

Planning Cycles

Planning must provide for defining objectives, assembling data, reviewing and analyzing information, determinating strategies, reviewing preliminary conclusions; and obtaining agreement of approach, finalization of strategies, and action programs which are to support them.

To do all of this a timetable is required. The more diversified the product line and markets served, the more complex this becomes and the greater the need for a planning cycle, which is the timetable that will be used in the development of the plan from start to finish. Differences exist in the sequence of events and in the establishment of specific dates, but in principle, application based on one variant or another of the planning cycle shown in Table 7 will be found in most institutions.

TABLE 7. *A planning-cycle timetable.*

Date initiated	Date for completion	Action	Responsibility
3/1	3/15	Planning Meeting 1: Initiation of planning cycle (1) Review corporate objectives (2) Assign responsibility for	Chief, marketing
		Preliminary marketing objective	Chief, marketing
		Preliminary sales budget	Sales management
		Preliminary profit budget	Product management
3/15		Preliminary objectives and budgets received	All responsible

TABLE 7. A *planning-cycle timetable (continued)*.

Date initiated	Date for completion	Action	Responsibility
4/1	6/1	Planning Meeting 2: (1) Approval of preliminary objectives and budget after discussion (2) Assign responsibility for finalization of preliminary objectives and establishment of following additional:	Chief, marketing or product management
		Marketing objectives and forecasts	Chief, marketing
		Sales objectives and forecasts	Sales management
		Profit objectives and forecasts	Product management
		Product objectives and forecasts	Product management
		Advertising objectives and budgets	Product management
		Technical or support objectives	Product management
		Preliminary strategies to support above	All responsible
6/1		Assignments from Planning Meeting 2 submitted for review and approval	Chief, marketing Product manager Sales manager
6/15	6/15	Planning Meeting 3: (1) Review and finalize assignment from Planning Meeting 2 after this two-week study (2) Arrange submeetings for review of areas requiring integration and possible conflict resolution. Revisions to be submitted to committee by June 25 for review prior to July 1 finalization	Chief, marketing Product manager Sales manager All responsible

TABLE 7. A *planning-cycle timetable* (*continued*).

Date initiated	Date for completion	Action	Responsibility

7/1	8/15	Planning Meeting 4:
		(1) Review and reconciliation of revisions
		(2) Finalization of objectives, strategies
		(3) Review of budgets
		(4) Assignment for development of action programs to support strategies
		  Sales
		  Profit
		  Product
		  Advertising
		  Technical
		  Commercial
			Chief, marketing
			Sales management
			
			Product management
			
			Sales manager
			Product manager
			Product manager
			Product manager
			Product manager
			Administrative

8/15	9/1	Submission of action programs.	Chief, marketing Sales manager Product manager
9/1	9/15	Planning Meeting 5: (1) Review of action programs (2) Review of plan status and recommendations (3) Intervening meetings for resolution of action plan conflicts or problems	Chief, marketing Sales manager Product manager
9/15		Submission of final action programs	Chief, marketing Sales manager Product manager
9/20		(1) Final approval objectives, strategies, budgets, action programs (2) Reassignment to all concerned for final draft preparation due Oct. 15	Chief, marketing

TABLE 7. *A planning-cycle timetable (concluded).*

Date initiated	Date for completion	Action	Responsibility
10/15		Submission final plan draft	All responsible
10/20		Planning Meeting 6: Plan review and finalization	Chief, marketing Sales manager Product manager
11/1	11/15	Submission of final draft	Chief, marketing
11/15		Final approval total plan	Management
12/1		Plan presentation to marketing and general management	Chief, marketing Sales management Product management
12/5		Plan distribution	All concerned

The specific dates given in the table are only meant to be indicative of general periodic cycles, approximate sequence of events, time allotted for component steps, and the early planning requirements found in all companies. The cycle often commences in the first quarter and extends well into the fourth. This is very time consuming and reflects a major company commitment, as well as that of all involved individuals, to the concept and its requirements.

Although this cycle consists of a series of six planning meetings involving representation from marketing management, which includes the chief of marketing, sales managers, and product managers, this is not to be considered restrictive since other representatives will also be called upon for their specific contributions. The basic planning committee only is seen as constituting this group. In addition, while the chief of marketing is always listed as conducting the meetings, this may in fact not be the case in those situations where plan development and coordination is left to the product manager. In the conduct of his planning responsibilities this is often the case, particularly in smaller companies where such elaborate planning cycles and integrated planning entanglements are not encountered. This phase then can be handled through committee. Or the planning cycle can basically be followed with the product manager contacting responsibility contributory elements and pursuing requisites directly. Whatever the approach, the same essential sequence will be followed; and information will be developed in this logical manner.

In developing a planning cycle, specific dates and serial activities must be based on corporate regulations and the implications of pre-existing financial, budgetary, or manufacturing requirements. In many companies this is the case and the plan's developmental stages will have to coincide with input needs in other planning areas. Where this is the case no serious problems will be encountered, provided these dates are known and taken into account when developing the planning cycle. This added complexity, and that of integrating the planning effort within the marketing group itself, clearly reveals the basic necessity for a planning coordinator and where possible a planning committee.

The planning coordinator or committee also perform another function: that of obtaining mutual commitment while the plan is in development.

Very often elements of the plan overlap in areas of responsibility. Sales will rely on product management for the products and conversely product management will need the agreement of the sales group for sales performance and expectation. Forecasts must take into account commitments of both, and moreover, the ability of manufacturing to produce and logistics to supply where needed. In the integrated approach during the planning meetings and at the intervening ones indicated, such resolution and mutual acceptance is obtained. Where differences are encountered they should be resolved before being introduced into the plan. Where resolutions cannot be effected at the committee or submeeting level, the chief marketing executive will have to, like Solomon, exercise his decision-making authority. What goes into the plan, preliminary or final, should be based on preobtained agreements and not on postplan decisions.

Such an integrated planning program will assure uniformity and complete coordination; it will also provide a plan which is logical, cohesive, and based on mutual commitment. While this may not be the only way to plan, it is surely one of the best. It is wise to remember that good plans do not just happen. They are the results of innumerable hours of discussion, work, effort, and especially coordinated activity. In order to plan effectively, the cycle and the philosophy of planning make one fact clear: It is necessary to plan to plan. Those who have the coordination responsibility should sit aside, think through their management and planning situations, and then plan their plan. Once planned, they should provide all those involved with a copy of the plan for the plan. Then, and only then, should they proceed with the plan itself.

Major Elements in All Plans

While the specific content of plans varies with their orientation, there are certain principal elements that are common to all. They are also the basic terms often encountered in the planning vocabulary, but surprisingly enough not completely understood by those who use them. One of the reasons for this is that all definitions do not agree, and so rather than split hairs, we have tried to develop some working understanding of these terms and their significance in the planning operation.

ANALYSIS

This, as commonly used, means dividing an entity into its components to assess their nature, relationship proportion, function, interactions, and dependencies with a statement of this assessment. As such analysis is vital to effective planning, it is a problem area since (1) information for analysis must be identified; (2) it must be obtained; (3) resultant data must be subject to analysis; (4) results of analysis must be prepared. One of the difficulties with analysis is that it takes time, but one of the faults found in many plans is that this time has not been taken; raw unanalyzed data is provided with no indication of its significance or interpretation. This should not be; any information contained in the plan should be pertinent and analyzed.

OBJECTIVES AND GOALS

These two words are considered simultaneously because they are often confused. Some authorities say they are synonymous, and to some extent they are. Others say they are close enough in meaning to be used interchangeably. Still others state that they are virtually the same, except that the word "objective" should be reserved for nonquantitative entities while "goal" is the preferred term for quantified finite representations. Of all approaches, the latter seems best. While the meaning of both is close, we should reserve objectives for non-quantitative and goals for quantitative expressions. If nothing more, this will keep matters clear. What are they? They are probably the most important single element of the plan since they represent the final distillation of corporate aims reflecting those achievements set by the company to assure continued growth and success. Therefore, they are of vital concern to all since they form the ends to be achieved and define the parameters within which the company will perform in a given time span. They constitute that which is to be achieved and are a measuring device against which performance can be determined. So important are the establishment of objectives and goals that separate treatment is later given to their selection, establishment, and use.

STRATEGIES

These are the basic approaches that will be taken for the accomplishment of objectives.

TACTICS

The specific actions contemplated in carrying out the strategy. Occasionally the literature will contain this word, but more often the term "action program" will be encountered.

ACTION PROGRAM

Those specific actions or activities that must be performed to accomplish strategies and objectives. They should be highly detailed and include three primary elements: (1) action to be performed; (2) date of action; (3) personal or departmental responsibility for initiation and completion.

ASSUMPTIONS

These are the premises on which the plan is based. They are important not because they are escape clauses for the planners but because they explain the basis on which the plan was constructed. If later prognostications prove incorrect reference to them indicates whether judgment was sound at the time determination was made. Planning assumptions should, as with information in the plan, be relevant and pertain to the business at hand. Commonly known facts and assertions do not need to be repeated in the plan, and only those variables essential to the business should be considered in any depth. This in itself poses many problems since identification of sensitivity factors is not simple. However, where they are not known clearly, their isolation and relative importance in the business operation should be one of the stated objectives of the marketing group. Once known, they must be periodically reexamined since they are, or may well be, variable variables.

OPPORTUNITIES

When examining opportunities one's rose-colored glasses should be removed. Imagination should be tempered by realism. In the optimism of opportunity identification there is a natural tendency to overlook the problems involved. For example, when the opportunity for a new product is contemplated, and sales and profit projections made, has the impact on existing business been determined? How much will be new as opposed to replacement sales? What existing products will be effected? What will the impact be on present profits? Every opportunity should be examined for its actual and potential problems. This does not mean that they have to be stated in the plan, but they should be known. Another problem in opportunity establishment is the identification of real opportunities for the company. Their selection is vital.

PROBLEMS

Problems should be closely examined for their possible opportunities. This does not mean that every problem can be transformed into an opportunity, but many will reveal unexpected possibilities. Such examination will also show that many imagined problems are just that, and analysis in the planning process will magically solve them.

Establishment of Objectives

Of all the plan's components, the objective is without peer and stands alone as the single most important factor. As we have seen, the objective is the statement of those corporate aims that must be obtained to assure continued growth and success. They are pervasive and represent the final condensation of all corporate elements into a finite expression of intention and attainment. They are the ends to be gained and the guidelines against which to measure performance.

Top management must fully appreciate the implication that these objectives convey within the corporate structure. Once the objectives are established, it is imperative that management endorse them and permit their implementation. This is, oddly enough, sometimes difficult for management to perceive; And without full subscription to the execution of objectives, the entire structure is undermined and accomplishment seriously jeopardized. This applies to corporate objectives, as well as those of marketing, sales, and product.

Nature and Type of Objectives

There is some confusion as to the number, nature, and variety of objectives that exist. Within any corporation there will be a multiplicity of what appear to be divergent recommended objectives. It is extremely important that management sort, distill, and derive from their input only salient objectives. This means that the corporation sets its own parameters and limitations in which goals are internally established. This perspective relates to the length of the planning outlook and is predicated on one, three, or five year outlooks, since these are the more common short, intermediate, and long-range planning periods.

The balance between time and specificity of objective is a requirement and must be further tempered in consideration of the objective itself. Some objectives are subject to quantification, others not. Some can be constructed with a high degree of certainty, others not. These factors must be applied in the derivation of the objective related to its nature. In this sense, we can distinguish between the following types of objectives and goals:

Corporate. Statement of the essential position that the corporation establishes for itself. These are usually quantified but often include unquantifiable elements. From an overall standpoint they clearly deserve consideration in the long-term planning perspective.

Financial. At the level of the marketing activity these are the most commonly encountered. They apply in long and short-term planning and are obviously quantified statements of the financial position to be achieved. The term "goals" certainly applies here.

In the statement of financial objectives, the following individual elements are usually identified and specifically quantified: profit (gross and net), sales (dollars and units), expenses, cost of goods sold, cash flow, assets, assets employed, liabilities, and return on investment. In the shorter-range outlook, the detailing of financial objectives is more extensive than in the long-range plan, which tends to report aggregates rather than the individual product.

Manufacturing. Statement of manufacturing objectives is very important particularly in industry-oriented companies. Capital requirements are quite significant and should be considered thoroughly, especially in the long-range plan.

Marketing. Objectives in marketing usually fall within major areas: sales, advertising, promotion, distribution; and depending on the nature of the plan their extent will vary. In short-range plans individual elements will be identified in detail, and in longer-range plans resort to aggregates will prevail.

Product. Here we separate product management objective from marketing only to clarify the relationship. While product management reports to marketing and must subscribe to marketing objectives, there are separate product objectives such as net profit, product control, and new product development that should be indicated. The distinction between specific product objectives, marketing objectives, and their interrelationships will be clarified in the next two chapters.

Technical. The establishment of technical objectives is one of the most difficult planning considerations. Technical objectives incorporating research objectives become exceedingly complex, particularly as we attempt to project them further into the future. Regardless of the difficulty, the attempt must be made, and many companies have developed elaborate procedures for such planning efforts. The commitment to planning and the establishment of research criteria and money is all important. It may not be possible to foretell specific discoveries, but it is possible to plan research areas, expenditures, and priorities.

Administrative. Primary objectives in administrative planning usually relate to financial statements through control of expenses or cost reductions. The emphasis given to administrative planning must be balanced within the framework of the company. This will often include intercompany requirements, personnel, and equipment budgeting.

While there are other types of objectives, these are the principal categories. We must now evaluate the technique by which objectives are selected.

IMPARTIAL CRITERIA FOR OBJECTIVES

In establishing objectives it is essential, considering their ultimate significance, that the right objectives be selected. Since establishment of the objective requires a certain subjectivity, it is important that an attempt be made to apply impartial criteria against which to test it. This will guarantee that the objectives developed meet certain specifications. The ultimate selection of objectives will reflect consideration of these elements even if they must be sorted from the many possible ones based on business judgment. This in effect means that only a few objectives should be cited. These are selected from many, but all have a rationality derived from objective criteria. The criteria to consider are:

Feasibility. Can the objective selected be accomplished by the corporation either as it exists or as it plans to exist?

Suitability. Is it actually economical to accomplish what is desired? Are the expenditures worth the rewards?

Realism. Is the objective real and do we truly wish to accomplish it?

Measurability. Certain objectives cannot be quantified but are nonetheless measurable. At the same time, a quantifiable objective obviously should be measurable, and it is a good index of validity to determine whether or not its realization can indeed be measured. If it cannot, its value is questionable, and the establishment of such an objective demands additional review.

Alterability. Is the objective flexible enough to be altered? Some objectives should be quasipermanent, but the capacity for change is inherent in effective corporate responsiveness and should be a consideration in objective assessment.

COMMUNICATING OBJECTIVES

Before any objective can be accomplished, it must be made known. Planning provides one mechanism for such dissemination. However, even before the plan can be initiated, management should convey its overall objectives so that the plan developed can reflect these concerns and support management intentions. While this is one more of those seemingly self-evident realities, there are companies that do not first develop their management objectives but derive them from the input of the supporting plans. This is rather like the horse after the cart, but if it works, all is well. However, it is questionable that such an approach, even if it works, is working well. If anything, planning is a logical process and should constantly be subjected to critical examination; it should also follow an order and sequence of operation suited to the company. Communications are central to the product manager's activities, and he should be vitally concerned with the plan and its dissemination.

Plan Format

The format of the actual plan will vary from company to company and should receive detailed consideration. The plan should be as brief as possible and follow a consistent approach. Where multiple plans are to be submitted for final assembly into one composite plan, for example, marketing plan into management plan, a predetermined format should be supplied to all planning elements. This will assure treatment of required subjects and facilitate subsequent review, analysis, and integration. To the recipient of the final plan it will also provide advantages in following the presentation.

Since the elements contained in each company's plans will vary greatly, it is not possible to provide examples that are too meaningful; however, in the chapter on marketing and product planning, typical formats for these two plans are indicated. In the overall planning activity, there are a few basics to be considered:

Use charts and graphs where possible to present information.

Do not present "raw" unanalyzed data.

Include only relevant information.

Predetermine length and do not exceed it; many plans are too long.

Be sure to include: executive summary, index, contingency plans where applicable, and control and review procedures.

Limit number of objectives.

Limit number of strategies.

Provide a neat, intelligible document.

Produce enough copies for total distribution.

Do not spare reasonable expense in printing and binding, since, like it or not, books are judged by their covers.

Where integrated plans are involved, the separation and integration of elements must be provided for. This can be quite problematical. Where one and five-year plans are being produced simultaneously, another decision remains to be made: Should the one- and five-year plan be included in the same document? There are two approaches to this: (1) they are inclusive; (2) they are separated.

INTEGRATED ONE- AND FIVE-YEAR PLANS

In this approach the five-year plan is totally integrated with the one-year plan. This means in a five-year planning cycle, Year One corresponds to the first year of the plan and then proceeds through to Year Five. In ensuing years the plan is updated by adding Year Six and Year Two then becomes Year One of the plan and so forth. In this system review and alteration are necessary, and no year remains constant. The plan as it stands becomes a reference for succeeding plans and, as such, it is catalyzing.

This technique is employed by many companies. It does have certain problems since the expense of preparation is more than that of separate plans. Because the one-year aspect is subject to more alteration than the longer range, portions of the total plan may be more affected than the entire one. Distribution also becomes a problem with the integrated plan since many companies, while not objecting to extensive internal distribution of their one-year outlook, do question the wisdom of distributing their long-range projections. This is a valid point and should be weighed in the balance.

SEPARATE ONE- AND FIVE-YEAR PLANS

In this approach the one-year plan is a separate document from the five-year plan. There are two ways of doing this. Planning for five years, Year One would be included in the five-year plan and the same elements removed and presented as a separate Year One plan. This overcomes alteration and distribution problems mentioned before, and places information in the hands of more people; it also provides a wider need to know the distribution base. In the other approach, Year One plan is separate and the five-year plan is separate, but Year One is omitted from the five-year plan which really projects five years after Year One. This amounts to planning for six years: the ensuing planning year and five years more. It has the same benefits as the separate planning aspect mentioned before.

There are advantages and disadvantages to either approach; management pays its money and takes its choice. But before leaving this question, there is another aspect of format that relates to separation, namely the separation of marketing plans from totally integrated management plans. This can also carry over to the concept of divisional and total corporate plans where multidivisional corporations with individual plans exist.

The rationale for such separation is security and the need not to know of total divisional or corporate intention and position. The arguments in favor of this separation are strong and reasonable, provided the necessary information is known by those involved in implementing specifics. There is nothing worse than the plan extant with little or no distribution. Where questions of confidential information arise to plague distribution, make the most of this simple but expedient solution: separate not only total plans—integrated management from marketing and corporate from divisional—but elements within the individual plans. If sales does not need to know profit, it can be supplied with only the sales planning aspect. This facile solution is not only possible, it is practical and will assure utmost distribution of the plan at all levels, something to be ardently strived for.

Plan Presentation

Once developed, the plan is usually presented first to management for final approval and then to sales, marketing, and others. In either case preparation for presentation is necessary. A poor package can make a poor product. It is therefore more than worth the time and effort to make adequate preparation for plan presentation in both instances. This should include a well-executed written plan with charts, slides, or even films as visual aids. After formal presentation, the time for distribution has arrived, and we should not stint. Either the total plan or those selected segments should be distributed far and wide.

Plan Control and Review

The plan itself is a control tool in that its objectives and budgets are devices for mensuration of performance. First and foremost, we must consider assessment of performance against plan. This is a review and control procedure. In such activities provision should be made for formal and informal assessment.

Periodic reports, usually quarterly, must be submitted on all significant factors: These should include:

Gross sales
Gross profit
Net profit
Expenses
Conformance to budget
Implementation of action programs
Attainment of objectives
Recommendation for alterations
   Sales
   Profits
   Forecasts
   Objectives
   Opportunities and problems
   Strategies
Alteration in business outlook
Review of business situation and conditions
Issues for management resolution

Each of these can be reported on an absolute, comparative, or exception basis. The latter has been found the most satisfactory in complex plans since it assures coverage of essential factors without undue time and expense in reporting that which is already on plan. When using the exception approach, tolerances should be established and quantifiable elements mentioned only where deviations are encountered. For example, plus or minus 5 percent sales variations would not be reported; over or under this limit, they would. Included in such reports should be recommendations for corrective action and expectations of such corrections. The review and control aspects of plan implementation are fundamental to the planning concept. Once issued, not forgotten, is the motto of the effective planning operation.

The Planning Concept Reviewed

The commitment to planning must permeate the company. It stems from upper management down but must be supported with equal vigor from beneath if it is to be successful. It is also a constant and ever-lasting effort and should be considered in this light since one plan does not planning make. With each year comes the annual and five-year plans plus all of their activities. When management contemplates introducing planning, it had best consider this persistent requirement. Planning becomes a fixed expense and a permanent obligation; it is not to be undertaken lightly.

The relationship of the product manager to the overall planning premise is apparent. His commitment to planning activities is vital in the development of the plan and its successful execution.

And one last factor in planning: now that you have a plan, use it. The purpose of the plan is not to gather dust on the bookshelf, nor is it to be locked away in some inaccessible file cabinet. It is a viable management instrument and should be used.

15

The Marketing Plan

MARKETING planning is an activity familiar to most practicing product managers. Because of management's ever-increasing commitment to planning, those who have not yet been exposed to the marketing plan had better familiarize themselves with this omnipresent management tool.

In creating a marketing plan, we try to put general planning principles into practice with the goal of accomplishing management direction. As we saw in the preceding chapter, the object of planning is to reduce major business objectives and the mechanisms by which they are to be achieved into a logical, concise statement. Such a statement is to serve as a guide to strategy and action predicated on predetermined objectives. In addition, it will serve as a yardstick for measurement of corporate, departmental, and individual performance.

This is a large order indeed. In considering the development of the marketing plan it is good to keep this utilitarian objective clearly in sight. The ultimate application of the plan is a pragmatic one, and the planning activity should not defer to scholastic, academic, or mandatory management.

319

Marketing Planning and Product Management

One not familiar with the planning process may well wonder why it is emphasized in a book on product management. In the preceding chapter it was mentioned that while a function of the marketing group, the actual development of the plan was commonly delegated to the product manager. If the product managers are to be faced with the responsibility for plan coordination or formulation, they should become thoroughly familiar with the techniques, objectives, and means of planning.

Second, even in those instances where the product manager may not have full responsibilities in the overall marketing plan, he will be called upon to contribute segments of the plan. Third, he may well be a member of a marketing planning committee, where a committee approach is employed; and he may find himself the chairman, coordinator, or a merely contributory member of the committee. In either event, he faces the same requirements in terms of planning knowledge.

These possibilities are far from unrealistic, nor do they represent concerns of the distant past or future. As many product managers know from first-hand involvement, planning is a thing of the present. It is to satisfy these "now" needs that product management must be deeply concerned with planning management. As an added consideration we must not forget that in the marketing plan itself we are trying to develop an approach that reflects all marketing concerns. Just as we have seen a radical change in the scope of marketing involvement, which has led to the modern marketing concept, so have the needs of planning and the structural requirements of the marketing planning operation altered. When marketing had specific concerns, plans reflected them; as managerial horizons expanded, so did the planning requirement. The result has been a more complex, interrelated, and externally-oriented marketing plan.

What this means in practice is that even those approaches employed only in the past few years have already failed to meet the needs of contemporary planning. Nor is there any reason to believe that this evolution will not continue. This is not so problematic as it first appears since it reflects the modern concern with dynamics and is indicative of the plan's reality. In order to be effective, plans must have the flexibility required in other segments of the business operation. If planning could not be altered, its value as a management technique would be seriously questioned. It is these very changes that validate the premise and its contribution.

From the product manager's standpoint, however, these impose the additional necessity that he maintain his familiarity with planning and keep up with new techniques. However, if the fundamental underlying essence of the planning rationale is grasped and the requirement for planning recognized, the problem is a long way toward solution. Having such a reflexive base, it cannot help but meet contemporaneous requirements.

What Marketing Planning Is All About

Just as the primary purpose of any plan is to formulate objectives that represent essential accomplishments and the means by which they are to be secured, the market plan deals with the development of similar elements but within the perspective of the market activity. Therefore, the contents of the marketing plan will, in most instances, follow closely the general planning guide provided in the preceding chapter. The same statements of objectives, strategies, opportunities, problems, action programs, plus review and control techniques will be required, but considered in the context of marketing requirements. Here the plan will also provide the base for performance assessments that were previously discussed.

The exact nature of marketing is imprecise, but from the marketing mix and the modern marketing concept emerges a contemporary assessment of both marketing and the requirements of the marketing group in terms of its own operational needs and its interrelations with other corporate areas. This means that the marketing plan must reflect these concerns in the same magnitude as the marketing group. In many companies, therefore, the only major planning document is the marketing plan, and interwoven in it are the elements of total integration to the extent of direct or indirect marketing requirements. This is not totally satisfactory since there remain many areas in which marketing is not that intimately involved, finance and research, for example.

The question then arises as to the adequacy of the marketing plan as the vehicle to obtain fully integrated management planning. The resolution of the problem cannot be achieved by simple formulas since the requirements of the planning company, the effort they want to expend, the financial allocations for planning and, most important, the objective of planning itself all must be determinants in the final planning activity. The resolution that has usually been effected is in those situations where integrated management planning on a larger scale is required. A separate management plan is then employed which either replaces the marketing plan or becomes the focus for various internal subplans such as marketing, research and development, financial, or administrative.

There is another sound reason for this latter approach. The traditional marketing plan has been of one year's duration. This is not inconsistent with marketing requirements, whereas in total corporate involvement the outlook must be longer and broader, hence the long-range plans of five or more years projection. While marketing has also come to realize the requirement for long-range planning and commitment, the implication of using the marketing plan only as the base for long-range integrated planning becomes even more tenuous and another reason for management plans.

In either case the marketing plan is obviously still required. In the first instance, marketing planning only, we may find two approaches to the plan itself based on duration, the one- and five-year plans being the most typical; in the second case, integrated management plan, we may find a one- and five-year marketing plan as a component of the five-year management plan.

As we saw in the planning overview, the nature and scope of the one- and five-year plans differ. This is a logical expectation since they differ not only in perspective but in purpose. This can be better appreciated if we show a comparative listing.

Marketing Planning Perspectives Based on One Year

Primarily concerned with immediate objectives.

Primarily concerned with immediate strategies.

Extremely detailed and highly quantified.

Individual products may be delineated in terms of sales goals, profits, costs, and technical performance.

Individual markets may be segmented and detailed quantifications provided in terms of potential market share.

Competition may be explored in detail.

While areas other than marketing are considered such treatment is limited and the focus is principally on marketing.

Action programs are a principal feature; they are precise, chronological and affix responsibility.

Budgets reflect the one-year outlook.

Distribution is wider.

MARKETING PLANNING PERSPECTIVES BASED ON FIVE YEARS

While concerned with immediate (one-year) objectives also cover and emphasize long-range objectives based on five-year and intervening periods.

While concerned with immediate one-year strategies also covers and emphasizes long-range strategies based on five-year and intervening period.

Not as detailed as the one-year plan in certain aspects but more detailed in others.

Quantification exists but often in aggregates rather than in individual areas; total sales to a market rather than by major products or lines; major products rather than on specific products.

Individual products are not usually delineated beyond the one-year period unless in the identification of major situations or research requirements.

Individual markets usually treated as aggregates or in major segmentation only.

Long-range corporate objects are heavily emphasized commensurate with budget and capital requirements.

Competition again only considered in aggregate and then from impact and potential in overall rather than the highly specific implications.

Areas other than marketing per se are given further elaboration here than in the corresponding one-year plan.

The marketing plan will reflect these general approaches depending on planning cycle and that other most important factor, the prevailing management philosophy. Let us hasten to clarify that in planning there is no one approach. The evolution of the plan, its contents, outlook, orientation, structure, detail, and organization must be suited to the organization and management situation. Therefore, while it is possible to generalize and even to be specific in planning recommendations, they should be considered just that, guideposts along the planning road. Taking them and tempering them with business requirements is part of marketing management skill.

Who Plans the Market Planning Requirements?

We have examined four approaches to marketing planning: separate and independent one-year marketing plan; separate and independent five-year marketing plan; marketing plan integrated in one-year management plan; and marketing plan integrated in five-year management plan. We now must determine who does the planning and how many of these plans are required.

To answer the first is relatively simple since we have already explored this question. The product manager will often be assigned responsibilities for marketing planning; then, either individually or via committee, he will develop the plan format, content, and subsequently obtain management approval. If working individually, which is not the usual case in larger companies, he will be responsible for making contacts and assignments that will develop all of the data required in the plan. In the committee approach he or the director of marketing will conduct meetings, the intention of which is to make assignments, review recommendations, and ultimately develop the plan. In this instance the assignment of chairmanship or direction of the committee will depend on the decision of the marketing chief, who may elect to delegate this to the product manager rather than himself.

In either event the product manager will be responsible for specific segments of the plan rather than its totality. His will be direct responsibility for the product plan component, covered in detail in the next chapter, and correlation of those aspects directly associated with the product or based on other specific assignments throughout the committee.

As we saw before, the committee approach is often employed where degree of complexity, extent of integrative requirements and "size" of business are such that this is not only desirable but absolutely necessary to be effective. This satisfies simultaneously a number of requirements, including one that will be dealt with in greater detail further on in this chapter—namely, obtaining commitment to the plan.

Where single orientation prevails with the product manager as coordinator, the problems of obtaining information, assigning planning responsibilities, and obtaining information and commitment becomes a time-consuming operation in terms of his personal expenditures. With these problems in mind we can immediately comprehend why the product manager must commit a major portion of his time to planning and structure his operation accordingly.

The second question posed regarding the necessity for all of these plans is more difficult to reconcile only because it is more controversial. The need for marketing plans remains essentially unchallenged; the need for management plans is also without reasonable doubt.

However, when we come to the question of requiring both, the waters become murky indeed. Where long-range plans are made on a management planning basis, then the major elements of the marketing plan required in the five-year outlook are obviously incorporated; but reflecting on the planning content guides between one- and five-year emphasis, it would appear that the majority of detailed information required for one-year plans would not be found in the later years of the five-year cycle. The justification of two plans—a one-year and a five-year marketing and management plan—then becomes an effective compromise between one-year and five-year requirements of the planning cycle and the organization and structure of the plan itself.

It is possible to have two separate documents, a one-year and five-year marketing plan and a one-year and five-year management plan. Conversely it is also possible to exist quite nicely with only one document, provided planning sophistication has reached the internal point where variations in content and requirement can be contained in the same plan without strife and controversy.

In such an approach the detail and perspective required in one-year planning is provided by supporting content and documentation. But as the planning years stretch out, the content, organization, and perspective are altered accordingly. This enables a simpler planning process, at least insofar as duplication of paper work is concerned; yet it satisfies the needs of both detail and lack of detail in the relative situations.

One added problem is, again, the question of distribution and access to the management plan. It is a justification of separate marketing plans to call attention to the confidential nature of the management plan, and the marketing plan. What this involves is the age-old question of how much do people want to know of the total business. However, even where this problem is posed, there is the simple expedient already proposed: that of segmentation and distribution of the segmented plan on the premise of "need to know." In structuring and segmenting the plan in this manner, everyone with an obligation to fulfill has a "need to know" his part, so be sure to tell him. One of the great benefits of planning is this identification of requirement and purpose, and also the knowledge of such dependency. The plan lets personnel know what is expected of them.

Obtaining Marketing Planning Information

One problem facing the neophyte planner is informational sources. The problem, however, is not the lack of same, but an overabundance.

Selectivity in sourcing and data inclusion is difficult, particularly in initial planning activities where there is a tendency to be superfluous, which leads to the several-hundred-page plan that many have seen but few have read.

This commonly encountered situation stems from a lack of internal planning experience, direction, and the failure to identify those elements in the plan that are really meaningful to the business at hand. The identification of source has already been provided in preceding chapters where reference to data sources were indicated relative to planning and other product management informational requirements.

Ascertaining what elements are important to the planning function can only be developed with experience. It is possible, however, to save a great deal of effort by planning the plan and giving this problem full recognition, as well as trying to determine that which controls, contributes to, directs, or influences the market, product, and company both internally and externally; from this can be developed a list of factors to be considered in the plan. Once these are known, data sources will usually be found to cover most of the external elements: gross national product, population indices, and economic projections.

The internally important elements pose another problem entirely. Here, we often find that the individual markets that particularly concern the company are not documented, and specific information is not externally available. This is as true for existing markets as it is for future ones.

A revelation that comes from planning is the experience of seeing just how much is not known about the market. What is sometimes even more surprising to planners and corporations is how little the company often knows about itself. Merely discovering either of these situations justifies planning, but there is an even greater peripheral benefit: These revelations often lead to resolutions, and the planning program becomes not only the internal source for identifying these internal limitations, but the area in which corrections are promulgated.

Returning to the question of obtaining specific information in regard to company activities: This can be accomplished through corporate market analysis groups if they exist, or through the services of professional market analysts. Another frequently used technique is to obtain the majority of data through the marketing group's own activities. Translated into practical terms, this usually means questionnaires to marketing and sales management which extend even to individual line salesmen. While there are arguments over the efficacy of this method, it is possible with proper guidance and interpretation to obtain meaningful data in a limited amount of time.

Once the information is obtained, no matter what the source, there is still the difficulty of assembling, interpreting, and analyzing it. This will be done by either the product manager, director of marketing, or the committee. Even this formidable task can be simplified if the informational requirements are carefully limited. As it is, even if a minimum amount of planning documentation is included, an unbelievable bulk of data will be forthcoming; anything that can be done to minimize this without jeopardizing the efficiency of planning is highly desirable and will pay dividends in providing more time for constructive planning.

From this we can say that while it is impossible to tabulate all the individual items of planning importance since they are so variable, we can list a few planning practicals when it comes to data selectivity. Second, we can add a word of cheer, for with this experience the task of selection and development becomes easier since earlier data provides a base which, while requiring refinement and updating, does indicate fundamental requirements. Also, as maturity in planning occurs, so do selectivity and cogency. The process of selectivity should follow these four steps:

1. Review existing data in company regarding the product, market, and general indicator and business sensitivity factors relative to the company's existing business and products, planned business and products, and existing and future markets. Also, review previous plans or planning experience, internal capabilities, external capabilities, and planning budget.

2. Determine, insofar as possible, indicators and sensitivity factors that affect business, market, product, and planning.

3. Locate data relative to internal factors and external factors (commensurate with budgets).

4. Retain all data developed for reference during planning, reference in future planning, development of planning data bank, and use in other management or reporting situations.

In the above items there are two cogent aspects:

Planning budgets. In the preceding chapter it was mentioned that planning is costly. Direct and indirect costs are involved, and in seeking out planning information this cost factor should be reviewed since one of the most expensive phases of the planning cost is in obtaining planning information.

Planning data bank. Unless there is a procedure developed, computer or manual, for retaining planning data in a planning bank, there will be a tremendous duplication of effort in succeeding years. The development of discrete data requirements and a planning data bank will save this effort. Moreover it can mitigate planning tedium since it can be employed for updating during the period between formal planning activities; it can be incorporated in other informational systems, and serve as a component in review operations, and it can be used as a source for other documents and reports.

Obtaining Plan Commitment

Let us be careful to distinguish between commitment to planning, which we have already considered in the preceding chapter, and commitment to plan. It is this latter, which involves subscription to the contents of the plan, that we are now concerned with. When the plan is in process, various goals will be established. If the product manager is coordinating the planning, he will seek out these recommendations and obtain commitment. Where a committee is operating, it will follow the same procedure.

There are differing schools of thought in this area, but fundamentally two basic techniques are available: the "up" technique and the "down" technique.

The Up Technique

Recommendations for objectives and goals originate from individual line managers and then feed up through the management pyramid until they reach the product manager or the committee. As they pass through each management echelon, they are modified, if necessary, based on the knowledge, experience, perspective, and managerial requirements of succeeding managers. These composite recommendations reflect the thinking not only of management but of the individual responsible for the lowest level of execution. There are many problems with the procedure: it is time consuming, difficult to control, requires extensive communication, and often leads to the development of unacceptable objectives.

Conversely, there is much to recommend it since commitment is inherent, provided upper management's modifications are not drastic and the final goals represent the original thinking of the participants. Even where modification is required by marketing management the imposition of final objectives is facilitated in receipt and execution since all concerned parties were instrumental in their derivation. Many companies are using the up technique, and it has been found to be reasonably successful. Implementation of this procedure depends on time available, personnel available, basic corporate objectives, and management philosophy.

THE DOWN TECHNIQUE

Specific goals are basically derived from the committee or the product manager's individual contacts. They are then distributed from the top down to all lower echelons and comment and commitment are then solicited. In this instance the basic goals are established, but upon review by lower levels can be discussed, and where required, modified. This approach has the advantage of saving time and effort, since only a few individuals are involved in the initial developments and comparatively few in subsequent review, resolution, and finalization. This disadvantage is primarily psychological, due to lack of identification in initial stages; or it may be actual, due to lack of first hand knowledge of market, potential, and the business situation.

While these may not be the only possibilities, they do reflect techniques that permit early integrated planning and commitment to objectives by participants. It is possible, of course, for the director of marketing in concert with his managers to develop the objectives and then present them as finalization of the marketing plan. They would later be distributed to responsible elements serving as dicta. This procedure is rapidly falling into obsolescence since it is in direct opposition to the basic tenets of contemporary management, which espouse involvement and mutual commitment.

If either the up or down procedures are employed, it is necessary to have a commitment from management. Both techniques require that modifications of objectives, either the preliminary ones flowing down or the constructed ones flowing up, be anticipated; and management and manager must be willing to come to grips with the problems that this might entail. Therefore, when it is necessary to alter an objective predicated on either up or down factors, there should be an atmosphere that will permit such alteration. Ultimately, it is management's responsibility to establish the optimal goal, and with this responsibility goes the authority. This means that where conflicts occur, the final yes or no rests with management. However, where commitment by involvement is possible, one of the highest plan acceptance hurdles is surmounted: by consensus comes commitment, from commitment, accomplishment.

Sequential Timing and Interphasing with Planning Cycles

Where plan elements are required either for development of the marketing plan itself, or where aspects of the marketing plan are needed for the integrated management plan, the plan coordinator must be concerned with the sequential operations required for his plan and the management plan. In the initial development of the planning cycle these factors should be considered and adequate preparations made to allow this intermeshing. This point is reiterated in the discussion of the product plan.

In interlocking plans, date information is needed. And the exact nature of the data required should be portrayed in the planning cycle, with the responsible personnel or departments indicated. In this way the timetable can be adhered to and major delays circumvented.

Use of the Marketing Plan

Specific uses of the market plan will, to an expanded extent, depend on the marketing operation: "expanded" in the sense that several of the major uses have already been considered and will apply universally. The use of the plan in providing commitment has an unquestioned application regardless of marketing management specifics. Identification of problems, opportunities, and marketing knowledge, or the lack thereof, have also been mentioned, as has its use as a mensuration device.

More specifically, however, marketing can use the plan or elements for developing of subplans for sales, product management, advertising, promotion, and test marketing. Each of these would be highly individual and concerned only with elaboration of detailed programs in these restricted areas. The plan can also be used for developing other reports and isolating major activity areas. It can serve as the point of initiation for additional market research, development, or analysis, for concurrent studies of marketing interests, and as a device for internal development.

Elements of the Marketing Plan

There is no right or wrong marketing plan, no right or wrong structure, format, or series of elements that should be in the plan.

There are only those approaches that meet the need of the specific marketing or management situation. However, there are certain guides or basic elements that in one form or sequence or another will be found in most marketing plans; these can provide planners with a point of departure. The following indicated elements should be so considered; they represent suggested items and sequence that can be altered to serve the corporate and marketing need. In employing them, or considering them for employment, it is wise to remember the four overriding criteria against which all plans should be tested in terms of content and cogency. Regardless of its structure, the plan should tell us where we were, where we are, where we are going, and how we are going to get there. If these four specifics have been satisfactorily dealt with, the plan will be valid, pertinent and useful.

Now we come to the elements of the marketing plan. Examining each of them further will give some indication of the total content and scope of the marketing plan. Naturally, emphasis in each area will depend on the use of the plan, the existence of an integrated management plan, and the managerial requirement.

EXECUTIVE SUMMARY

This should be a short one- or two-paragraph document containing the plan's most important points. It is usually restricted to statement of financial objectives and the principal strategies to achieve them. It serves only to provide a succinct recap of the plan's most important features.

TABLE OF CONTENTS

This is exactly what it says it is; and while seemingly trivial, there is no greater frustration than hunting through the marketing plan to find what you want.

INTRODUCTION AND PLAN SUMMARY

The introductory part is to a large extent an extension of the executive summary. Guard against making it too long; aim for one page and provide only major elements: sales goals, profit goals, major strategies; and, in the one-year segment, major action programs may be important. Elements of the budget are also appropriate. The summary segment deals with an indication of the plan's content, scope, and organization. As years succeed each other, this becomes less important unless there are significant changes in the market or in planning.

REVIEW AND ANALYSIS OF THE PRESENT MARKETING SITUATION

This section serves the dual purpose of examining "where we were" and "where we are." Bear in mind that the recipients of the plan are not as familiar with the marketing activity of the corporation as is the writer of the plan. The purpose of this segment is to acquaint them with this information. The historic position of the company provides the base from which activity and position derive.

Care should be taken to provide analysis, which is often lacking because of overfamiliarity with the subject by plan writers. To state that the company's historic position in terms of market share has been 10 percent is not sufficient unless with this is the analysis of what significance 10 percent conveys. Is this good, bad, or indifferent performance? What of competitors? What are reasonable market-share expectations? These and similar facts provide the means by which the statement of past and present position is made meaningful.

PROBLEMS AND OPPORTUNITIES

These are most important statements and should include detailed documentation of the problem and its significance. To cite a problem is not enough unless it is put in perspective. Its significance, possibilities of correction, and cost of correction all must be indicated. Conversely, opportunities, unless expanded upon, are also relatively inadequate. There should be an analysis of the opportunity's significance and its possibilities for corporate exploitation.

OBJECTIVES AND GOALS

In the previous chapter we dealt with these at great length. There is no necessity to repeat it all, but it is worthwhile to emphasize the importance. There is no single more significant area than the statement of objectives; and even more cogent is its derivation. In the plan one practical fact is to state objectives clearly and concisely. Be certain that they are understandable and understood. Quantify where possible, and keep the number of stated objectives or goals to a realistic, practicable limit.

STRATEGIES

As we saw in the preceding chapter strategies are broadly speaking the "hows." Be sure that every objective or goal is supported with one or more strategies, and submit the strategies to careful scrutiny.

BUDGETS

The budgetary problem is so well known, there is no need to elaborate. Fit the budget statement to meet the established corporate requirements.

CONTROL AND REVIEW PROCEDURES

No plan can be established and then disregarded. This defeats both planning and managing. Provision should be made to review the plan periodically. Such review should report major elements, sales, profit, major action programs, and possible plan revisions. Bear in mind that as the plan changes, the reporting base can also change. If the base changes, accuracy of performance against plan is lost since reports will be against revision rather than the original. This is satisfactory provided annual review is made against original and revised plan to ascertain performance against both. Many companies report comparisons against both in every reporting period.

PLANNING ASSUMPTIONS

These, being tagged on at the end, may appear relegated to comparative oblivion. This is not correct; structurally they are viewed here as appendixes. The planning assumption is not an actual element of the active plan, but it does help provide the base of many discrete date projections.

ACTION PROGRAMS

These are considered as appendixes because of their significance in day-to-day operation. And in those situations where there is a distribution problem, the action program package can be readily separated from the body of the plan and individually distributed.

Contingency Planning

Not much, if anything, is seen regarding contingency planning. The reason for this is that no one does too much in the way of actual formal contingency planning. A contingency plan is a "what-if" type of plan; if the expectation of some particular strategy is not achieved, it provides an alternative strategy. Similarly, actions, opportunities, research objectives, or any other planning element could be employed as the basis for contingency planning.

While it is impractical to provide for every contingency, there is a place for such planning in highly speculative areas. Also, where sequential events depend upon succeeding activities, contingency planning provides alternative directions or action predicated on variable results from the intermediary steps. Therefore in those situations where such important "risk" areas exist, so should contingency planning. This is a relatively new aspect of planning and deserves further exploration. As precision in management is attained, less contingency requirements will be necessary; but they should be used consistently wherever multiple possibilities prevail. For our purposes, it is sufficient to note the availability of the technique and consider its use in specific situations.

Relationship to Product Plan

In the next chapter we deal with the separate product plan. This can be found as either a discrete document or a component of the marketing plan. Both approaches are considered, and no specific elaboration of this aspect is provided. One point to keep in mind is that where no separate product plan is prepared, the elements of same are interwoven in the marketing plan, and product-oriented specifics are included in the respective sections of it.

Presentation

Once the information required in the plan has been determined and the elements to be contained finalized, the above sequence or some satisfactory variation can be followed. However, it is important to carefully consider the above presentation, format, and layout. Many excellent plans have been poorly organized and executed. The effort expended in developing the plan warrants professionalism in printing, graphics, and presentation. This applies to the "book" or the plan presentation made orally or in writing to management and marketing.

Distribution

It cannot be overemphasized that the plan to be employed must be known. One of the major values of a marketing or management plan is to provide everyone with a concise explanation of what the company wants to do, how it wishes to do it, and what each individual or department is expected to accomplish.

From what has been said there can remain little doubt regarding the importance of marketing planning, the commitment necessary for effective planning, the requirement in time, money, and resources for planning, the necessity for constancy in the planning effort, and the relationship of product management to the planning activity. There is no limit to the importance of planning and the uses of the plan. It remains for the planners to live up to the promise.

16

The Product Plan

A RELATIVELY new concept is the separate development of a product plan per se. This document can stand on its own merits as a working tool for product or marketing management; and it can, in its entirety or by element extraction, be incorporated into the marketing plan. The generation of a separate product plan is based on the increased complexity of product management and the vital corporate concern expressed toward the product effort. Whether the plan is used for internal purposes in the marketing group or as a basis for integration into the overall planning endeavor, its structure is similar, and its value more than compensates for the required effort.

Obviously, the responsibility for such a plan falls directly to product management. Its detailed execution will depend on the organization and the status of the product-management group. Where only one product manager is involved, he will be called upon for preparation of the entire plan and, possibly, the coordination of the entire marketing plan. Where multiple product managers are involved, assignment of responsibility will depend upon their reporting relationships. Where they report to the chief marketing executive directly, they may also have to compile individual reports, which he will assemble and integrate. Where numerous product managers are present, they will report to a product director who will be responsible for the overall product plan and will assign specific individual product planning responsibilities to managers. They will then have the task of preparing the product plan for their brands, products, or lines; and he will integrate them. In such a situation, an extension of the planning cycle will have to be made consistent with preparation and assimilation of the product subplans into the product plan and subsequently the marketing plan.

The purpose of the product plan is to provide analysis of the product effort and to establish objectives, strategies, and action programs that are specifically oriented toward the product requirements. These must reflect concerns of marketing, sales, manufacturing, engineering, research, development, test marketing, advertising and promotion, since all are involved in the relationship of product to marketing reality. The product plan is also the place for development of the gross profit plan and the net profit derivation. This is a further example of the requirement for cycle integration.

From this it is immediately apparent that many of the requirements for product planning are similar. Much of what must be determined for the marketing plan is also important for the product plan and, conversely, what is developed for the product plan has application in the marketing plan. As stated in marketing planning, we do not plan the market, only the marketing activity. In product management, we must also maintain perspective; we do not plan the sale, create the profit or the market, but only that activity related to product that can support the sale, profit, and marketing effort.

Why Separate Marketing and Product Plans?

At first glance it may appear that the preparation of separate product and marketing plans is a duplication of effort. Where a relatively small product line and a compact organization exist, this may be so; however, in large companies with several hundred products in several different product lines, one or more of which are intended for distinct markets, the complexity of the plan for products alone is formidable. Couple this with the elements of the marketing plan and other interphased documents, and it becomes obvious that the most the plan could contain are extractions of major objectives, strategies, new products, and budgets, plus the identification of principal opportunities and problems. All could not be extracted, nor, for that matter, could the incorporation of action programs even begin to be attempted.

Therefore, while requirements of the marketing plan might be satisfied by including only these bare essentials, what of the requirements for operational effectiveness within the product group itself?

It is also worth noting that a similar situation exists with sales, advertising, and promotion, where separate operational plans derive if size and content militate against total inclusion in the former documents.

Thus we see that the reasons for separate plans stem from: (1) Product group need for formalization of action programs and total planning involvement; (2) Practical limitations of space and content in marketing and management plans; and (3) Integration of product management activity in the total planning effort.

Sequential Timing and Interphasing with Planning Cycles

Where·the separate product plan is to be developed, requirements for distribution and planning activities within the product group should be provided. Where the product manager is the coordinator, this is reasonably simple, and he can make the required provisions. Where he is not, at the first planning meeting he should be asked to determine time requirements and submit cycle recommendations. This, together with the requirements for the total plan, will be combined by the planning committee or the coordinator; from this the appropriate scheduling can be determined.

Another approach is to establish the schedule for submission and then leave the implementation within the product group to the product manager. If this is the case, he can develop his own internal cycle and develop requisite data. Either technique will result in the same accomplishments. Specific information for the marketing plan will be forthcoming along with a more comprehensive product plan.

Uses of the Product Plan

Once advocated and developed, what then? To what use is the separate product plan put? These, too, are valid questions. If for no purpose, then why bother? The answers more than reconcile such reservations.

First, the product plan is implemented on its smaller scale exactly as the more pervasive marketing or management plan. It provides the same control and review procedure as do its bigger brothers and similarly establishes objectives and strategies for the product activity. As such, it provides all the benefits and problems inherent in the planning premise. Again, in large-scale operations with all of the products and concerns, this is a real contribution.

Second, the distribution of the detailed products plan is not limited to the products group, just as the detailed sales plan is not restricted to the sales department. It is through the interchange of these extensive documents within the marketing group that harmonious blending of plans and actions is possible. At this level, interphasing occurs along with detailed planning to coordinate product and account; product and manufacturing plant; product management support calls and sales efforts; technical support and product management direction. It is here that special-emphasis products can be identified, key products developed and promoted, test marketing developed, and research recommendations promulgated.

The application of the product plan is limited only by the imagination of the product group manager, product manager, sales manager, marketing director, or the company.

Elements of the Product Plan

The product plan, like the marketing plan, has specific components. When considered specifically as a product planning operation, the perspective is quite limited. Only those concerns that directly relate to product are included, since in those situations in which specific product plans will be developed, we already encounter a degree of progress and sophistication in which a marketing plan will also be prepared; hence the broader requirements in the marketing plan will already be provided by the product manager in his capacity as coordinator. He will provide information that encompasses his managerial duties in full scope. Alternatively, this information may be obtained directly from responsible elements via assignment made in the marketing planning activity as indicated in the preceding chapter.

And so the components of the product plan have a very circumscribed perspective. In contradiction to the normal product management outlook, we turn introspective and are preoccupied with only the product function.

Thus, the following elements are of immediate concern. They provide a working outline of a typical product plan, one we shall refer to later in an example of a model product plan. Remember, however, all of these items need not be present in any given plan.

Product-oriented business outlook.

Product-oriented objectives or goals.

Product gross profit plan, by line and by specific products.

Product opportunities by product line, individual products, market segment, a new product, a key product, a potential key product.

Product problems: commercial, technical, profit, supply, manufacturing, competition.

Product strategies: commercial, technical, profit, supply, key product, key market, potential key product, potential key market, new product, test marketing, product modification, pricing, competitive.

Needed products.

Budgets, for product group, advertising or promotion.

Product action programs: commercial, technical, advertising, promotion, sales, test marketing, new product, key product.

Action programs: commercial, technical, profit, supply, key product, key market, potential key product, potential key market, new product, test marketing, product modification, pricing, competition.

In the last element, action programs, each item is separately listed. But these are often concurrently involved since the basic orientation is by product. It is the selection of actions relevant to product that becomes the criterion for action, unless it supports a nonproduct strategy.

For example, when delineating action on a specific product, advertising, promotion, commercial, technical, and other actions will be incorporated, and the total is the action program for the product. In other instances, the action may be on one specific activity; for example, profit improvement. The order and nature of events will be based on this and may include specific products, as well as general factors pertaining to the total profit improvement activity.

Product Orientation

As was said, the entire structure of the product plan is based on a product orientation. This is a perspective that differs radically from the customary, and one may well wonder at the exact meaning of the approach. Reference, however, to the above tabulation of elements and the product management hexagram, as well as the tools and techniques of product management, will quickly illustrate the specific product related planning requirements. It will also explain the whys of separate product centricity.

In order to do this effectively, however, the product manager should reflect on the purposes of the plan, which are essentially the same as the purposes of any planning function, and the use to which the plan will ultimately be put. Planning on this level, as seen, can serve a dual function: supplying information for the integrated plan and forming the nucleus for annual activity at the product management level in the ensuing year. Since this is the case, the planning cycle in the product plan must also be altered to correspond with the use.

If we are making two plans on two plan bases, one for incorporation in the larger integrated planning activity and the second for our internal application, we must reconcile these planning requirements with the short and long-range aspect of the marketing plan. In most cases, these later plans will be of one and five year's outlook.

The differences are even more important when the question of product planning arises. How valid is it to make a detailed five-year product plan with all supporting action programs delineated for a five-year projection? The solution to this problem once more returns to operational logic. There is little need nor much gain in such detailed planning for this long a time. Then the product plan to be used in conjunction with one and five-year marketing plans is redirected. The emphasis reflects the requirements we have already examined in considering this same problem in context of the marketing plan. While the outlook and specificity of the one-year plan is replete in detail, in the five-year projection we deal more with aggregates and less with specifics.

And so in product planning, the one-year product plan for internal use will be completely detailed; the input for the one-year plan on the integrated level will usually be restricted to: objectives, principal strategies, profit goals, new products, budgets, major opportunities, and problems. The five-year internal detailed product plan is not necessary, and the input for the five-year integrated plan then follows the direction of the data supplied for the one-year plan; but again it is more related to aggregate figures, key elements correlating with the identifications made in the integrated plan itself.

When conceived of in this manner, it is apparent that the application of logic and common sense is the salvation of the planning process. The entire premise, built on a logical base, strives for application

TABLE 8. *Product plan.*

	Internal		Marketing		Management	
	1-year	*5-year*	*1-year*	*5-year*	*1-year*	*5-year*
Business outlook	Detailed	Major	Major	Major	Highlights	Highlights
Objectives	Detailed	Major	Detailed	Major	Highlights	Highlights
Profit	Detailed	Aggregate	Detailed	Aggregate	Detailed	Aggregate
Opportunities	Detailed	Major	Detailed	Major	Highlights	Highlights
Problems	Detailed	Major	Major	Major	Highlights	Highlights
Strategies	Detailed	Major	Major	Major	Highlights	Highlights
New product recommendations	Detailed	Major	Detailed	Major	Detailed	Major
Budgets	Detailed	Aggregate	Detailed	Aggregate	Detailed	Aggregate
Action programs	Detailed	Major	Major	Major	Highlights	Highlights

of these dictates from initiation to completion. The level of planning should be commensurate with the practical applications of the plan.

To summarize these various product planning requirements, we can arrange them as in Table 8. Naturally, carryover of elements from one to five years' consideration, particularly as inputs into the five-year management plan, is predicated on the necessity of the element being projected forward from one year to the next; and there are many situations in which planned activity does extend over several years. However, since there is a funneling-down effect in the contents of the five-year plan, only what is meaningful for commitment should be included in the plan itself.

Similarly, where this tabulation indicates developing information for an internal product plan based on a five-year projection, and it was previously stated that such a plan would not or should not be developed for internal use, this is not a contradiction. What is implied is consideration of this planning requirement as it relates to informational necessities: data supplied by product management to management for inclusion in the five-year plan.

Therefore, while a certain amount of data will be required, it will not necessarily be expanded into a full-blown, full-scale internal product plan. However, we must take cognizance of the need for developing this information in order to schedule time and plan our own planning activities.

A Model Product Plan

Having just examined a modicum of product planning theory, it may be helpful to provide a product plan model in which these elements are incorporated. Since space does not permit a full plan to be developed here, we can indicate the skeleton and merely hint at the physiognomy that constitutes the total. It will, however, indicate the principles and some of the many individual components. The model (Appendix B) is based on a hypothetical company and must in no way be construed as representing any particular situation. With this firmly in mind, we can set the hypothetical scene.

The name of the company is the Imaginary Marketing Corporation, and it offers five principal product lines. Each line consists of several products and in total they number some 900 separate items. Profitability varies from line to line and product to product, but is known for each item. The corporation is integrated, has its own research, development, and manufacturing capability, but is primarily marketing oriented. Gross sales have been on the increase at an average rate of 9 percent per year, and corporate objectives have been furnished for the one- and five-year planning cycles. Gross profit averages 35 percent and has improved measurably in the last five years since the introduction of product management. Having this information, the product manager, who has been with the company for three years, has been requested to prepare a product plan to serve two purposes: It must constitute an internal annual operating plan for product development; and it must provide input data for one- and five-year marketing plans.

At this point it will be useful for the reader to look through the model plan in the appendix and then to refer back to it in the course of reading the rest of this chapter.

Implementation of the Plan

Using the product plan as a guide, we can see that the product manager would use the overall plan to estimate his performance quantitatively and qualitatively. To him, the most valuable of all would be the action programs. In this example, an action plan format was employed, which provided not only a comparison of action to strategy and objective, but included a working check-list for insertion of the date that action was commenced and completed, as well as space for a summary of result. This elevates the plan to a meaningful, working document that can be put to practical everyday use. If nothing else, this approach will force constant reference to the plan and its implementation, which is one of the principal objects of the plan and planning itself.

Referring once more to the model plan, the elements for 1971 implementation are clear and fully documented by appropriate action programs for the one-year period. The general indication of strategies and objectives that would prevail throughout the planning period, as well as identified opportunities and problems, is also provided.

In reviewing the plan with marketing management, the requirements for incorporation into the marketing or management plans can then follow, predicated on this information. Typically, the principal and salient factors illustrated in the tabulation previously provided would be used. Using our model, the following would be illustrative of the objectives, strategies, and other elements that would be used in the integrated plans:

Objectives
    To support planned sales.
    To achieve planned profitability.
Strategies
    Comprehensive response to competition.
    Emphasis on key product and key market marketing.
    Optimization of sources.
    Sale and promotion of most profitable products.
    Systems and process selling.
Needed products
    New electronic device for sensitivity recordings.
    Consumer goods version of existing industrial products.
    Counteroffering to ABC companies' line.
Budgets
    Product group.
    Advertising and promotion.

In this way, it can be seen that from the entire plan developed for use within the product group, only the most significant points are extracted and used in the integrated plan. Naturally, the degree and detail of interphase will vary from company to company; and in some instances, the entire plan may be completely incorporated into the marketing plan, but summarized when included in the management plan. Whichever the technique, the principle will be found essentially constant in practice.

The effort expended in preparing the product plan should also be considered in the total environment of product management. Earlier in the book it was mentioned that all product-oriented efforts were essentially educational and that because of the diverse nature of the job itself, no scrap of information ever went to waste. This is not to imply that any effort in planning is wasted. Rather, there is just the additional, happy thought that above the direct application of data developed in planning, there is also the benefit of more than 1,001 other pieces of information obtained, sorted, analyzed, and indelibly imbedded in the mind of the manager. There it lies ready and waiting for that time when it may be the key required to unlock some product management door.

PART SIX

The Future

17

The Future of Marketing

PRODUCT managers may wonder why we start with the future of marketing rather than that of product management. The answer is quite simple: To approach the future of the product manager and the concept of product management, we must be deeply concerned with what the gods portend in their unfathomable wisdom for marketing. Unless there is some revolution yet unseen and totally illogical, the future of both is inseparably intertwined, and as grows marketing, so grows product management.

Looking forward, however, requires that we look backward and sideward first. To some extent we have already examined the past and from it have ascertained what created the milieu from which the modern marketing concept evolved. In so doing, we also gazed at the present and found that like management techniques, marketing has not remained static. It too has developed to the point where the classic marketing concept has been substantially modified to encompass the activities and responsibilities requisite in undertaking marketing in the contemporary business atmosphere. These developments were not incidental but the consequence of an awareness that dynamic changes in market and products would lead to new requirements for "doing business." This evolution carries far-reaching implications. It

349

provides full appreciation of scientific and technological advances as they apply to the consumer, the market, the product, methods of manufacture, alterations in the conduct of business, the needs of the market place, and the necessity of integrated business management. It also indicates the revelations of behavioral sciences that must be applied if the marketing effort is to be successful.

All of these multifaceted considerations carry with them a host of additional implications and contribute both restrictions and opportunities. It is, however, only from recognition of their influences that the structure of the future marketing effort can be projected. It is apparent already that the requirements of the marketing effort differ vastly in contemporaneous business activities from even such a short time as ten years ago. This is the result of accelerated scientific and technological developments, coupled with sociological changes. These two phenomena are now recognized to be self-catalyzing, and their interrelations will create the market of the future. Added to this is the external influence of the marketing organization as it responds to and generates effects in both of these dimensions.

Characteristics of Business in the Future

Economists, sociologists, academicians, and business savants are unanimous in their opinion that the extent, nature, and rate of the technical and social revolution will accelerate exponentially. This indicates that despite attempts to assess marketing ten, twenty, or fifty years hence, specificity is impossible. But generalities do provide reasonably accurate indicators that relate to the technological, market, and business operation. Each must be assessed in relation to its application in effecting many of these dimensional parameters and their integrated influences.

From this it is immediately apparent that we can identify certain characteristics of business in the twenty-first century.

Recognition of market's influence on marketing.

Creation of new markets.

Necessity for new ways of doing business.

The development of new business.

Impact of a changing economy.

Impact of a changing technology.

Impact of a new sociology.

Future development and refinement of scientific management.

Ability for greater internal and external control.

Increased legislative influences, product, environmental, and commercially oriented.

Increase in relative size of market.

Increased size of companies.

Increased emphasis on planning.

Increased consumer education.

Greater effects of automation in terms of business management,
business operations, and business usage.

Tremendously rising costs of research and development.

Tremendously rising costs of business operations.

Radical restructuring of the economy.

Increased competitive pressures.

Increased necessity for risk minimization.

Increased necessity for forecasting.

Dramatic rise in market research and market identification requirements.

Radical revision in management structures.

Increased complexity of products.

Any of these elements in themselves would be formidable; but
taken in combination, they portend an expense and complexity of
business far beyond our present day involvements, which are themselves vastly more costly and complicated than those encountered in
preceding years. All of this necessitates recognition for total corporate
involvement to effect economic survival and growth in the markets of
the future.

The Increasing Role of Marketing

From this evolutionary process, it is apparent that the marketing
activity will increase in importance, viability, and vibrancy since it is
essential that product and company are integrated to meet as well as
create demands in the marketplace. This involves far greater emphasis on integrated and coordinated functions within the company,
as well as increased market responsiveness and greater ability for accurate determination of market requirements. The challenge, therefore, will be to assemble, analyze, and integrate a dramatically increased information base and to then develop products and methods
for marketing them commensurate with the need and the customer.
This involves an ability to respond to market requirements and to
develop new products, as well as new ways to market these products.

The very size of market and companies will obviously create both internal and external complications. Marketing now, through product management, performs an integrative function. And the necessity for this will increase as does the market, the company, and its anticipated complexities. Assuming, therefore, that this fundamental role will remain within the sphere of the marketing group it is immediately apparent that there is a bright light within the crystal ball. This illumination reflects the brilliance of the outlook and marketing's relative position in the business management family.

Just as marketing now touches base with all operational and functional business areas, it shall continue to do so. Its relationship to market analysis, identification, and cultivation has in recent years been stressed and will in ensuing years carry even additional importance. Recognition of back integration, from market to company, will become one of the single most important functions of the future marketing organization. The second will be need analysis, and the third, the creation of new imaginative and dynamic marketing techniques.

In sum and substance then, we can say that market's zenith is yet to come. Future marketing successes, like the golden apples, merely await the plucking.

18

The Future
of Product Management

As we have already seen, the future of product management is intricately interwoven with that of marketing. Historically, product managers reported either to general management or higher management echelons. As further refinements ensued and with the alteration of marketing's roll in the management and direction of the corporate effort, the product manager attained his present reporting relationship and became an effective member of the marketing team.

From indications relevant to the future complexity of both market and marketing, there is little reason to doubt that marketing will continue in its function with even greater emphasis on coordination, integration, responsiveness, planning, identification of opportunity, and market exploitation; commensurate with this is the continued centrality of product. The concept of product management has, then, developed primarily as an outgrowth of the recognition for centralization of these responsibilities.

Future outgrowth, therefore, holds no question as to the need for increased recognition of these requirements and additional provisions for their accomplishment. The question that does arise is whether product managers will continue to function as they presently do, or indeed whether product management itself will remain constant. To give full credence to present possibilities, it must be acknowledged that the philosophy of product management is by dint of its own youthfulness still far from completely proved. The test of time has yet to be met.

Alternative Future Approaches

Looking to the past and comparing it with the present, one cannot help marveling at the relative progress of product management and, moreover, the refinement and solidification of the concept and its functions. This, in management sciences, is indeed progress. It is, if nothing else, indicative of a validity in time and place. To project the future based on contemporaneous value is not valid.

To many practicing product managers, this may appear heretical and, to those not at present engaged in product management, equivocal. This is not the case, for as a personal assessment, optimism is mandatory. Unfortunately, it is simpler to be subjective than objective. Therefore, in attempting objectivity, it is necessary to admit the possibilities of major alternative approaches in the future. Two of the most likely are that product managers will report directly to corporate management, or that the concept will be restructured with further emphasis on coordinative responsibility.

There are already indications that one or both of these may be the ultimate outcome since some critics of the system have vociferously rendered strenuous reservations concerning the ability of any one individual to deal completely with the innumerable ramifications and disciplines with which the product manager is involved. Examining these two possibilities further, we could envision structural and consequent operational implementation in several contexts.

In considering the approach in which product managers report directly to corporate management, we can readily see that the product manager would be separated from direct responsibility within the marketing group, and his primary reporting authorities would be via corporate or overall business management. The reasons for this are, of course, inherent in the requirements we have already considered regarding product management activity, coordination, planning, and relations with corporate functions. With a prognosis of more stringent concerns in each of these areas, the obvious need is for a person in whom are vested coordinative, integrative, and allied responsibilities. These are activities that the product manager is more than familiar with and which he by experience and historical position can perform. Why then divorce him from the marketing effort where such requirements will yet be manifested? Marketing will have its own objectives. And these will, by virtue of its expanded participation in the total direction of the corporate enterprise, be more closely allied to the perspectives of total corporate management objectives. But while this may be the case, marketing must maintain its own, somewhat more circumscribed perspectives; in the final analysis its duties are related to just marketing and not the total integration of the business.

As business expands then, and larger, more complex corporations develop markets that become fragmented and larger, will marketing not have its own obligations? And can these be adequately fulfilled and still allow the product manager to function as a coordinator when his own particular product problems become magnified? The reply to this query is probably no.

This is not to demean the importance of marketing; indeed we have already acknowledged the anticipated increase in responsibilities of marketing, both within its own rights and as a factor in total corporate direction. However, it does do justice to the problems that will be essentially marketing oriented and which will consume that majority of the product managers and all those involved in developing, planning, and sustaining the marketing group in order to meet challenges and to realize attainment of marketing and profit objectives.

The possibilities of altering the reporting relationship of product management from marketing to general management are predicated here on assessment of the nonmarketing responsibilities in which product management is now involved, and in which it will become increasingly involved in the corporation to evolve. If these intercorporate nonmarketing interphasings are considered, as opposed to the directly marketing related responsibilities of the product manager, it must be acknowledged that a substantial portion of this time is spent in planning and coordinative responsibilities that are not a direct responsibility of marketing. It is only from this standpoint that the premise is promulgated of redirecting the authoritative relationship.

Now that we have examined this approach more thoroughly, it must be acknowledged that it does not satisfy the requirements for integration and direct product management that would still exist within the marketing group, regardless of its status in the corporation. So while there remains the clear developmental alternative, if such an evolutionary course were to be pursued, it would carry with it the very definite implication that product managers would still be required at the marketing level; and it might reflect a dichotomy wherein corporate responsibility with emphasis on certain responsibilities presently assigned to product management would be within the realm of the corporate integrated function; others more directly associated with the marketing activity would remain under the auspices of a product manager who would continue to report to the marketing director.

Now let us consider the restructuring of the concept, with a further emphasis on coordinative responsibility. It has already been stated that business is becoming more complicated, harried, and hectic. Couple this with exorbitant operational costs and the pressing requirements for insurance against new product failure; the coordinative activities of the past pale when contrasted to those of the future. One of the primary reasons for product management's present position is due to necessity.

It is, therefore, not difficult to envision a future situation where product management responsibilities are redefined to the extent that marketing will either divest itself of certain integrative responsibilities or become increasingly responsible. If this trend prevails, it is not unrealistic to postulate the possibilities of subdividing product management responsibilities to the extent that the coordinative responsibility would be vested in a separate position. Or we may continue to see future development of product group or marketing directors whose primary responsibility will not be that of the management of the product per se, but individual product managers reporting to them. There are strong indications that this approach is already finding acceptance, and of the two possibilities, this is the one that appears most probable.

Stabilization and Flexibility

From whichever vantage point we consider the theory of product management, whether it be predicated on present implementation or extended in either of the two variants indicated, product managers and management should take heart since there is no implication or question of the value, contribution, and necessity for continued emphasis and further growth of the product management concept. Structural limitations and reorganizational considerations do not invalidate its values.

Considering the youthfulness of the concept, possible structural alterations are not unexpected. This is also to be anticipated because of change. If the marketing activity is to be sustained, it must be flexible; if it must be flexible, the components of the marketing group must reflect this flexibility. If this capacity should be anywhere demonstrable, it should be in the realm of product management, since if either the position or the man cannot respond to variations in the market and in the means for attaining success in such markets, the purpose of marketing and the function of product management is self-negating.

Product management has already demonstrated this capacity for change. The very fact that the direction of product management has altered—product directors, product group managers, product coordinators—is attributable to this inherent responsiveness. Flexibility within the concept also demands selective application and emphasis of elements in those particular segments of the function where selectivity will reap rewards. This implies adaptability, another test of utility, which the ideology, technology, and reality of product management have repeatedly confirmed. All these standards have been met, but time must still elapse before structure, responsibility, and reporting relationships ultimately solidify.

If the concept of product management is left unadulterated to the basic extent of retaining flexibility and remains centrally concerned with the six key functions already discussed: product, market, planning, forecasting, profit, and coordination, it cannot help but retain its viability, responsiveness, and individuality.

Responsibility and Authority

One more conflict should be reviewed, an entity that may never be fully resolved: the conflict between responsibility and authority. This has been approached here through implementation of an authority responsibility index: a solution that may not satisfy all but can, if nothing more, provide some illumination in one dark corner. But what of this problem in the future? With marketing taking an even more decisive role and with greater dependency on right decision, what of the poor but righteous product manager? Can he be expected to continue operation merely as the bastion of gross profit and the ubiquitous coordinator? The answer to this is not clear. Much depends not only on the man, the circumstance, and the product, but on the actions and reactions of the management team.

In a general sense, major authority shifts are not anticipated; the balance will most likely be retained. This is not caused by lack of confidence or ability, but is another indication of the position's requirements and technique. Too much authority contradicts the product manager's function; consequently, his future will primarily mirror his past.

Marketing and product management will in their ultimate analysis continue to be concerned with many functions that now consume their time and talents, although emphasis on individual components will shift. The principal problem of trying to put round companies in square markets will remain. As time goes by, the problem will expand with company and market, leading to the need for increasing ability to accomplish this imperative.

The future is never clearly known. The past and present provide tantalizing hints, but surprises always exist. And that is for the best. More relevant is that regardless of specifics, the unfulfilled product management vision that we started is no longer unfulfilled. Visionary, yes, but no longer a vision.

APPENDIX A

Three Typical Job Descriptions

Product Manager

The Product Manager is responsible to the Vice-President–Marketing for the overall supervision and efficient operation of the Marketing Division Product Sales Departments in a manner which is compatible with obtaining the maximum volume of profitable sales.

He is charged with executing policies, procedures, and programs, as established by the Vice-President–Marketing.

RESPONSIBILITIES AND AUTHORITY

Within the limits of his approved program and the company policies and control procedures, the Product Manager is responsible for, and has commensurate authority to accomplish, the fulfillment of his assigned responsibilities. He may delegate to members of his organization appropriate portions of his responsibilities, together with proportionate authority for their fulfillment, but he may not delegate or relinquish his overall responsibility for results or any portion of his accountability.

ACTIVITIES

1. *Management Responsibilities*
   a. Establish, consistent with the policies established by the Vice-President–Marketing, those programs and procedures for each Product Sales Department which will assist the field organization in obtaining the optimum volume of profitable sales of each division's products.
   b. Review and approve sales quotas recommended by the respective Product Sales Managers before submitting these recommendations to the Vice-President–Marketing for approval.
   c. Continually evaluate competitive conditions, technical advances, and market potentials, recommending extent of participation, design changes, and both short- and long-range product development.
   d. Supervise and assist individuals reporting directly to him, delegating proportionate authority to carry out their assigned responsibilities.
   e. Assist in the formulation and establishment of advertising, marketing, and sales promotion programs for the company's products.

361

f. Coordinate large job and/or systems activity and negotiation.

g. Exercise general supervision through the respective Product Sales Managers over the operation of the Product Sales Department, including selection and administration of personnel involved.

h. Establish and maintain a uniform product service procedure which will provide product service by the divisions or manufacturing plants consistent with the best interest of the company and its customers.

2. *Control and Financial Responsibilities*

a. Review and approve expense and capital equipment budgets, as prepared by the Product Sales Managers, before submitting these budgets to the Vice-President–Marketing for approval. He is responsible for operating within approved budgets.

b. Approve all expenditures, as prescribed by other established policy, not exceeding limits imposed by the Vice-President–Marketing.

c. Provide for necessary protection of company property within his control.

3. *Marketing Responsibilities*

a. Establish, consistent with the price policies set by the Vice-President–Marketing, the criteria by which the Product Sales Managers establish the price levels for their respective divisions' or manufacturing plants' products. Obtain Manufacturing Division or Manufacturing Plant Manager's approval of prices offered below the established minimum price level.

b. Assist, through membership on the Distributor Policy Committee, in the establishment of distributor policies and channels of sales, including selection and approval of distributors.

c. Coordinate Product Sales Departments' activities with the Marketing Division Managers to obtain the maximum effectiveness of the overall marketing effort.

4. *Product Planning and Engineering Responsibilities*

a. Review and approve each Product Sales Manager's program on new products to be marketed and desired modifications to existing products.

b. Keep abreast of developments and manufacturing programs directly related to product planning, advising the Product Sales Manager when alternative action should be taken.

c. Collaborate with Marketing Division Managers to obtain maximum effectiveness of promotion plans involving products.

d. Assure the maintenance of an effective and efficient application engineering staff, within each Product Sales Department, capable of meeting the marketing requirements.

    e. Determine, in conjunction with the Product Sales Manager, what action is required to correct field problems arising out of product failure, quality, or customer service, working out corrective measures with the appropriate members of the Manufacturing Division or Manufacturing Plant.

    f. Establish training program at Headquarters Sales Department for sales personnel, as well as for distributors and customers.

5. *Personnel Responsibilities*

    a. Develop and maintain a sound oragnization in each of the Product Sales Departments.

    b. Submit recommendations for personnel changes and salary adjustments to the Vice-President–Marketing for approval, in accordance with established procedures.

    c. Conduct periodic appraisals which will judge the performance and potential ability of those employees reporting directly to him. Assume responsibility through delegated channels for similar appraisals being made of other supervisory personnel.

    d. Encourage and assist in the best possible communication with all employees to secure an informed, cooperative, and efficient organization.

RELATIONSHIP TO OTHERS

1. *Vice-President–Marketing*
He is accountable to the Vice-President–Marketing for fulfillment of his functions, responsibilities, and assigned duties.
2. *Managers–Marketing Division*
He will maintain close liaison with the Marketing Division Managers to insure the optimum coordination between headquarters and the field marketing organization.
3. *Marketing Division Staff*
He will collaborate with other members of the Vice-President–Marketing's staff to insure that the Division is meeting the commercial requirements consistent with profitable operations.
4. *Division and Manufacturing Plant Managers*
He will work closely with the Managers of the Manufacturing Division and Plants to insure compatibility of the Marketing Headquarters Departments with their operations, objectives, and Company goals.
5. *Vice-President–Manufacturing*
He will coordinate with the Vice-President–Manufacturing with respect to Product Planning and Product Development activity commercially desirable to meeting Company objectives.

Product Manager [*]
Tar & Chemical Division

RESPONSIBLE TO: Sales Manager

BROAD SCOPE OF ACTIVITY

1. To acquire and maintain a high degree of knowledge of the markets and industries in which assigned products are sold.
2. Supervision and coordination of commercial sales activities of assigned products as a staff function.

SPECIFIC RESPONSIBILITY AND AUTHORITY

A. *Sales and Business Development*
   To acquire and develop an understanding of, and be familiar with, specific markets and industries which could become major users of assigned products.
   1. To develop, recommend and coordinate marketing programs leading to the expansion of profitable sales volume of assigned products.
   2. To innovate ways to expand Koppers' business opportunities through development of new markets or uses for assigned products and through the addition of new products to satisfy customers' needs.
   3. To make sales calls with Sales Representatives and/or Districts Sales Managers to get firsthand information on trends and conditions in the market and/or industry and to aid the Districts in their sales efforts.
   4. To attend sales conferences, association meetings, conventions to promote sales of Koppers' products and services.

B. *Planning*
   1. To originate, develop and recommend marketing programs and techniques designed to give Koppers a position of stature and leadership within the industry and/or market for assigned products.
   2. To develop and recommend sales objectives for assigned products within specific markets or industries, including sales volume and profit forecasts.

[*] Courtesy Koppers Company, Inc.

3. To develop and recommend plans and programs to achieve assigned goals.

C. *Supervision*
1. To assist the Sales Manager in the training of Sales Representatives; this involves
    a. Selling techniques.
    b. Uses of assigned products.
    c. Competitive situations likely to be encountered.
    d. General market picture of assigned products.
2. To coordinate and facilitate the exchange of information between sales districts, Product Development Department and between units of the Sales Department.
3. To coordinate activities of the districts for assigned products, involving
    a. Sales coverage.
    b. Customer relations.
    c. Customer complaints.
    d. Product performance information.
    e. Improvement of Sales Representatives' effectiveness.

D. *Administration*
1. To recommend merchandising policies for assigned products within specific markets and/or industries, such as
    a. Sales prices.
    b. Terms of sales.
    c. Discounts.
2. To continually study the potential and actual demands for assigned products and their profitability. To recommend to the Sales Manager
    a. Products which should be dropped.
    b. Improvements to present products which are required to expand present markets.
    c. New products which can be profitably integrated with the present line.
    d. Levels of inventories to be maintained to assure proper customer service.
3. To analyze the activities of competition on assigned products and keep management informed on the following:
    a. New competitors.
    b. New competing products.
    c. New merchandising policies.
    d. New prices.
    e. New sales promotion programs.
4. To prepare special studies and reports in connection with assigned products, as may be requested by the Sales Manager.

E. *Programs and Budgets*
   1. To collaborate with the Sales Manager in the preparation of three-month sales estimates and the annual and three-year sales programs for assigned products.
   2. To review sales, by industry and customer, for the purpose of determining progress toward sales goals for assigned products.

F. *General*
   1. To assist the Manager, Advertising and Sales Promotion, in the selection, planning and evaluation of advertising and sales promotion programs.
   2. To collaborate with the Manager, Advertising and Sales Promotion, in the preparation of technical sales literature.
   3. To coordinate his activities for assigned products and cooperate with other Koppers Divisions or Departments in matters of mutual concern.

G. *Authority*
   To operate within the limits of authorized policies, pricing schedules and procedures.

MEASUREMENT OF PERFORMANCE

1. The strengthening of Koppers' position in the specific markets and industries.
2. Volume of profitable sales and its relation to quota and programs for assigned products.
3. The soundness of policies and procedures recommended to the Sales Manager.
4. The initiative and imagination reflected in ideas for new sales and business opportunities.
5. The cordiality of relations which exist between the Product Manager and other units, both within and outside the Corporation.

Group Brand Manager
A Food Products Company

BASIC RESPONSIBILITIES

Under the general direction of the Director of Marketing, is responsible for providing overall guidance, coordination, and direction in the marketing of all products in his assigned product group to achieve stated profit and marketing objectives within the framework of Division and Company policies, budgets, and long-range plans.

SPECIFIC DUTIES

1. Develops and recommends to Director of Marketing overall objectives and strategies, both near- and long-term, for the marketing of his assigned product group, in support of objectives and strategies of the Division.

2. Reviews and counsels Brand Managers in the development of volume, share of market, and profit objectives for their assigned products, together with complete marketing plans and programs for the achievement of those objectives; insures coordination of plans and programs within and beyond his assigned product group.

3. Oversees the development of the most profitable line of products within his assigned product group, through planned introduction of new varieties and regular review and suspension of unprofitable varieties.

4. Collaborating with the Director of Marketing Research, develops and maintains a continuous program of research and analysis to obtain information essential to the effective marketing of products in his assigned group.

5. Oversees and counsels with his Brand Managers in the development of sales and share-of-market forecasts for products in his assigned group, together with the analysis of sales and product performance reports.

6. Oversees and counsels with the Brand Managers in establishing and maintaining continuous programs of coordinated commercial research for their assigned products to develop and interpret factual information regarding consumer needs and preferences, competitive conditions, market position, and industry trends and trade practices.

7. Oversees and counsels with Brand Managers in developing advertising plans and programs for their assigned products, in line with approved advertising policies and budgets and in coordination with advertising plans and programs of other products and product groups.

8. Oversees and counsels with Brand Managers in the development of coordinated merchandising and promotion plans, schedules, circulars, and materials for their assigned products.

9. Oversees and counsels with Brand Managers in their development of advertising, merchandising, and other expense budgets for products and activities under his direction, presenting consolidated budget recommendations for management approval.

10. Insures proper planning, scheduling, and coordination in the development, testing, and market introduction of new and improved varieties and packs for his assigned product group.

11. Oversees and counsels with Brand Managers as they maintain prices, terms, and discounts for products in his assigned group at competitive, profitable levels; recommends changes in line with company policies, sales, profit objectives, and applicable laws and regulations.

12. Keeps continuously informed of industry and trade developments, makes periodic field sales and factory visits. Analyzes trends and recommends changes, as appropriate, in production and distribution arrangements for his assigned product group; participates in professional, industry, and trade association meetings and other activities.
13. Keeps continuously alert to ideas for new varieties, new products, and other new developments that are potentially applicable to business, referring such ideas through appropriate channels to the New Products Department for evaluation and development, if merited.
14. Presents overall marketing strategy recommendations for his assigned product group at the Annual Strategy Meeting, introducing Brand Managers for individual product strategy presentations.
15. Selects, appoints, trains, periodically counsels, evaluates, and recommends changes in personnel status of Brand Managers and other employees assigned to his direction.
16. Maintains contact with key General Office and field sales personnel and with important customers to follow up on marketing programs and to keep informed on needs of the sales force and on marketing conditions throughout the country.
17. Periodically reviews customer and consumer complaints and suggestions concerning products in assigned group and oversees Brand Managers response and follow-up.

APPENDIX B

Model Product Plan

1971–1975 Product Plan
The Imaginary Marketing Corporation

Drafted September 1970 by Mr. I. M. Wise, Product Manager

Approved:

_____ V.P.—Marketing

_____ V.P.—Sales

_____ Executive V.P.

_____ President

1971–1975 Product Plan
The Imaginary Marketing Corporation

Contents

1971–1975 Product Plan
The Imaginary Marketing Corporation

Executive summary

The products department plans gross profits of x percent in 1971, predicated on planned sales of \$ x mm in this period. This will increase to y percent aggregate gross profit in 1975, based on gross dollar sales of \$ y mm, which represents an increase in average profitability of z percent and, \$ x mm sales. This is x percent above anticipated market performance and constitutes an x percent gain in average performance over the preceding five years in both product and sales dollars. These continued improvements will be obtained by primary emphasis in 1971 on:

Increased sales of product line A.

Increased control over low profit items.

Effective liaison with manufacturing, developing additional supply and profit capability.

Projected improvements in critical plant processes.

Withdrawal of several items in product lines C and E.

Implementation of key-product marketing concept.

I BUSINESS OUTLOOK

Predicated on last year's performance, we enter into the new year from a position of continued growth that reflects outstanding performance in our economic and marketing sectors. These are admittedly in contradiction to the national economic indexes and past general business performance. Considering the virtually unanimous prognostications for caution in the overall economy—increased effects of inflation, "tight money," continued governmental controls to curb inflationary tendencies, lower reported net earnings, lower inventory to sales ratios, moderate rate of new housing starts, and anticipated rise in cost of living—all indicators portend a continuation of the present, unsettled business and economic outlook, we are in a unique position. There is every reason to believe that this basic situation will prevail over the planning period (1971–1975) with little major resolution. All of these considerations must temper our enthusiasm and require careful monitoring of the market, particularly in those segments where our products are now sold.

Despite these indications our own projections, relating as they do to past performance under similar conditions, still indicate good performance, and our anticipated gross sales and profit increases will continue at a slightly higher level. Contrasting this to national performance and those of other specific market segments, this means that we will outperform both the national averages and the market. This outlook is based on the following assumptions:

1. Continued use of product line D in government contracts.

2. Improved process and supplies of product line E which has application in several consumer sectors projected to exceed current position and sales.

3. Continued consumer requirements in critical basic products which unless a major economic setback were to occur, would still sell at levels correlated to population increase.

These elements lead to the conclusion that despite the economic downturn and projections of similar performance in industry and the national economy, our position will reflect advances at the rates and to the levels indicated.

II OBJECTIVES

1. To support planned sales indicated in Table 1, Appendix I.

2. To achieve plan profitability by product line, indicated in Table 1.

3. To reduce, consolidate, and maintain product line with xxx products in 1971 and yyy products in 1975.

4. Control products via:

Selection of profitable key and potential key products for major marketing emphasis.

Elimination of low profit profits.

Use of market, product, and profit life-cycle analysis.

5. Improve marketing response: identification and analysis of competitors and competitive situations as well as the development of appropriate countermeasures and strategies.

III PRODUCT OPPORTUNITIES

Primary opportunities lie in the following areas:

1. Sales of product line A to consumer or industrial markets.

2. Profit improvement in product line D via:

Packaging alteration.

Mass sales in bulk.

Revision of process.

3. Emphasis on product line D for government contracts. This is projected to continue from 1971 through 1976.

4. Modification of products in line C.

5. Development of new products for growing industrial requirements in electronic medical instrumentation.

6. Revision of new product introduction techniques to be implemented in 1971.

Specific action programs to implement activities relative to these opportunities will be found in the appendix.

IV PRODUCT PROBLEMS

1. Cost of product line D. Already opportunities for improvement have been indicated and action programs initiated for such correction in 1971.

2. Competitive pressure on product lines A and E:
   Price.
   Supply.
   Market attrition.

3. Size of product line.

4. Average profitability in product line B.

5. Manufacturing delays requiring possible plant expansion. Recommendation and terms of reference have been included in the manufacturing and engineering plan. (See separate Manufacturing and Engineering 1971–1975 Plan.) Product management has been working closely with manufacturing and engineering in the development of this study, and long-range consumption requirements have been considered, as well as potential return on investment. This new facility may also provide increased capacity for production of additional products in several other product lines.

V STRATEGIES

Objective No. 1
To support planned sales indicated in Table 1.

Strategies
1. Comprehensive response to competitive strategies and actions.

2. Exploitation of technical service at all levels, including:
   Support calls.
   Demonstrations.
   Instrumentation.

3. Release of new products, detailed in Appendixes I and II.

4. Increase advertising and promotion on:
   Product line A.
   Product line D.
   Specific key and potential key product, indicated in Appendixes I and II.

5. Expand on key market approach.

6. Attain position as primary supplier in government contracts on selected electronic equipment.

7. Improve sales forecasting techniques.
8. Implement closer liaison with operational and functional areas.
9. Restudy distributorship possibilities.

Objective No. 2
To achieve planned profitability by product line indicated in Table 1, Appendix I.

Strategies
1. Optimize sourcing
    Internal.
    Purchased products and materials.
    External contractual manufacture.
    Imports.
2. Continuous review and analysis of costs of manufacturing, packaging, shipping, and warehousing through liaison with responsible groups and agencies inside and outside the company.
3. Sale and promotion of selected profitable products.
4. Emphasis on product mix selection.
5. Systems selling.
6. Closer inventory control.
7. Direction of research activities in higher product items via establishment of profitability goals.
8. Improved forecasting techniques.
9. Establishment of minimum individual product profit goals.

Objective No. 3
To reduce, consolidate, and maintain product line: xxx products in 1971 and yyy products in 1975.

Strategies
1. Elimination of products not meeting minimum profit goals.
2. Elimination of slow-moving items or those below established sales minimums.
3. Careful screening of proposed new product additions and assurance of conformity to minimum sales and profit goals.
4. Disposal of obsolete and slow-moving inventories.

Objective No. 4
Control products via
    Selection of profitable key and potential key products for major marketing emphasis.
    Elimination of low-profit items.
    Use of market, product, and profit life-cycle analysis.

Strategies
1. Analysis of sales distribution by
    Product line.
    Product subgroups.
    Individual products.
    Markets.

2. Market Analysis of product and product lines, including potential versus actual performance.

3. Improve sales motivations relating to individual products.

4. Implement computerized life-cycle analysis.

5. Improved forecasting via computerized procedures.

6. Increase product control functions, based on established frequency, periodic review.

Objective No. 5

Improve marketing response: identification and analysis of competitors and competitive situations plus the development of appropriate counter-measures and strategies.

Strategies

1. Continuous evaluation of competitor products.

2. Development of specific counterproducts.

3. Develop long-range product competition action and reaction pattern.

4. Incorporate competitive considerations in new product development.

5. Include competitive considerations in need analysis and input into research.

6. Develop systems or processes to prevent competitive ease in duplication.

VI   NEEDED PRODUCTS

Analysis of existing markets and products (ours and competitors') reveals the need for the following. This assessment also reflects the need for projection predicated on the created markets. Those marked with an asterisk are included in the impending research plan, since after discussion with marketing and product management (New Product Committee), tentative agreement has been reached.

  * 1. New electronic device for thermal sensitivity recordings.

  * 2. Consumer goods version of existing industrial products.

  * 3. Counteroffering to ABC companies' lines.

    4. Basic research project in miniaturization of alpha circuits.

Specific details of research programs will be found in their aforementioned report. Quantification of sales potential and profit analysis will be found in Table 2, Appendix I, along with specific "need" profiles as presented to research.

VII   BUDGETS

Detailed budgets for the planning period have been prepared for product group operation and advertising and promotion. They will be found in Table 5, Appendix I.

VIII   ACTION PROGRAMS

Action programs developed in support of indicated strategies are contained in Appendix II.

IX   CONTROL AND REVIEW PROCEDURES

This plan will be subject to the same quarterly performance control and review procedures indicated in the 1970 marketing products plan, with no revisions.

Appendix I
1971–1975 Product Plan
The Imaginary Marketing Corporation

TABLE 1. *Planned gross sales and profit by product line 1971–1975.*

		Sales					Profit					
		71	72	73	74	75	71	72	73	74	75	
Product line	A	$									%	A
	B											B
	C											C
	D											D
	E											E
	Total	$									%	Total

TABLE 2. *New products to be released in 1971.**

Product	Date of release	Planned sales	Percentage planned profit
New version of Product 21 in Line C	3/15/71	$xxx	x
Consumer goods version of Product 5 in Line A	4/25/71	$xxx	x
New addition to Line E	6/10/71	$xxxx	x
Modification of Product 17 in Line B	8/15/71	$xxx	x
New product in Line D	9/10/71	$xxxx	x

* Detailed action steps relative to each of these products are located in Appendix II.

TABLE 3. *Needed products.*

Product	Profile	Planned sales	Percentage planned profit
New electronic device for thermal sensitivity recording	Sensitivity range plus or minus 000 Size Shape Specification Tolerances Market price Components Market Competition	$xxx	xx
Consumer goods version of existing industrial products in Lines ACD	Same commercial and technical considerations as above	$xxxx	xx
Counteroffering to ABC companies' lines	Same commercial and technical considerations as above	$xxx	xx
Basic research project in miniaturization of alpha circuits	Same commercial and technical considerations as above	$xxxx	xx

TABLE 4. *Product group expense budget.*

Salaries	1971	1972	1973	1974	1975
Existing personnel	$	$	$	$	$
Added personnel		+$	+$	++$	++$
Administrative expense	$	$	$	$	$
Equipment expenditures	$	$	$	$	$
Miscellaneous expenses	$	$	$	$	$
Total	$	$	$	$	$

TABLE 5. *Advertising and promotion budgets.**

	1971	1972	1973	1974	1975
Advertising expenses					
Product Line A	$				
Product Line B	$				
Product Line C	$				
Product Line D	$				
Product Line E	$				
Product 73	$				
Product 74	$				
Product 18	$				
Product 16	$				
Institutional	$	$	$	$	$
Subtotal	$	$	$	$	$
Promotional effort					
Two-for-one sale	$				
Name the product	$				
Contest	$				
Miscellaneous	$				
Subtotal	$				
Total	$	$	$	$	$

* Specific dates of planned advertisements and promotional activities for 1971 are indicated in Appendix II action programs. No specific assigned expenditures are indicated for 1972–1975 based on present policy of not planning specific advertising programs other than on a one-year base.

TABLE 1. *1971 action program.*

Objective 1	To support planned sales as indicated in Appendix I				
Strategy 1	Comprehensive response to competitive strategies and actions				
	Responsi-bility	Date to be initiated	Date to be completed	Date initiated	Date completed	Result

Initiate competitive product reporting system; to be issued

1st quarter	Prod. Mgr.	1/1/71	3/25/71		
2nd quarter	Prod. Mgr.	4/1/71	6/15/71		
3rd quarter	Prod. Mgr.	7/1/71	9/25/71		
4th quarter	Prod. Mgr.	10/1/71	12/24/71		

with intervening supplements when requirements dictate

Competitive price report form to be developed and
employed in future competitive pricing situations:

Design form	Prod. Mgr.	1/10/71	2/1/71
Approve form	VP Mark.	2/1/71	2/10/71
Distribute form	Prod. Mgr.	3/1/71	3/1/71

Seminar on competitive practices relative to
Product Line D

	Prod. Mgr.	4/1/71	6/1/71
	VP Mark.	4/1/71	6/1/71
	VP Sales	4/1/71	6/1/71

Completion of competitive product name
cross-index

Design	Prod. Mgr.	1/1/71	2/10/71
Approve	VP Mark.	2/11/71	2/19/71
Compile	Prod. Mgr.	2/19/71	8/15/71
Distribute	Prod. Mgr.	9/1/71	9/1/71

Bibliography

Bowersox, Donald J., et. al., *Physical Distribution Management: Logistics Problems of the Firm*. New York: The Macmillan Company, 1968.

Brion, John M., *Corporate Marketing Planning*. New York: John Wiley & Sons Inc., 1967.

Buzzell, Robert D., *Mathematical Models and Marketing Management*. Boston: Harvard Business School, Division of Research, 1964.

The Computer in Advertising. New York: Association of National Advertisers, Inc., 1965.

The Computer in Marketing. New York: Sales Management Magazine, 1966.

Cook, Victor J., and Thomas F. Schutte, *Brand Policy Determination*. Marketing Science Institute, 1968.

Copulsky, William, *Practical Sales Forecasting*. AMA, 1969.

Developing a Product Strategy: Planning-Production-Promotion. AMA Management Report 39 (1960).

Evans, Gordon H., *The Product Manager's Job*. AMA Research Study 69 (1964).

Frey, Albert Wesley, ed., *Marketing Handbook*. New York: The Ronald Press Company, 1965.

Grayson, Robert A., and Reynold A. Olsen, *Marketing and the Computer*. AMA, 1967.

Haas, Raymond M., *Long-Range New Product Planning in Business*. West Virginia University Foundation, 1965.

Howard, Marshall C., *Legal Aspects of Marketing*. New York: McGraw-Hill Book Company, 1967.

Karger, Delmar W., *The New Product*. New York: The Industrial Press Inc., 1960.

Konopa, Leonard J., *New Products: Assessing Commercial Potential*. AMA Management Bulletin 88 (1966).

Kotler, Philip, *Marketing Management: Analysis, Planning and Control*. Englewood Cliffs, N.J.: Prentice-Hall, Inc., 1967.

Lynn, Robert A., *Price Policies and Marketing Management*. Homewood, Ill.: Richard D. Irwin, 1967.

Magee, John F., *Industrial Logistics*. New York: McGraw-Hill Book Company, 1968.

Marketing Harnesses the Computer. AMA Management Bulletin 92 (1967).

Marting, Elizabeth, ed., *New Products/New Profits*. AMA, 1964.

———— and others, ed., *Effective Communications on the Job*. AMA, 1963.

Maw, J. Gordon, *Return on Investment: Concept and Application*. AMA Management Bulletin 122 (1968).

Moore, Russell F., *Law for Executives*. AMA, 1968.

Murdick, Robert G., and Arthur E. Scharfer, *Sales Forecasting for Lower Costs and Higher Profits*. Englewood Cliffs, N.J.: Prentice-Hall, Inc., 1967.

Pessemier, Edgar A., *New-Product Decisions*. New York: McGraw-Hill Book Company, 1966.

Robinson, Patrick, Jr., *Promotional Decisions Using Mathematical Models*. Marketing Science Institute, 1968.

Smith, Paul T., *Computers, Systems, and Profits*. AMA, 1968.

Stern, Mark E., *Marketing Planning: A Systems Approach*. New York: McGraw-Hill Book Company, 1966.

Talley, Walter J., Jr., *The Profitable Product: Its Planning, Launching and Management*. Englewood Cliffs, N.J.: Prentice-Hall, Inc., 1965.

Uman, David B., *New Product Programs: Their Planning and Control*. AMA, 1969.

Wainwright, C. Anthony, and John T. Gerlach, *Successful Management of New Products*. New York: Hastings House Publishers, 1968.

Wallenstein, Gerd D., *Concept and Practice of Product Planning*. AMA, 1968.

Working with Other Departments. AMA, 1969.

Index